# CHILD WELFARE, IN A CHANGING WORLD

A.K. Rizwi

**MOHIT PUBLICATIONS**
NEW DELHI (INDIA)

*Published by*
**MOHIT PUBLICATIONS**
4675/21, Ansari Road, Darya Ganj,
New Delhi-110002
Ph.: 23255141, 23284136, Fax: 23280611
E-mail: mohit_publication@rediffmail.com

**CHILD WELFARE, IN A CHANGING WORLD**



First Published 2008
ISBN-978-81-7445-421-8



[The responsibility for the facts stated, conclusions reached, etc., is entirely that of the Author. The publisher is not responsible for them, whatsoever.]

PRINTED IN INDIA

---

**Published by Mohit Publications, New Delhi and Printed at Delhi**

# CONTENTS

# PREFACE

Social work, however, may be carried on in connection with these social institutions. In that situation it varies widely in both quality and quantity. Case work in child guidance clinics, for instance, has a highly technical body of theory and practice. In contrast, the problem of adapting the principles of social work to juvenile probation and "training school" work has not yet advanced far, although juvenile courts, a probation system, and institutions for delinquents exist in almost all states. Social work services are provided by only a few school systems, and social work in connection with organized recreation has only begun to be developed. As to social work in connection with the medical aspects of child welfare, not much has been done that distinguishes medical social work with children from that with adults, although medical social workers are being increasingly used in children's clinics. For this reason and other it has seemed best to postpone the description of the medical and psychiatric aspects of child welfare social work until a later chapter, where it will be combined with that of work with adults, and to describe, first, the social work carried on in schools and recreational organizations, and, next, that which is carried on with delinquents and other children who do not conform to social regulations.

**Author**

# I

# SOCIAL WORK IN THE FIELD OF CHILD WELFARE : ECONOMIC AND FAMILY ASPECTS

As has already been pointed out, the most important of children's needs are provided for through the family, so much so that when family facilities are lacking or parents and other relatives discharge their duties very inadequately, social custom always provides means for offsetting at least the most gross of the deficiencies. In modern American society numerous supplements to or substitutes for inadequate family life have been developed, some of them directed largely to its economic aspects, others concerned chiefly with its other functions. The types of assistance with which social work activities are most likely to be associated are the following :

1) Financial assistance to children in their own homes
2) Assistance to parents and children regarding other aspects of their home life
3) Foster care in day nurseries, child-caring institutions, and private homes

We shall consider each of these general forms of assistance separately in order to show how the social work function is discharged in connection with each of them.

## Social Work in Financial Assistance Programs

The sources of financial assistance for families that cannot carry out their economic responsibilities toward their children have already been described, and it has been noted that children whose fathers are dead or out of the home have been traditionally considered a class requiring and deserving special attention. In earlier years family welfare societies and other private charitable organizations provided financial or material aid over long periods of time to many cases of this type, put with the growth of "mothers aid" of "pension" schemes under state and country auspices and their more recent counterpart, the federally subsidized aid-to-dependent-children program, family welfare agencies have been enabled to give up most of their long-time relief work and to concentrate their attention on other services. Since at the present time by far the largest source of financial assistance in behalf of needy children who, as the Social Security Act puts it, "have been deprived of parental support or care by reason of the death, continued absence from home, or physical or mental incapacity of a parent" is the aid-to-dependent-children program, we shall concentrate attention on it in this analysis of the part the social work has to play in helping to make the relief aspects of child welfare activities useful to clients.

As has already been stated, about seventy million dollars are paid out and nearly 800,000 children are served by this program annually. The average amounts granted per family vary widely from state to state, for each state sets-up its own rules, subject only to certain minimum standards that must be met before the federal government will match its funds. In February, 1938, for example, the average amounts paid per family ranged from \$ 10.41 to \$ 60.39 in the various states, the average being \$ 32.02. Similarly, there is wide variation in eligibility requirements. Some states will grant this form of assistance to a needy father so that he may engage a housekeeper if his wife is dead, out of the home, or physically or mentally incapacitated; some will supplement the earnings of a physically handicapped father; consideration has been given by some states to the adoption of a policy of supplementing a needy mother's part-time earnings. In many states, however, these funds are available only for the care of children who are fatherless and whose mothers or other very close relatives remain at home to care for them. Since these provisions and policies vary so much from state to state and from time to time, we shall make no further attempt to be specific about them.

In Chapter X we came to the conclusion that the providing of financial assistance is not in itself social work but that social work services may be profitably employed in connection with it for various purposes, chief of which is that of rendering relief helpful, both psychologically and materially. Much the same questions as those discussed in that chapter arise with regard to the place of social work in the aid-to-dependent-children program. Social work is facilitated there because of the greater possibility of uniformity of policy, for–as contrasted with general relief–the administration of aid-to-dependent-children must by law be carried on through a single state agency if the federal subsidy is to be secured. Locally, however, the agencies dispensing this sort of assistance vary widely and include such authorities as courts, poor boards, and local public welfare departments. Nevertheless, the Federal Social Security Board now exercises some control over the persons who actually carry on the work, for the 1939 amendment to the Act says that state plans must "provide such methods of administration (including methods relating to the establishment and maintenance of personnel standards on a merit basis....) as are found by the Board to be necessary for the proper and efficient operation of the plan."

In the earlier chapter it was shown that social work in general relief programs is sometimes conceived as being the equivalent of family welfare work under public auspices. The relation of this concept to the theory that poverty evidences individual fault or incompetence was discussed, and the prevailing point of view regarding the distinction between relief and family welfare work was described. This distinction was seen to lie not in the needs of the clients (for doubtless many people in all economic strata have difficulties in their family relationships for which they might profitably seek professional assistance) but in the problems that bring them to the agencies and in the services the agencies are set-up to render. The scope of a relief worker's activities must doubtless be wider in a rural than in an urban setting, for there he may be the only source of social work assistance in matters of family welfare. Even so he must be clearly aware of what function he is performing in each case, lest his control over a family's source of income put him in a position of undue control over the rest of their lives.

### The need for case work in judging eligibility for aid to dependent children

This same question regarding the scope of social work arises with even greater urgency in connection with the program of aid to dependent children. Here we have a system of financial allowances based on the proposition that no child shall be deprived of his home by reason of poverty alone. This principle is less a declaration of human rights than might at first be thought, however, for its converse is that a dependent child may be denied this form of assistance if his mother or other responsible relative is considered not fit to care for him–even though that lack of fitness is not such as would be judged neglect in a court of law. Most of the present state laws no longer have rigid requirements about the "character" of the relatives in charge of the children for whom aid is requested, but they do say that such children shall live in "suitable" homes.

There is much to be said pro and con that requirement. In behalf of it is the fact that money is given for the children's benefit, and there must accordingly be some assurance that it will be used to that end. Against it is the fact that the requirement may be a means of denying assistance to some children because their relatives conduct is not such as conforms to the dispensing agency's standards, and that it may result in the kind of surveillance of their activities and limitation of their right to conduct their lives as they see fit that is not provided for in the other branches of the relief system. Discussing the interpretation of the factor of suitability in the eligibility requirements for aid to dependent children, the Director of the Bureau of Public Assistance of the Social Security Board wrote in 1939:

In some parts of the country laws and plans, which in themselves would permit a liberal interpretation of aid to dependent children, remain limited in application because of hampering opinions and attitudes.... It is the day-to-day operation–and its immediate and continuing effect upon children and their families–which clothes this legal framework with reality. And here, although real progress has been made, much remains to be done.

. . . Thus, for instance, it sometimes seems to be assumed that if a parent fails to measure up to a particular social pattern, the community may wash its hands of all responsibility for caring for the children. Or, if the community does accept some responsibility in such cases, it may still attempt to tie strings to the assistance offered: transfer from general relief to aid to dependent children may proceed as if it were a matter of "promoting nice families." Parents whose behaviour is looked at askance may be given to understand by inference that assistance may not be available for them unless they mend their ways. . . .

A special aspect of this problem is that of community attitudes toward illegitimate children in need of assistance.... No state with an approved plan has legal provisions which would exclude such children . . . but even where aid is given to such children, the conditions imposed may often close the door to any really constructive solution to the family problem. It is, for instance, impossible for a child to receive aid in some states, in cases of desertion as well as illegitimacy, unless the mother takes court action against the father.

As long as suitability of the home remains one of the eligibility requirements, however, it seems especially important that the passing of judgement in individual cases should be entrusted to those who are trained to evaluate the intangible factors that may enter into it. It is in this area that social workers have much to offer, for one of their special competences is to assess personal factors and to take into account the emotional values that, in spite of apparent material and even moral inadequacies, parents and relatives may have for their children.

In addition to passing upon the eligibility for aid to dependent children, a case worker frequently helps an applicant to decide whether he or she really wants to accept that kind of assistance. Involved in that decision is not only the question of whether "charity" (as the applicant may regard it) is distasteful but, often more important, whether the mother wants to abstain from employment and continue her parental role in the absence of a husband.

**Arguments regarding the provision of other case work services**

Once eligibility is decided upon and the applicant has decided to accept the assistance, the question arises of the further case work services to be made available by social workers in the aid-to-dependent-children program. We have previously discussed the place of social work in general relief programs and have seen that its main function, as conceived by many social workers, is not that of rehabilitating families (as though poverty and unemployment necessarily evidenced incompetence in the management of family affairs) but that of trying to make the giving, receiving, and withholding of relief a constructive experience for the clients and, consequently, a useful expenditure of funds by taxpayers. The same argument may be used in connection with the program of aid to dependent children, although it may be that applicants are less likely to feel socially disgraced by having to resort to this type of assistance than by being the recipients of general poor relief.

The fact, however, that the assistance is given specifically to benefit children and that it is likely to continue over a long period of time is frequently used to justify a broader program of case work services in connection with it. Involved also is the question of whether aid to dependent children is a relief of a "welfare" service, in the narrower meaning of the term, and much of the dispute about what social work services are to be afforded turns upon it. The courts have ruled that the mothers' aid laws that preceded the present system were welfare rather than relief measures. Nevertheless, aid to dependent children was classified by the Social Security Act as one of the public assistance services, and provision for help with other aspects of children's welfare was put in a separate category. The question, however, is not one to be answered finally by reference to legal rulings or administrative organization but rather by an analysis of the function the institution serves. We shall not attempt such an analysis here, however, but merely point out the contrasting conceptions of the place of social work in the system.

As illustrative of the position of those who maintain that social work in the aid-to-dependent-children program should be devoted to the promotion of children's total well-being, some statements of representative authorities may be cited. In 1940 the National Association for Aid to Dependent Children, a private organization devoted to the promotion of better standards and methods of administration in the work, listed the following as its conception of the purposes of the aid-to-dependent-children program:

1. To preserve normal family life for children in danger of losing it.

2. To preserve kinship ties where these are desirable for the children concerned.
3. To provide financial security by a regular, adequate allowance in the home which will offer opportunities for family planning, for expression of individual taste, and for protection of the family's status in the community.
4. To make available to families aided, through the agency or other resources in the community, health services, parental education, recreational outlets, vocational counselling and placement to the end that such families may become self-sufficient at the termination of the aid.

For the furtherance of those purposes the Association held that certain "service aspects" of the program are required. These service aspects include:

1. Liaison services between the home and the school in the interests of the child's proper school adjustment.
2. Vocational guidance and placement of older children.
3. Medical and surgical care for members of the family, including the disabled parent.
4. Assistance to families in securing proper housing.
5. Expert advice on life insurance conversion, property holdings, and the like.
6. Individual or group instruction in meal planning, buying, food preparation and preservation, nutrition, child care and training and other arts that enter into home making.
7. Assistance to families in securing wholesome recreation such as memberships in character-building agencies, summer outings, and the like.

Along the same line the Director of the Bureau of Public Assistance once wrote: "Important as they are, determination of eligibility and the granting of allowances are only the first steps. Continuing service and guidance in helping families meet the many problems confronting them are equally essential if aid to dependent children is to fulfil its purposes.... The purpose of all our efforts. . . is adequate and constructive help to each child and each family in accordance with individual needs."

The argument is a persuasive one, for it is well known that associated with poverty are many other conditions unfavourable to child welfare. But these conditions also exist in many families that are not on relief rolls, and to those who regard aid to dependent children as a relief rather than a "welfare" measure it seems highly questionable whether the receipt of financial assistance should put a family in a special category with regard either to other services or to supervision of other aspects of their lives. With respect to the latter, parents' rights to deal with their children in their own manner are limited by statute in many ways, but the social worker administering a relief scheme is not the proper enforcement officer. Similarly, resources for aiding mothers in the care of their children are available to some extent and should be increased. It seems, therefore, that it lies within the duties of a social worker in a relief program (whether one of general relief or one of relief to specific categories of people) to bring cases of illegal neglect to the attention of the proper authorities and to give to clients who need the desire it information about and assistance in securing the use of other social resources affording help of various kinds. But the social workers in a relief program should undertake the same kind of service as that afforded by family or child welfare agencies to which clients come on their own initiative or use in accordance with their own choosing seems to many social workers a mistaken conception of their function.

This conclusion is an application of what might be stated

as a general case work principle: that objectives of relief and rehabilitation should not be combined unless they are expressly so understood and accepted by the client. To be more specific, on the legal side, aid to dependent children is granted when application for such assistance is made and certain conditions laid down in law or administrative regulations are found to obtain in a family. It would therefore be an infringement of a client's legal rights if he were denied continuance of assistance because he did not take advantage of other services that were offered, such as having his children's tonsils taken out or sending the children to summer camp. Probably aid would not be discontinued for that reason, but the thought that it might be discontinued could be equally damaging psychologically to a client (enhancing either his dependency upon the social worker or his resentment against him); and clients might well have such fears if social workers both dispensed financial assistance and urged upon clients these other forms of service that they thought were for the children's good.

## Examples of situations in which case work may be needed

If the object of securing for the children the most favourable environmental conditions possible is renounced, what are some of the other problems (in addition to those of determining eligibility and the continuing need for relief) that occasion the use of social workers in this program? To answer this question in detail would require many concrete examples, but a few situations can be described in general terms.

First, there are problems centring around the calculation of a budget. Among them are the following. The amount of aid–within the limits prescribed by law–to any particular family is based upon the family's income and other resources and the children's requirements for food, shelter, clothing, and other necessities, and, usually, medical care. The maintenance requirements of the relatives who are providing a home are not included, although general overhead expenses–such as those for rent, light, and heat–may be taken into account. The calculation of a budget to cover these items may be a rather complicated procedure which might be thought best entrusted to a specialist in household planning. It has been found, however, that best results are secured–in terms of co-operation and the preservation or development of that sense of responsibility on which so much of constructive family life depends–when clients take an active part in such planning and calculations. To secure their participation and to clarify what part in the budget-planning process is their responsibility, and what part belongs to the representative of the agency, often requires special knowledge of individual psychology and group customs, and special skills in the establishment of human relationships that are among the technical assets of a trained social worker.

Again, along the same line, budgets have to be continually adapted to changing needs. Then, too, questions frequently arise as to what the money may be spent for, what–if any–limitations on a family's activities the receipt of this form of aid imposes, what actions on its part will result in a change in the size of allowance. For instance, aid to dependent children is not available to physically or mentally handicapped children unless they can qualify on the same basis as other children, nor is it given for the assistance of children who are in institutions. On the other hand, temporary residence in a hospital does not disqualify a child. A family may need help, therefore, in deciding whether to have a mentally defective child committed to an institution or to use, for instance, a sanatorium for a tuberculous child who might be cared for at home. This question and many others have to be answered on an individual basis; and if the impression of arbitrariness of decision is to be avoided and the relatives' sense of participation in the planning is to be maintained, there is much need for case work skills.

In the course of this planning and its attendant discussion, the children's relatives (perhaps the children themselves, if they are old enough to participate) are likely to want to talk about other problems and needs. With some problems that do not involve the use of outside resources or that involve the question of whether or not to use such resources, a case worker can give immediate aid, his services in this area being of that "counselling" nature that has been illustrated in Case 12. In other situations, resolution of the difficulties may require the use of other organizations–schools, hospitals, recreation centres, churches, social agencies, such as those affording child placement or family welfare services, and so on; and the knowledge of how to use these services and how to avoid taking the responsibility for their use away from a client (thus depriving him of his customary status as a person who makes his own arrangements) again calls for case work skill.

Another kind of problem that usually comes up for discussion centers around when to lessen or discontinue aid. The relatives with whom the children live (a mother, frequently, or an older sister or a father who is partially incapacitated) may want to work outside the home; there may be a question of whether or not the children should continue to attend school after the age of sixteen; the mother may be considering remarriage.

These and numerous other situations come up for discussion and for decision about allowances. All in all, there is much scope for the kind of services that social workers are specifically trained to give. Through their use, the receipt of aid in behalf of dependent children can often be rendered a more socially constructive experience–both to the relatives and to the children–than might be the case if the assistance were given in a mechanical manner and without that individual adaptation to clients' needs and desires that case work affords.

### *Social Work Regarding the Welfare of Children in their Own Homes*

In addition to programs that have been instituted for the financial assistance of children who are handicapped by both poverty and the loss or incapacity of a parent or parents, there are those whose aim is to meet the needs of children whose family life is unsatisfactory for other or additional reasons. It was shown above that in the early days attention was centered chiefly upon children who suffered from neglect or abuse or other extreme handicaps to their physical or social well-being. With improvement in social and economic conditions (the establishment of a free and compulsory school system, better medical and recreational facilities, provision for the relief of financial distress–in sort, better social organization for meeting basic needs), the number of cases of this type has probably decreased, though there are still enough of them to require considerable work on the part of courts and welfare agencies. In the meantime social concepts of what constitutes adequate home life for children have altered (for the better, we are of course inclined to think), and child welfare organizations have accordingly broadened their programs to take into account many children who in earlier years would not have been thought to be in need of their services.

The services to be described in this section of the chapter are those that have to do with the social welfare of children in their own homes. Originally organizations carrying on what is now called "protective" work with children centered much of their attention upon removing children from home. As has been shown above, the children's aid societies put their agents to work in the slum areas of large cities to seek out vagrant children and to prevail upon parents who did not or could not give children adequate care to take advantage of the free homes the organizations offered to provide. Other organizations followed suit, some of them setting up childcaring institutions instead of placing children in foster homes. With changing ideas, however, as to the importance of family ties, the emphasis of the work of many organizations has shifted to giving assistance to parents and children in their own homes with various problems of family life, including those that earlier were deemed severe enough to necessitate breaking up families.

**Types of agencies and programs**

The organizations affording this kind of help are of various kinds. Family welfare societies do much of this sort of work, although application for their services is usually originally made on the basis of general family needs rather than those of individual children. Children's aid societies also engage in this work. Some of them limit their assistance to helping applicants decide whether they do or do not want to place their children in foster homes, and refer them to family welfare agencies for further help if a decision against placement is made. Others give more varied forms of aid. In the more strictly "protective" work (that is, services specifically designed to protect children from the damaging effects of bad home conditions) the humane societies,societies for the prevention of cruelty to children, juvenile protective agencies, and the like play a prominent part. Then there are organizations devoted to special categories of children–the illegitimate their mothers, adolescents, migrants, and others. And, for rural areas, there are the "child welfare services" financed in large part by funds provided by the Federal Social Security Act.

"Protective" work under private auspices began with the establishment of the New York Society for the Prevention of Cruelty to Children in 1875, its special function being conceived as that of prosecuting cases of cruelty and neglect and securing the punishment of the responsible adults. In some cities and states (the organizations soon began to operate on a state-wide basis) the agents of the humane societies, as they came to be called, were given police power and often had at least semilegal control over the children who became wards of the state. Protective work on behalf of adolescent girls and unmarried mothers and their children was also early organized, the services of these agencies including the provision of temporary "shelters" and homes. In addition to work on individual cases, protective agencies devoted much attention to the improvement of community conditions, both through private efforts and the promotion of legislation. Through their work public attention was directed to the need for eliminating "baby farms" and various forms of child exploitation, for regulating dance halls, and for removing other moral and physical hazards to children and young people. As juvenile courts, women's police bureaus , and other legal agencies for safeguarding children's welfare became established, however, need for these activities on the part of privately financed organizations decreased, and the protective agencies began to give attention to the less extreme forms of child neglect and exploitation and to provide case work services.

For many years activities in the field of childcare and protection were largely confined to urban areas, although some children's aid societies and protective agencies operated on a state-wide basis. Some states and counties provided services in behalf of neglected and ill-treated children through their public welfare departments, some of them having divisions or bureaus especially devoted to child welfare. In most rural counties, however, juvenile courts and poor law officials were they only source of assistance to children, and they usually provided only meager financial aid or maintenance in inadequate childcaring institutions or ill-supervised foster homes.

Improvement in this rural situation is being achieved, however, under the "child welfare" provisions of the Social Security Act. Under that Act $ 1,510,000 is appropriated annually for the "payment of part of the cost of district, county, and other local child welfare services in areas predominantly rural and for the developing of state services for the encouragement and assistance of adequate methods of child welfare organization in areas predominantly rural and other areas of special need." The services thus financed are described as being for the "protection and care of homeless, dependent, and neglected children, and children in danger of becoming delinquent." Eligibility for their help is not dependent on financial circumstances, and assistance is offered to children and their families without regard to economic status.

In consequence of this federal subsidy there has been a considerable expansion of state child welfare programs. In 1936, for example, only twenty-seven states had child welfare divisions in their public welfare departments, while by 1940 the number had increased to forty. In that latter year a sixth of the counties in the country were providing social services to children under public welfare auspices, forty-five thousand children being served by about five hundred professional workers. This is still not a large program, it is true, but it is said to be unusually successful in bringing to light numerous previously unsuspected problems of child health, family neglect, inadequate housing and nutrition, and poor parent-child relationships.

Under these public child welfare services, wider activities than those customarily provided by individual agencies in urban centers are carried on. The clients include children who require foster care, those who present conduct problems in school or community and so are regarded as "in danger of becoming delinquent," mentally defective and physically handicapped children for whom arrangements for treatment or custody need to be made, as well as children whose home conditions appear to be disadvantageous to their welfare. Most of the work of the agencies, however, has to do with children in their own homes rather than with foster care. In this they differ from many privately financed, urban agencies, much of whose work centers around placement in foster homes, or the provision of care in shelters, detention homes, and other kinds of children's institutions.

**Types of services**

With such a variety of agencies at work in the field of "childcare and protection," as it is called in social work parlance, it is rather difficult to generalize about their services, even in the limited area of work with children in their own homes. Broadly speaking, however, several types of services may be distinguished. There is, first of all, strictly "protective" work–that is, services that are aimed at securing children against neglect, abuse, or exposure to unhealthful or immoral conditions. It has been found that such unfortunate conditions are not always either deliberately or carelessly created by parents but are often the result of ignorance or misfortune or lack of adequate resources. Accordingly, it is held that just as children should not be removed from home because of poverty alone, so, too, foster care should not always be secured even in cases of apparently unwholesome home conditions. Instead, some protective agencies try to help parents work out plants that will meet at least the minimum needs of the children.

Such protective services are usually entered upon at the request of somebody outside the family. Schoolteachers may report that children are uncared for; neighbors may complain that children are mistreated; the police may intimate that they will take action unless conditions are remedied. The protective agencies, therefore, start upon their activities in a very different relation to their clients from that which is usual in social work. As a matter of fact, their work is often not social work at all but rather that of legal authorities. When, however, they do engage in social work and undertake to help parents provide more adequately for the welfare of their children in their own homes, they cannot avoid the authoritative position in which their agency's function places them. Their responsibility is that of securing proper care for the children, and they cannot retire from the case-as a family agency worker would–if their services are not desired by the parents. Even in such a situation, however, basic social work principles may be observed (the client's right to privacy, and the right to make his own decisions and to live his life as he pleases within the limitations set by law), and families may frequently be helped to work out plants that are in keeping with their own desires. Case 14 illustrates this aspect of protective work and includes the writer's comments upon it.

***Case 14***

The Waldrons were referred to the S.P.C.C. after a conference of interested agencies. There was every evidence of neglect but nothing specific that could be brought into court. There was a large mixed family by the previous marriage of each parent and by the present partnership. Home conditions were terrible, and the children dirty and ragged. Mr. Waldron was, however, unwilling to place his children and resentful when approached.

Before the worker could state more than her name and agency when she called, Mr. Waldron shouted that she should stay out of his affairs. The worker replied that she had been asked to call because of the children. The community did not feel that they were receiving proper care. Both parents began to talk at once, Mr. Waldron saying that it was a lie, Mrs. Waldron screaming and sobbing that it was the truth. It seemed to the worker that "she had been keeping this to herself and that the relief to pent-up emotions was brought about by the worker's entry." After a while the worker said that there seemed little doubt that they were having trouble, and she wondered what they were going to do about it.... Implicit in her statement was the demand that something be done, yet she did not presume to tell the Waldrons what they should do. Only if they did nothing would the worker assume authority and insist that the children be cared for somewhere.

Each parent blamed the other and proposed dividing up

the family. The worker did not question this but said she would call in a week to help make what plan seemed best. When she did so she found them already beginning to move toward a solution of their problem. Each saw improvement in the other. Mrs. Waldron could recognize that her husband's physical condition was making things harder for him. He is turn showed a real effort to come to grips with the situation. As the case worker put it, "He hated to be condemned by the agency.... He did not want his wife to leave but if she felt she must, she could do so. The present conditions were not fair to the children, but he did not know how to make them better.... If he felt placement was the best plan he would not care, but he was not sure yet."

The worker continued to call to discuss the difficulties with the Waldrons. At the end of four months the home seemed to be running on a fairly even keel and Mr. and Mrs. Waldron were showing increasing affection for each other.... The children benefited by the calmer atmosphere in the home and were happier and better cared for. The worker, who came into the home unwanted, even resented, was now a welcome visitor to whom Mr. Waldron proudly showed his new pigeon-loft, by which he hoped to increase his income.

How was this accomplished ? The personality and professional integrity of the worker undoubtedly had much to do with it. She was not disturbed by Mr. Waldron's anger, she was not drawn into their quarrel, she was able to let them express themselves freely and yet remain friendly and interested. But perhaps it was her clear understanding of her responsibility, both to the community and to the Waldrons, that helped most. Could they not acknowledge her right to insist on adequate standards for the children just because she did not insist on the way that was to be achieved ? On that basis they could accept her help and begin a reorientation of themselves around the focal point of the children's care.

Another kind of service that social agencies afford to children in regard to their family life is that of supervision and planning in the mother's absence or when she is inadequate, physically or mentally. Typical cases are those in which the mother is dead and an older child is trying to keep the family together; those in which the mother is not capable of carrying on her normal duties but there is a strong sense of family solidarity among the children; those in which the children are in special need of the mother, even though she is not a very adequate person.

Another service is that of counseling with adolescent children concerning the difficulties they face in adjusting to the demands of family life. Among cases of this type are those of children who have run away from home, those who are contemplating such action because they find life at home so unpleasant, those who are regarded by their families as antagonistic or un-co-operative or inexplicably sullen, remote, or silent.

Finally, there are many cases in which the service of the social agency consists chiefly in planning with parents and children (or perhaps only with the parents if the children are very young) regarding how to deal with the problems that living together involves. Frequently such cases come to the agencies' attention because the parents are considering foster care for the children, feeling that they can no longer cope with the difficulties. Fairly representative of the way a social worker may be of assistance in such cases is Case 15, in which it will be seen that the social worker's ability to appreciate the clients' feelings and to help them to try out their solutions to the problem resulted in reinforcing the strengths in their relationship with each other.

***Case 15***

Mrs. Minter telephoned the Children's Bureau, saying that the high school principal had said we might be able to help her. It was about her stepdaughter, Joan, aged sixteen.

She had taken care of Joan since April (it was now November) without any assistance from Mr. Minter, and now he had written Joan that he wanted her to come and live with him. Mrs. Minter said he was not a proper man to have Joan. He deserted them last spring and has never written to anybody but Joan since. Mrs. Minter had insisted that Joan write and ask him for money. He replied by saying Joan should come and live with him. Mrs. Minter said that Joan knows what kind of man her father is and that she would be safer and get her three meals a day if she stayed with her stepmother instead. Mrs. Minter continued by explaining her financial status (she runs a small cafe in an industrial district of Los Angeles) and her difficult situation since Mr. Minter left, for he had encouraged a rowdy lot of people to patronize the place and had got into legal entanglements over his employment practices. She, however, was beginning to make a go of the restaurant now, but she needed Joan to help her, and Joan would do nothing but wash a few dishes.

Mrs. Minter continued her monologue by saying that Joan had lived in England for some years after her mother's death, and it was a mistake that eight years ago she and Mr. Minter had sent for her to come and live with them. Mrs. Minter has always had to fight her battles alone. She isn't getting help from anyone, even Joan. Things would not have been so bad if Mr. Minter had not taken to drink after their marriage. She blamed much of her situation on that, as well as on his weakness and poor character, and feared Joan might inherit his alcoholism. Then–as though she had said too much against Joan–she added that Joan has her good points, they are often confidential with each other, and people tell her that she is sometimes too strict with Joan. She gave some examples of this but justified herself by showing how her strictness had saved Joan from misfortune. After further description of her hard lot in life (she had once been a certified public accountant) and the present unsatisfactory conditions under which she lived, she asked whether the worker could help her keep Joan (they are company for each other, and she could give Joan a good home if only she could get some money out of Mr. Minter) and work out a financial plan.

The next day the worker called and found the family in a shabby restaurant, furnished with a long wooden counter and cheap stools, a few booths, and a couple of tables in the middle of the room. A girl behind the counter inquired in a unfriendly manner what she wanted and gestured to a girl sitting at a table behind the door, "There's her daughter. You can talk with her." Joan, an attractive adolescent dressed shabbily but in good taste, had apparently not been told about the worker's expected visit. The worker gave her name but not her business and asked to talk to Mrs. Minter. Joan, with a rather hard, grim expression, went to the black of the building and appeared with Mrs. Minter, who–contrary to expectations–was pleasing in appearance, courteous, and fairly at ease. She asked the worker to come to the back of the house and told Joan to come too, saying, "This concerns you, Joan." Joan looked started, shrugged her shoulders, and followed. The interview took place in a very small bedroom, which was the only other room in the house.

Mrs. Minter turned to Joan first. "I asked this lady to come out from the authorities and talk to you, Joan. I want to have things settled once and for all. I want you to make-up your mind today just what you want to do about things." Joan sat rigidly on the bed, a hard, impenetrable look on her face. She glanced at the worker, who smiled reassuringly, but she looked quickly away again and gazed at the floor. Mrs. Minter hurried on to say that things would not be this way if it hadn't been for Joan's father. She repeated some of yesterday's story and emphasized what an expense Joan had been to her, adding that she thought Joan didn't appreciate what she had done for her. Joan turned quickly and said huskily, "I do, too!" To which Mrs. Minter replied, "You have a funny was of showing it !" For some time the interview consisted of Mrs. Minter's telling of Joan's misdeeds and

Joan's defending herself. Then Mrs. Minter returned to a description of Mr. Minter–the desertion, the legal troubles, and so on–after which her talk slowed down and she began to cry.

After a pause, the worker said, "How terribly unhappy you two people are ! So much has happened to both of you that it is no wonder you get on each other's nerves. You have both badly hurt by the same man, and it is very hard to take it. Some things are so hard to face because they are so disillusioning." Both Joan and Mrs. Minter looked at her in surprise. Mrs. Minter responded by saying that she had once loved Mr. Minter and what a blow it was when he took to drink and spoiled their home life. She tried to think of reasons for his behaviour–perhaps he got into the wrong company, perhaps she had nagged too much. . . . And then to see him treat his own daughter that way; it was more than she could bear. It was always she who insisted that he give Joan money; it was she who was interested in Joan's welfare. And then he went off with that waitress. She felt sorry for Joan and wanted to see her happy. There are so many things that Joan wants that she can't give her. Joan complains that they don't have a home and family life. God knows she would like to have that kind of home too ! If she could get her affairs straightened out and rent a small apartment, things would be much better. Maybe she had been unusually cross lately. It was a matter of being worried about finances and Joan's behaviour, and she had been sick too. She showed the worker her angry-looking varicose veins and told of how her nerves often hurt so badly that she could scream. Then, too, she doesn't trust her employees or her customers; she is sure they walk off with food and money when she is resting. That is why she had hoped that Joan would work in the restaurant and help her. If Joan goes with her father she will be very unhappy. He may still have "that woman" with him, and she won't give Joan a good home.

The worker responded, "You certainly have enough to

make anybody unhappy. Have you talked these things over with Joan ?" No, said Mrs. Minter, she never had. She wasn't one to talk about her feelings much. Besides, she didn't think Joan cared. "I thought it was better not to let her know I was upset. She might lose her respect for me." The worker remarked that she thought Joan was an understanding person but she supposed both of them were so preoccupied with their own worries they didn't have much thought about discussing matters. She then turned to Joan and said she must have had things to irritate her too–no home to which she could bring her friends, not the kind of clothes she wanted, not much energy because she was growing so fast. Perhaps the men customers were annoying sometimes. Then, too, maybe she felt lonely, and maybe it hurt her to hear Mrs. Minter talk that way about her father, even if he had left them. She wondered that Joan thought about her father's invitation to her to join him.

During this recital of her possible woes Joan lost her hard expression and finally said with feeling that she didn't care what became of her now. She had been fighting most of her life for a home and people who wanted her. She is sick of sticking her chin out and getting it smacked. She is not going to say what she wants. The worker can make any arrangements she pleases. The worker responded by telling Joan about the agency. It doesn't force people to do things; its aim is to help unhappy people to work out the plans they think will bring them greater happiness. Under no circumstances should Joan and Mrs. Minter think she was there to "push them around." She wanted to be their friend and to help them work out their misunderstandings. She looked directly at Joan and said quietly. "You don't have to be afraid of me, Joan. I like you and want to help you." Joan smiled. It seemed hard for her, as though she had not smiled for a long time.

Mrs. Minter then asked Joan to give the worker the latest letter she had received from her father. The worker said that letters are personal things and maybe Joan would rather just tell her about it, but Joan handed the letter to her. It turned out to be well written. Mr. Minter called Joan "dear" and "sweetheart," told her her regretted her unhappiness and his present inability to send he money, told her to keep her chin up; as soon as he got steady work he would send for her.

When Mrs. Minter had left the room the worker remarked to Joan that a letter like that must be a help. Joan began to cry and said she couldn't forgive her father for having gone away. Things were so different when her mother was alive. In response to the worker's suggestion, she said he shouldn't have married again; she could have taken care of him. He shouldn't have sent her to England. He never drank when he lived with her mother. It was all Aunt Mabel's (the present Mrs. Minter's) fault. She couldn't let him alone but kept nagging him and driving him crazy. "The lady he went away with was a little like my mother." Joan was talking in low tones now. She said it was true her father probably wouldn't give her a good home. She had always liked Aunt Mabel, who was fine in everything except about her father? She had tried to give her things and had even gone without necessities so that Joan could have fun. She is sick and unhappy now. When she is well things are different.

When Mrs. Minter returned, the worker suggested they talk over possible plans. She said maybe they needed a vacation from each other for a while; if so, she might be able to arrange for a temporary home for Joan. Joan and Mrs. Minter inquired further about the possibility, and Joan wanted particularly to know whether she would have to work for her keep. The worker told of both work and boarding homes but said she thought the latter would be better right now. Then she said that an alternate plan would be for Joan to go to her father, and a third would be to stay where she was and try to work things out with the worker's help. If a boarding home were decided upon, there would be the question of finances. Since Mrs. Minter couldn't pay, they would have to find out whether Mr. Minter would make a contribution or whether the agency would be willing to help them. Mrs. Minter replied that her legal matters would be straightened out soon, and she would know better where she stood. In the meantime they would talk things over.

When she worker left, Joan said, "I sure am glad you came," and Mrs. Minter followed her to the door to tell her that she thought she understood Joan better now. The worker suggested that since Joan is growing up, Mrs. Minter should try to be more of a companion than a mother to her. Mrs. Minter replied that Joan was still immature and needed a strong hand over her but that she would try to be more companionable with her.

Within the next two weeks the worker called to leave some clothes she had found for Joan. Mrs. Minter was in a hospital for some days and Joan was away at the time of each visit. After Mrs. Minter's return home she was found to be very angry with Joan and insisted that the worker take her away immediately. The interview consisted of a recital by Mrs. Minter of all the things Joan had done wrong while she was in the hospital and a defence by Joan of her activities, Joan. The last time Miss Jones was here I thought her talking had done you some good but I see you don't intend to pay attention to anybody. I have taken all I'm going to from you. "Now you can get out !" After a protest from Joan that she too was sick, the worker said it seemed to her that they had come to the parting of the ways for the present. It might be, however, that this was due to Mrs. Minter's illness and the fact that the cafe business was going poorly–both of which would make Mrs. Minter find caring for Joan particularly hard. She would suggest, therefore, that they try a boarding home for Joan for one month before making a final decision; and she turned to Joan to ask her what she thought of that.

Joan burst into tears and said she didn't care what happened to her. She was tired to struggling for things. She had been just as sick as Mrs. Minter, and she had tried to do her share of the work. All she wanted was a home where she didn't have to live on schedule. She was sick of having to get up at six in the morning, not being able to sleep at night because of the noise in the cafe, and not having a place to bring her friends for a little fun and conversation. The worker said she would go ahead and see about a home for Joan for a month. She would also write to Mr. Minter, but perhaps Joan would like to write to him first and tell him about the plans. Finding a home would take a couple days. Mrs. Minter agreed to try to make a go of things over the weekend.

A good home in a nearby school district was located, and the worker telephoned to tell Joan about it. She did not sound very enthusiastic and said that, although she would do what the worker wanted, she would rather wait till they heard from her father. Mrs. Minter then came to the phone and told in a friendly manner of how changed Joan had been since the last visit. She apologized for her temper display at that time and said she guessed she had just been worn out and desperate. She too wanted to wait with arrangements till Mr. Minter was heard from, and she added that she would be pretty lonely without Joan. The worker said she understood how things were and agreed to postpone plans.

A few days later Mr. Minter wrote to the agency offering to pay for Joan's board. Mrs. Minter, on being told about this, was rather angry, saying that if he could afford to do that he could give the money to her; this proved that what he really objected to was her keeping Joan. With this letter the worker agreed and suggested that they therefore had better go ahead with the temporary boarding-home plan. Mrs. Minter then accused the worker of trying to take Joan away from her, said she would use this letter in court to get money out of Mr. Minter for Joan's care, and so on. The worker told her that under no conditions would she give her the letter to use in that way and pointed out that such action would so antagonize Mr. Minter that he would do nothing further to help them work out plans for Joan. Mrs. Minter calmed down a bit at that, said she saw the point, and promised to think things over before taking action.

The same day Joan telephoned to the worker to say that she had decided that she would say with her stepmother for the present, since she needed her so much. Asked whether she really meant this or was only saying what her stepmother wanted her to say, Joan replied, "I really mean it. In spite of everything I'm fond of Aunt Mabel, and I don't want to go away from the only home I've known." The worker told Joan that she was not trying to force any plan on her and that she and Mrs. Minter should get in touch with her if they had any further need for her help. Mrs. Minter then came to the telephone and again apologized for her remarks. She said she had been thinking matters over and wondered whether the worker could write to Mr. Minter and tell him that so much of Joan's unhappiness was due to lack of money. Perhaps he would be willing to send it to them instead of to a boarding home. The worker agreed to write such a letter.

A few days later a call revealed a much more satisfactory situation in the Minter home. Mr. Minter had sent Joan ten dollars, which she was using to purchase clothes. Mrs. Minter attributed that to the worker's letter, but the worker assured her that she had not yet written. That made it all the better, said Mrs. Minter, and she went on to say that they were grateful for the way the worker had helped them to make plans. "You seemed to understand, and you didn't make us do things," she said. Mrs. Minter was now optimistic about her business. She had two new waitresses, the customers were coming back, Joan was working in the cafe and saying she was glad she had not left home, and plans were on foot for getting a small apartment.

Later a letter to Mr. Minter brought a cordial response. He continued to send Joan money, which–in Mrs. Minter's opinion–she spent wisely. Mr. Minter said that he thought that Mrs. Minter and Joan were really fond of each other and that he had told Joan that he would not take her away as long as she liked living with her stepmother. He had advised Joan to get in touch with the worker if things went wrong. The worker in her final call emphasized her willingness to be of service if setbacks occurred. Mrs. Minter closed the interview by telling about the plans for the new apartment and saying, "We are going to fix it all up nice and then we will invite you out to see it."

### *Social Work in Connection with Foster Care Facilities*

In spite of the fact that money is available for aiding dependent children and that agencies provide parents and relatives with various forms of social work assistance in regard to problems of childcare, it will already have become apparent that there are many situations in which foster care for children either must be resorted to or is preferred by parents. A child may, for instance, require foster care because his parents or relatives cannot secure enough money to maintain the home in the way they desire, because they are ill and cannot afford to pay for his care, because they do not want him or cannot manage him, because he has no parents or relatives who are both able and willing to give him a home. Sometimes the need is for a permanent home, in which category adoption is to be included; sometimes only temporary care is required, the extreme of which is to be seen in the facilities day nurseries afford.

Foster care is provided in various ways, ranging from informal private arrangements through which parents and foster parents find each other to those involving court action and the state's permanent custody of the child. The types of social agencies that provide foster care for children–either through foster homes, childcaring institutions, or a combination of the two–are also numerous. As classified by the Census Authorities they are: state, county, and municipal welfare departments; child-placing departments of juvenile courts and long-time detention homes; state, county, and municipal agencies and institutions; fraternal, religious, and non-sectarian agencies and institutions doing child placement work or giving institutional care; family agencies with special children's departments; maternity homes which keep children after the mothers are dismissed from care. Excluded from this list, although also providing substitute homes for special types of cases, are institutions for delinquents, detention homes for short-time care, and institutions for the physically or mentally handicapped. Day nurseries should also be included, since they substitute for homes on a part-time basis. With such variation in auspices it is not unexpected to find that philosophies and policies about foster care differ widely and that it is difficult to generalize about programs and methods. We shall accordingly, not attempt to make anything like a complete survey of the work, especially since our primary interest is in the part that social work plays in connection with it.

### *Day Nurseries*

Whether social work service is considered necessary by day nursery administrators and for what purposes it is employed depend largely upon what the chief objective of day nursery care is held to be. Day nurseries were originally designed to provide daytime care for the young children of employed mothers who otherwise would have had to leave them at home under inadequate supervision. Later the children of mothers who were ill or otherwise incapacitated were admitted to nurseries, the objective in providing care for them being essentially similar. Under this custodial conception of the nursery's function, day nursery administrators are not likely to see much need for the services of social workers, for the chief criterion for a child's admission to a nursery is the mother's need for this form of assistance, as judged by her employment status, income, and absence of other means of caring for the child. The day nursery's service consists of trying to keep the children clean, well fed, well supervised, and happily engaged in activities. If the children do not respond well to such care or the parents are dissatisfied, administrators of day nurseries of this type are not likely to feel the need of offering them further services, although some few supply social workers to look more closely into the children's home conditions.

A very different conception of day nursery care is held by those who regard the nursery chiefly as a part of a program for improving family life. Under this conception the chief purpose of the nursery is held to be that of helping children and parents who are experiencing difficulty in family relationships to live more harmoniously together. The fulfilment of this objective is regarded as the joint task of the day nursery and the family welfare or children's agency; hence these nurseries are likely to look to the other agency for case work assistance. Social workers are used by such nurseries both to help the administrators decide which applicants are most in need of the nursery's facilities and most likely to benefit from them and to carry on case work with the parents in regard to family problems while the children are being aided by the nursery's program of activities.

Very different from either the custodial or the family welfare conception of a day nursery's purpose is that which makes the nursery's prime aid that of furthering the growth and development (social and psychological as well as physical) of each individual child. This educational objective day nurseries are held to share with nursery schools; in fact, in the opinion of some authorities, the distinction between the two types of organizations is very slight, being chiefly one of the economic status of the parents and the greater variety of services that need to be made available when mothers have little money and are employed all day long.

When case workers are employed by day nurseries that have this educational aim, their work with parents is likely to be of a very different nature from that of family case work. (Their point of view and methods would appear to be applicable to childcaring day nurseries also, for many of the same questions in regard to their use and procedures would arise in the parents minds.) In their interviews with applicants, for instance, these case workers are not concerned with seeking evidence of difficulties in family relationships or judging whether daytime care of the child away from home would prove beneficial. Instead, they are, on one hand, determining whether the child is eligible for day nursery care and, on the other, trying to give the applicant some idea of what is involved in using the nursery as means of solving his difficulty in providing care for his child. The admission procedure and the nursery's requirements (vaccination, daily physical examination, fee scale, and so on) are explained. These facts, which might be stated in a routine manner by an admission clerk, the case worker recognizes have different ramifications for each applicant, and the case worker uses them as concrete means of giving the applicant an opportunity to decide whether day nursery care is what he really wants. The applicant's decision will be furthered by a case worker's description of the nursery's activities and by his observation of them. In addition, the case worker tries to give the child a share in deciding whether to join the nursery group. Through these interviews the case worker will be able to sense something of what sort of person the applicant is, why he is seeking the nursery's help, and whether he is likely to be able to make use of what it offers.

If these discussions eventuate in the child's attending the day nursery, the case worker will be available to the parents for discussion of other questions connected with the nursery and the child's and the parent's use of it. For example, the nursery may use unfamiliar methods of disciplining children, may have routines for eating, sleeping, and playing that are different from those the children are accustomed to at home, may impose restrictions on attendance because of minor illnesses, and so on–all of which matters parents may want to discuss, protest, or at least have explained. Mothers may have continuing doubt as to whether to use the nursery or care for their children at home. Ability to pay the fee agreed upon (the amount charged is usually based upon a family's income) may alter from time to time. Discussions about these and other matters connected with the child's or parent's use of the nursery are believed to be best left to a case worker, for they often require careful individualization if the parent is to make his decisions in a way that is most helpful to the child.

An example of this kind of work is provided by the following extract from a case record of a child in a day nursery. It shows show a case worker may help to make even a child's withdrawal from a nursery a constructive experience both for him and for his mother. The worker was able to do this, it will be noted, because she was keenly aware of how this mother and child would be feeling about the situation: the child wanting to remain in the nursery and yet also wanting to please and comfort her mother; the mother wanting to have the child at home and yet fearing the nursery workers would disapprove of her plan.

***Case 16***

Fritzy was placed in the nursery when she was fourteen months old, and she was four and one-half when Mrs. Harmon took her out. Mrs. Harmon always resented the fact that she had to work because her husband could not support her and the children as she wished. Fritzy liked the nursery and was making great progress in the group. At the same time she was deeply concerned about the strain between her parents and was especially sensitive to her mother's moods. Mrs. Harmon had indicated several times that she might try something other than working, but always the security of her wage and her need for a higher living standard and Fritzy's wanting to stay at the nursery carried her decision.

In June, before she took Fritzy out finally, she planned with me for Fritzy to stay at home for the summer vacation with her and the eight-year-old boy. Mrs. Harmon wanted this to be only a partial leaving, wanting to bring fritzy to play with the children every afternoon. She was able, however, to accept a real break for the summer, and Fritzy knew a week before she left that she was to go. In September Mrs. Harmon came back to apply for entering Fritzy again. She asked our help with Fritzy's eating problem but almost immediately took the problem outside to their private doctor. Fritzy was well adjusted in the group again but Mrs. Harmon gave little indication of making much use of the experience.

Mr. Harmon came to the office early one morning to say that Fritzy was staying at home now. The superintendent asked that Mrs. Harmon come in to see me, which she did in the afternoon. Mrs. Harmon had Fritzy with her (this was her first day out) and I don't know when I have seen two more forlorn-looking people. Mrs. Harmon was almost in tears and Fritzy stood beside her patting her arm. Mrs. Harmon told me that she was really sick and that she would have to stop work and stay at home. She went into a long story, telling me exactly what was wrong with her. When she had finished I made no comment. After considerable pause, she burst out, "Of course, that's not exactly what is wrong with me. It's my nerves. The doctor says it is." I said that it seemed to me that she really wanted to stay home and keep Fritzy with her. With much feeling she said yes, she did; she wanted to stay home right now and she wanted to keep Fritzy home right away.

Tears came to her eyes when she said that we had raised Fritzy and she had never had her. It suddenly dawned on her that next winter Fritzy would go to public school and she would never have a chance to stay at home and have Fritzy there all day long. She is willing to live on bread and water so that she can stay home and have her baby there like other women do. I said I thought that his seemed more important than having the clothes she liked and the apartment. I commented on the fact that she dressed herself and Fritzy with a great deal of taste and that she certainly had a flair for decorating her home. This pleased Mrs. Harmon very much. She added that of course she could not have these things unless she worked, but now she knew that she could do without them, at least for a while until Fritzy goes to public school.

I said I thought that perhaps Fritzy would like to come to the nursery this week and have a going-away party at the end of the week. Fritzy was already beginning to feel better, and with this her little face just beamed. She left her mother and climbed up on a big chair in the middle of the room. Swinging her feet she told me in great detail about the going-away party for Angela which was in the early part of the summer and the one for Mary Jane in October. She knew why each child left and what they were going to do at home. Angela was going to help her mother scrub floors and get a new baby to play with. Mary Jane was going to the country to live and have a cat and a dog and chickens. Mrs. Harmon said that she hadn't realized until now what leaving meant to Fritzy. Then she turned and asked Fritzy if she would like to stay in the nursery this week and have a party on Friday. She explained to her that she would bake her a cake and come to the party with her. I asked Fritzy if she would like to stay in the nursery today. She smiled and nodded, and I went to get Miss Olson. When Miss Olson came to the door Fritzy ran to her happily, saying that she was going to stay in the nursery this week and have a party; then she was going to stay home and help her mother.

After Fritzy left, Mrs. Harmon told me that she had had no idea that Fritzy's staying at home meant so much, or for that matter, that leaving the nursery was very important for her. She had only been thinking about herself. She was glad that she came in today. I said I thought, too, that perhaps she would feel better having it this way. She was sure that she would and she was glad that I thought it all right for her to stay home and keep Fritzy at home. She knew that Fritzy learned a lot and liked to come to the Junior Kindergarten.

All week the nursery schoolteacher and the group leader talked with Fritzy about her staying at home with her mother and about the party she was going to have on Friday. She did not take her nap on Friday but stayed up and helped the adults set the tables and decorate. She wore her party dress which the other children called her "going-away" dress. Mrs. Harmon came with the cake. It was decorated in pink and white and had Fritzy's name on it. Mrs. Harmon told me proudly that she had made the inside of the cake pink and white also.

Mrs. Harmon told me how Fritzy had talked all week about leaving; she thought she now really wanted to stay at home with her. Then Mrs. Harmon talked about Fritzy's sudden change in feeling toward Sue Balderson. Until this week she had seemed to hate Sue but now she was planning to give Sue she two birds on her cake. Mrs. Harmon supposed she wanted to "square up" before she left. Leter Fritzy give the birds to Sue with great ceremony and it was hard to tell who was the more pleased, Sue or Fritzy. Fritzy helped her mother cut the cake and Miss Olson helped Fritzy serve all the children. When they had finished eating, the children gave Fritzy a little set of tin dishes to take home with her. The expression on her face indicated that she had reached her peak. She turned to her mother and asked to go home but on second thought decided to let Sue play with the tea set a while. Her mother waited for her and talked with me about how pleased she was with the way the cake turned out and how much she was looking forward to keeping house and having Fritzy with her. I thought that this seemed a happy ending for a long coming to the nursery. Mrs. Harmon was able to express her feeling that she was so glad that it was like this. Once during the afternoon Mrs. Harmon referred briefly to her illness, immediately was much embarrassed and changed the subject. She invited the group leader to bring the children down to see Fritzy's Christmas tree. In the midst of loud and happy goodbyes from the children, Mrs. Harmon and Fritzy left. It was hard to believe that they were the same people who were in my office on Monday.

It will be seen that the case worker's service here consisted in helping the mother to discontinue her use of the nursery's services in such a way that she felt comfortable about doing it and did not need to resort to illness as an excuse. This was obviously of great help to the child, for the little girl had sensed her mother's indecision and unhappiness and was torn between desire to remain in school and desire to comfort her mother by accepting her plan for leaving. In arranging for the child to remain an extra week and plan her going-away party, the case worker not only made it easier for the child to round out her nursery experience and to leave happily but reaffirmed for the mother the nursery's approval for her decision to withdraw the child. In these ways the case worker carried out the general function of social work : to help individuals to use a social institution and thereby to help the institution fulfill its purpose more effectively.

### *Childcaring Institutions*

As in day nurseries, the place of social work in childcaring institutions is a disputed question. It is said that in 1935 there were no social workers on the staffs of half of the childcaring institutions in the United States and that very few of the social workers who did hold such positions were professionally trained. This situation may be partly due to the fact that for years institutions have been somewhat in disrepute as a means of caring for children other than those who are in special need of close supervision, such as certain groups of delinquents or some mentally defective or physically handicapped children. So widespread is the preference for foster homes they many erstwhile childcaring institutions have been converted into "study homes," from which children are placed in boarding homes after a period of observation. In recent years, however, the opinion has been gaining ground that some children are better served by institutions than by foster homes. This is now thought to be particularly true of adolescents, since they are likely to be in a stage of development in which they resent parental restrictions and respond better to congregate care with others of their own age group.

At present childcaring institutions may be classified into three main types. First, there are those old-fashioned ones that operate under conceptions about foster care that were formulated in the last century; it is seldom that they do much deliberate individualizing in their work with children. Second, there are institutions that are an adjunct to a placement program; and third, there are a few institutions that have been organized, or reorganized, in accordance with modern psychological theories and that limit their intake to children who are thought to be in special need of the kind of care they can provide. Whether or not a childcaring institution has social workers on its staff and how it uses their services depend largely upon which of these categories it belongs to.

The administrators of many childcaring institutions consider their duties fulfilled when they have determined that the children who apply for admission meet the eligibility requirements (for instance, that they have no other source of support, or that they are needy orphans of Masons in good standing, or that their fathers were soldiers or sailors or belonged to whatever other specially designated class the institution was established to serve), and when they have provided the children with adequate shelter, food, clothing, and instruction. Other administrators, however, want to know about the previous circumstances under which the children who come into their charge lived and about their general training, habits, and personality–not only to help them decide whether the children are illegible for care but to give them some understanding of the children's behaviour in the institution. Such administrators are likely to employ social workers to gather this information, especially if they think that more than the asking of simple questions is required.

That such investigations can be a part of social work, according to our conception of social work's function and methods, will be clear upon a little consideration. On the one hand, they are an indirect means of helping the individual children to utilize the institution, for the information so secured may be later used to individualize their treatment. On the other hand, such investigations enable the administrators and the rest of the staff to discharge the social function of the institution more effectively. As to methods, when effectively carried out, this social investigation aspect of social work requires that careful individualization and that consideration of the peculiar nature of the difficulties a client encounters in specific social relationships which is a characteristic of the most highly developed forms of social work. As a matter of fact, it will be found that social work in connection with each social institution, including that of the family, started with this service of social investigation, and it was only after some time that its other services developed or were found to be useful.

Once added to the staffs of childcaring institutions, social workers are likely to be also used for what was originally called "aftercare work" (that is, to make arrangements for the children's leaving the institution, for finding them homes, jobs, perhaps recreational resources, and so on), as well as for keeping in touch with the children's families while they are in the institution's care. Here again, as in the case of social investigation, there is great variation in the spirit and the methods with which the work is carried on. It may be of a very routine character, limited to seeing that relatives are informed about a child's health and progress in the institution and that they know when he is returning home, making sure that a job is available and adequate living quarters are provided–all of this without much regard for the individual differences among the people concerned. Aftercare work may, on the other hand, consist of a real attempt to help the relatives with these and other matters, such as the problems they face in having a child away from home or having him return to their care, or in understanding his desires and needs and his reactions toward his experience in the institution and toward themselves. In these and other ways social workers in childcaring institutions may help to facilitate a child's social adjustment away from home and make his transition to life at home and in the community easier and more beneficial.

In some childcaring institutions social workers play an even more prominent role. They may be used as "intake workers," their job in that capacity being not only to form an estimate of the children's needs that the ability of the institution to meet them, but to give the relatives an opportunity to ask questions and decide on the basis of a description of the institution's regulations whether they want to use its services. These workers are likely to interview the children also, both in order to give them share in the decision about leaving home, and in order to prepare them somewhat for life in the institution.

Then, too, social workers may work directly with children while they are in the institution. There they have a twofold service to offer. They are available to the children for discussion of questions regarding their home situations or other aspects of their social relationships outside the institution–both currently, during their stay in the institution, or in regard to future arrangements. They also offer the children an opportunity to talk about the difficulties they encounter in their social relationships in the institution itself. In both of these ways, it will be seen, social workers are clearly carrying out their primary function of helping individuals to make use of a social institution's services, for it is likely that many children can profit more from what the childcaring agency has to offer (education, recreation, some of the benefits of home life) if they can be relieved of worry or confusion about other aspects of their lives.

### *Foster Homes*

The early history of placement in foster homes and the place of social work in connection with it have been described in the preceding chapter. There it was shown that social work in the field developed in response to the discovery that delinquent and near-delinquent children need something more than new homes to overcome their antisocial tendencies. Children's aid societies early found that individual consideration had to be given both to the peculiar character of each child's situation and behaviour and to the choice of a home for him and to his supervision in it. This kind of individualized service was soon recognized as of value to destitute children also, with the result that social work in connection with child placement became firmly established.

It is to be noted, however, that the finding of homes and the placement of children in them are not in themselves social work. This is a service that can be carried on in a mass manner (as witness the wholesale gathering up and transportation of homeless children to the Middle West that characterized the early work of the New York Children's Aid Society) or for profit, as is the case with individuals or organizations that supply babies and children for adoption. In either case the social welfare of the children may be promoted; but social work beings only when to the childplacing facility are added those activities that help the individuals concerned (the parents, the children, the foster parents) to make use of it.

Child placement organizations that are deemed to be social work agencies do not consider it their task to supply lists of available foster home to parents seeking care for their children, nor do they confine their work to effecting contact between people who want homes for their children and those who want to supply homes. Instead, in accepting children for either temporary or long-time placement in foster homes, they themselves assume responsibility for the children's care, sometimes requiring that the relatives' giving over of responsibility be made a matter of court record. That relationship having been established, child placement agencies that are engaged in social work center their attention around fulfilling the consequent obligations to the children and helping them, the parents, and the foster parents with the problems that arise out of this substitute-family situation. The services of such agencies, therefore are confined to people who want to give their children over, temporarily or permanently, into somebody else's care, who want to relinquish certain aspects of their responsibility for them. An important part of social work in connection with child placement accordingly consists of explaining to the adults concerned the conditions under which the given agency accepts children, the responsibilities it assumes and those that are left to the parents or relatives, and of discussing with them whether they want to use the agency's services under those conditions.

### Examples of typical situation in which fosterhome care is sought

Before considering further the activities of social workers in a child placement program, we shall present some examples of the kinds of situations in which people seek this sort of assistance. The cases described are representative of those that came to the attention of an urban children's aid society in about 1930. It will be noted that neither destitution, neglect, nor delinquency was involved in these cases. Destitute children still exist, of course, in spite of the aid-to-dependent-children programs, for there are families that either are ineligible for that sort of assistance or do not want to use it, and there are children who have nobody who can assume responsibility for their care. Destitute and neglected children, however, usually become wards of the state through court action and are placed in foster homes or institutions through its agents. State authorities may, of course, carry on their activities in accordance with social work principles, but some differences in work to be done arise because many wards have no homes to which they can return. As to delinquent children (and those who are considered "problems" by reason of home influence), placement in foster homes is frequently used for them also, but in the cases that involve court action, additional problems for fostercare agencies are involved.

The gamut of problems that bring children to the attention of childplacement agencies is as wide as all of family life. Some idea of their diversity and consequently of the variety of services needed to meet the difficulties is suggested by the following cases. The first is illustrative of that great number in which the presence of the child is believed by the parents to be the cause of their domestic disharmony. Although other reasons, usually financial, are also adduced in such cases, this is the crux of the problem.

### *Case 17*

This case was referred by a friend of the wife with the explanation that the young couple were in financial straits owing to the husband's having to work for a much lower salary than he was accustomed to, and that it seemed best for the wife to work to maintain the standard of living. This would involve boarding the baby, and the wife would appreciate advice as to finding a suitable home.

The wife, a young girl with a good deal of charm of personality as well as prettiness of features, began by saying, "Of course I hate to give my baby up now that he is so cute but I think that if you could place him in a home where he would have good care, it would be the best thing." Then, within a few sentences, she said, "It is the interference of his people that has nearly wrecked things for us. They wanted him to marry a society girl with plenty of money, and they just couldn't see me at all." The care of the baby had been the greatest source of friction. "It is funny afterwards, but it hurts at the time when he says the baby hasn't had a good meal since last June when his mother got it for him." She would feel worse about it if it were not so absurd when the baby weights twenty-five pounds, has had toxin-antitoxin and everything recommended by the baby health station and *they* think he's a fine youngster.

Then followed discussion about the lack of money, the poor apartment, which was the best they could afford, the lack of fresh air for the baby. The social worker asked the mother whether, if money did not enter into it at all, she could be happy at home taking care of the baby. The mother said she would like to do it, but when everything she did was criticized it made her nervous. She thought she would feel better to have some outside contacts. "I'm not ninety years old yet and I do like a good time." She said she and her husband never go out together, although her mother would take care of the baby. He thinks she should have no interest in going out. Then, after more discussion about the boarding home arrangement, she said in reply to the social worker's question about whether her marriage meant much to her that she had hoped that if the baby were having good care her husband would be satisfied and they could patch up their difference.

The next case is the kind in which a child interferes with the parents' other plans, so that they want the child taken care of by outsiders for the time being. Adoption is not desired, nor would financial assistance solve the problem. If it is argued that such people ought to "be made" to take care of their children, the answer is that nobody can force them to do it, that there is no law against people boarding their children, and that these are not cases of neglect in which a court could exercise authority.

***Case 18***

The mother came into the interviewing office stepping daintily, a slight figure with artificially gold hair in short curls around her face, delicately drawn eyebrows of a darker color, straight-looking grey eyes, and an engaging smile. She was becomingly dressed and was wearing a close-fitting toque and short black for jacket with ermine collar.

As she sat down, the mother smiled and said, "I have the sweetest little baby in the world, and I want the best home that can be found for him, just as a temporary plan till I can have him with me. My family do not approve of boarding him at all, but I've thought it all out and I'm sure I'm doing the best thing." The baby was four weeks old, was "healthy and lovely" and she could pay ten dollars a week board for him.

When she was asked why her family objected to her plan she said, "Well, you see, you can't understand how I feel about the profession. I was just getting started on Broadway last May when I got pregnant, and while I would not have missed having the baby for anything, I want to go on with my work. My family just can't understand what it means to me. It gives me something I've always longed for and that satisfies me all through. My folks came from up in the country, and they don't see things my way. . . . My plan is to take the baby in six months, after my husband and I get settled, I get a job on Broadway, and we get a good maid."

The social worker asked how the father felt about the plan. "He agrees with my family," the mother said. "He would like me to give up the stage and can't understand why I can't. He wants to get an apartment right away and a good maid, but he doesn't understand that a baby cries at night some. I couldn't look after a baby nights and work, and neither could he stand to lose sleep. He doesn't realize that so I do, now that I've been home with baby two weeks."

Then there are many families, like the one in Case 19, in which the parents, because of unemployment, low wages, health considerations, and so on, cannot provide the kind of home they think a child needs. They are devoted to their children, willing to contribute financially to their care, but not able in their present economic circumstances to maintain a suitable home.

***Case 19***

Husband and wife came to the agency together. The mother told the first part of the story. "Well, you see, my husband has been out of work a long time and we had a home and lost it, and the boy got sick and I took him to the hospital. They said he had tuberculosis of the glands of the abdomen and sent him to a convalescent hospital, where he's been for six months. So now the baby [it turned out he was twelve years old] is ready to come out, but there is no home to come to. I live where I work [as a telephone operator in a hospital] and *he* lives with his sisters." At this the father broke in to say that the boy looked "wonderful" and that he did not want him to lose it all. At home he would not eat, and "if I didn't give in to him, the Mrs. would." Where he is they have trained him to routine and he's got to keep it. "I want him to be out in the country, about forty miles out, maybe, where there's a good school, because, you see, he will have to make his living by his brain (and he has a good one too) and where he can play outdoors with the boys after school and come in and be in bed by eight o'clock at night."

"What about your situation ?" asked the worker. "I'm living on charity," he replied, with a considerable force of bitterness. "I'm walking the streets. I bunk in at my sisters' where I sleep in the parlor and do most anything to get along, but I'am not saying that it is comfortable. It doesn't matter about me. Only about the boy. I'm registered with the Emergency Unemployment, and I can have work when the boy becomes a charge on me. You see, as long as the hospital out there takes care of him I'm a single man. *I can* go sleep on the Bowery. I have promise of work in the park for three days a week at $ 5.00 a day as soon as the boy comes out."

The father said he was "one of those white-collar workers,

chasing a pen for twenty-two years." He had worked for the same company for many years. The mother got $ 50 a month and maintenance as a telephone operator in a hospital, and there was another son, seventeen, who was just about able to support himself while living with his grandparents.. This boy worried the parents a bit by going out nights, but Samuel, "the baby," was called by his mother "a beautiful soul" and by his father "a boy that everybody likes."

In contrast there are parents who really want to be rid of their children. The reasons are many. It may be because they cannot manage them, because the children interfere with their lives, because for many reasons, clear and obscure, they dislike the children and think they will be much happier without them. Among such cases are some unmarried mothers, such as the one in Case 20.

***Case 20***

The mother, a young Negro girl who seemed very nervous, said she had a child, two months old, that she wanted to "put away" for a year or two so that she could get work and support it. She wanted to get a place in service with living, since she had been laid off at the hat factory. She hesitated, and then said, "My sister would support me as far as that goes, so there is no trouble about that." About her parents she first said they were dead, then told that they lived far away and didn't know about her having a baby without being married. "You see they are very strict and have social position at home and I couldn't have them disgraced."

She had come to New York to live with her sister and go to college and attended evening sessions last winter. Her sister and brother-in-law were not urging her to put the baby out but she had thought it over and decided it was best. Her sister has lived in New York for five years and has friends with whom she should not be disgraced. In a year or two she might marry the baby's father. He is not married and would marry her, but she can't decide to do so. "He passed a remark

I didn't like, and I don't think I care to marry him," she said in explanation. To the social worker she seemed an immature school girl, uncertain of what she wanted or could do, more conscious of her family's fine standing and of the disgrace to them than of anything else.

As a last example Case 21 is cited to stand for that type of case in which a home is broken up by discord or desertion and the parent who is left with the children must find some way of having them cared for while he or she earns money for their support.

***Case 21***

The mother said that she has tried again and again to live with her husband because she cannot manage the support of the children alone, but it is impossible. She is so worn out with the terrific strain of it that she can go on no longer. She started divorce proceedings last May when he was living with another woman and giving her money for the children so spasmodically that she could not count on anything. She took him to court, but he continued to be impossible about payments, and for lack of money she had to drop the divorce proceedings. She finally made complaint that she was receiving no money and he was sent to the county jail for six months. "Did he care anything about that ? Not in the least. He snapped his fingers at them all." . . . Later he came to her and asked her to take him back. The children were glad to see mother and daddy together again and he promised to help her to make a home. But it didn't work. Now they are to separate finally.

The mother worked as a canvasser for a laundry company, earning $ 15 a week. She shared an apartment with another woman, whom she paid $ 10 a month to look after her two boys at lunch time and after school. As to her plans, the mother said she was utterly at the end of her rope, physically and nervously. Many days she has collapsed while getting ready for work. After a long day of walking she finds housekeeping and proper care of the children impossible. In applying to the agency she was asking for some temporary plan until she could "get on her feet." Her hope was that she would get a better job, a cheaper apartment, or that her husband would contribute some money. She kept asking, "Do you think it is right for me to board my children ?" She said she dreaded placing them because "people who take children just want money. They have no interest in the children." When told of the agency's plan of searching for good foster parents and working with them in supervising the children, she said, "Do you mean you find people with love in their hearts for children ?" And she later asked, "Would I have *anything* to say about their care ?"

Five cases can give only a hint as to the variety of situations which make people think it would he better that their children live somewhere else than at home. We have given no examples of those numerous cases in which the child's own conduct and the influence of the home situation on it is the point at issue, nor of those in which the parents are so grossly negligent as to the brought to be attention of legal authorities. Nor have the cases in which there are no parents or suitable relatives been mentioned, nor those in which the children themselves are eager to get away from home. These and many others make-up the clientele of agencies that work in the field of foster care.

## Two schools of thought about child placement work

To return now a description of the activities and objectives of social workers in connection with child placement programs, it will be found that there are two main schools of thought about the matter. The one is in the social work tradition that reached its height in the writings of Mary Richmond. The other bases much of its practice on the psychological principles that have been formulated in more recent years.

The main objective of childcare, according to the first

group, is to provide an environment–physical, psychological, and educational–that will develop the children's potentialities to their fullest capacity so that the children will grow up to be thoroughly self-reliant adults. Such an assumption of responsibility requires that the social agencies have well-trained staffs, excellent equipment, facilities for obtaining all manner of information about the children's lives and potentialities, and complete control over their circumstances.

Agencies working under this philosophy use both institutions and foster homes as means of caring for children. They try to determine very carefully which sort of environment will be best for the individual child and sometimes keep each child for a time in a "study home" in order to learn to know him well before choosing his foster home. On the whole, they are inclined to prefer foster homes to institutions, as coming nearer to duplicating the family life of which the child is deprived, but it has been found that some children, particularly older ones, do better under congregate care.

The similarity of the social work carried on by these agencies and that which characterized the work of most family welfare organization until recently is seen in the mass of informations about the children which is collected: long histories about their parents' past lives, the reasons for the family breakdown, the relatives whose help might be enlisted, their personalities and economic resources, detailed descriptions about all aspects of the children's lives–medical, educational, social, psychological–and the findings of doctors, psychologists, and psychiatrists about their present status and future potentialities. Similar inquiries are made into the personalities and social and economic circumstances of the people who apply for the position of foster parents. When all this information is gathered together, a great effort is made to evaluate the child's needs and to find the foster home that will most precisely meet them. The old slogan, though not nowadays so frequently expressed, still obtains: that there is one best solution for every case and that it is the social worker's responsibility to find it.

Underneath all of this are several assumptions about child nature that seldom come to the surface of the worker's consciousness. One is that children are too young to take any responsible part in the making of plans about their welfare. Another is that they are only temporarily affected by unpleasant events, such as leaving their home, and that they quickly forget in a pleasant atmosphere. A third is that if they do not respond favourably to "good" care, they are to blame, and if things go badly enough, the agency can wash its hands of them. This latter point of view has been somewhat modified by the recent infiltration of psychological concepts, but, by and large, these do little more than give a name–like "maladjusted" or "neurotic" or "psychopathic personality"–to a condition long since recognized. When psychological theory does greatly modify practice, the foster care agency may attempt to "cure" the children of the psychological disorders, either through the case workers' efforts or through adding a psychiatrist to the staff. By this means the agency seeks further to assure that the children will grow up to be self-sufficient adults and takes even more responsibility for that outcome.

All of this is perfectly logical and praiseworthy (as are also the other systems of childcare if their underlying assumptions are judged to be correct) and is so much in line with what most of us believe about the purpose of life that it is at first difficult to see what improvement could be made in it. If, however, one can free himself from thinking in generalities and tries to put himself in the place of the individuals–parents and children–concerned, it will be clear that the work of a foster care agency can be conceived in much different terms.

Those who form the second school of thought among foster care workers hold that the agency is set-up to give and called upon to give help with present, often emergency, situations to people who retain responsibility for managing their own lives. Even when the agency is made the legal custodian of a child, it does not actually take a parent's place. The agency performs certain parental functions–provides shelter, food, clothing, the cost of medical care, and indirectly supervises education and recreation–but not even the foster parents whom the agency secures can take the parent's place in every respect. They cannot make the children their own (the attitude of people in the community toward even adopted children bears witness to the fact that a status is acquired by kinship that cannot be simulated), nor can they usually be depended upon to stand by the children through all vicissitudes. A child deprived of a family for whatever cause lacks certain advantages that cannot be supplied through other sources. A modern foster care agency accepts this fact and the assistance it offers is based upon it. It does not hope to do away with the disability.

When the work of the agency is conceived in these terms, emphasis is not put upon the future and the preparation of the child for it (which would involve planning about and controlling all aspects of a child's life) but upon giving assistance to parents, children, and foster parents with the practical aspects of the present situation and the doubts and perplexities which arise out of it.

Underlying this conception of function (justifying, in a sense, the apparent retreat from the assumption of greater responsibility) is the psychological principle that each individual contains his own dynamic of growth, which others cannot direct but only foster and strengthen. Parents as well as foster care agencies are limited in what they can do for a child, but both biological and social factors make the parent's part in the growth process much the greater. The agency's part, assigned to it by a court or requested by parents or relatives, is to give professional help in a situation in which a blocking of growth is threatened by a child's loss of position in a normal family group. Sometimes this loss can be averted, as when parents, after talking matters over, decide to use other methods of dealing with the difficulties. More often it must be accepted, and the agency's task then is to work with all parties in the situation–parents or relatives, child, and foster parents–in order to help them meet as constructively as possible the problems that continuously arise in regard to the child's changed status.

**Kinds of case work services afforded**

To be somewhat more specific, let us consider some of the kinds of service which these agencies offer to the various parties in the situation. Take first the parents, who under compulsion of law (as when they are adjudged neglectful or their children delinquent) or circumstances (such as those of ill-health, marital discord, poverty, or death) or their own desire come to ask for temporary or permanent care for their children. To parents who are not compelled by law to part with their children, the agency workers fist offer counsel about the matter. Parents come to a child-placing agency angry or afraid or sorrowful or rebellious, but few of them are certain that foster care is what they want. The social worker gives them an opportunity to talk about this in an atmosphere in which they are neither blamed nor pitied, and the idea of possibly parting with a child is regarded as one a reasonable person can entertain. What is involved in such a plan is discussed, and the parent is helped to feel out whether this is something he thinks he wants to do.

The parent is aided in this endeavor by certain realities of the situation. It may be, for instance, that he must agree to go through with the court process of committing the child to the agency's care and arrange with the court about the amount he will contribute toward the child's support. (The court may order payment through state or county funds if the parent is unable to contribute.) He probably has to let the agency select the foster home or institution in which the child is to be placed. He must agree to the agency's decisions as to how often he may visit the child and to what extent he may share in the child's rearing. In brief, the agency offers its services on certain conditions, and the parent in thinking through these conditions–and later in experiencing them in actuality–is enabled to test out whether he really wants to part with his child.

With the child the agency worker usually has more frequent contact, though the parent, too, is often seen frequently. The child, like the parents, is faced with what is almost necessarily an unpleasant situation? Few parents wholeheartedly want to give up their children, and probably even fewer children want to be given over to the care of others. The child, however, usually has less choice than the parents about this situation, nor does he have any more control than they do over what kind of foster home is chosen for him. To be in such a predicament is obviously painful, and the social worker who understands children knows that all she can do directly with the child is to help him find his way of adjusting to it. That even very young children can be helped to understand what is going to happen (and, sometimes, why) is, however, one of the discoveries of those who have worked with them in this way.

In her continuing contact with a child a social worker has many things to discuss with him and to do for him. The agency, typically, supplies his clothing, decides upon his school arrangements, provides medical care, supplies money for "extras" and, in general, shares with the foster parents many parental duties. Authority for moving a child from one foster home to another likewise rests with the agency, but it is held that in order that all these things should contribute to the child's good, he must have a share in deciding about them. Likewise a child's adjustment to a foster home is a continuing process. One distinction between a child's being placed under agency auspices and independently (as when, for instance, his parents find a foster home for him) lies in the fact that the agency affords the child professional assistance with the problem that arise out of that situation. Most children probably could work out an adjustment through their own efforts (those numerous children who were indentured or placed in wage homes by the early children's aid societies generally did so), but the modern foster care agency takes a part in the process and through giving a child a chance to talk about accomplishments and difficulties doubtless facilitates the process and helps to make it more beneficial to many of the children.

With the foster parents also, the agency maintains a continuing relationship. In the first place they are chosen by the agency, usually not for one particular child but as people who seem to be the kind who like children and can be helpful to them. Many practical questions have to be discussed during the selection process, and the social worker has to judge, out of intangible, perhaps even more than tangible, bits of evidence, what kind of person this is who is applying to take children into his home.

If, however, the search for ideal foster parents has been discarded because the agency no longer seeks the perfect environment that will fashion children according to ideal standards, it is not necessary for the social worker to know "all about" the prospective foster parents but only enough to judge whether they seem to have a genuine interest in children and are likely to be able to work with the agency in the care of the children entrusted to them.

Once a child is placed in a home, innumerable questions always arise. For most of these the social worker does not so much supply answers (does not act as a supervisor of a foster parent's activities, as one who is an expert on all aspects of childcare and management) as give information on the practical matters that lie within her knowledge and an opportunity to talk about the puzzling aspects of the others. The social worker has, of course, the continuing responsibility to see that the child's needs are being met as well as possible, but this is accomplished not by telling the foster parents how to carry on their job but by assisting them in doing it in their own way, and removing the child from their home if that way proves unsatisfactory.

Such descriptions give only a hint of what is involved in working with parents, foster parents, and children when temporary or permanent placements must be made. The relinquishing of responsibility for a child's total development, the abandoning of the goal of making him the kind of person the community thinks he ought to be has not meant any lessening of the difficulty of the job of the child placement worker. Instead, this work of "helping a parent and child to separate temporarily of permanently," of "placing an actual child in an actual foster home whose concrete needs and limitations must also be taken into full consideration," and of "sustaining the placement responsibility in relation to the community as a whole" calls for the highest degree of skill and understanding, and conviction and courage.

# II

# SOCIAL WORK IN THE FIELD OF CHILD WELFARE: SCHOOLS AND RECREATION

In the preceding chapter some of the difficulties that children encounter in family life were considered, as well as the kind of help that social work affords in overcoming them. The welfare of children in secured, however, not only by their belonging to families that can meet their needs, physical and psychological, whose help they can put to effective use, and in which they can play their expected roles. The lack of such advantages often creates in children an inability to operate well in other group relationships, but it is not the sole cause of that condition or the one around which social workers' efforts always center. For the full development of their capacities and for the securing of the full advantages of group life, children have to be able to make use of the services that schools and medical facilities offer, and they have to be able to join with others in recreational groups and to be law-abiding citizens. This proposition, can, of course, be stated in the reverse with equal validity. Adequate facilities for education, recreation, and the care of health must be provided for children, and social conditions must be created that promote the likelihood of their being law-abiding. It is not the task of social work, however, to provide these facilities (though the profession has the duty of showing why they are needed) but, in part, to direct children and their relatives to them and, in greater part, to help children to be able to use their services.

Social work, however, may be carried on in connection with these social institutions. In that situation it varies widely in both quality and quantity. Case work in child guidance clinics, for instance, has a highly technical body of theory and practice. In contrast, the problem of adapting the principles of social work to juvenile probation and "training school" work has not yet advanced far, although juvenile courts, a probation system, and institutions for delinquents exist in almost all states. Social work services are provided by only a few school systems, and social work in connection with organized recreation has only begun to be developed. As to social work in connection with the medical aspects of child welfare, not much has been done that distinguishes medical social work with children from that with adults, although medical social workers are being increasingly used in children's clinics. For this reason and other it has seemed best to postpone the description of the medical and psychiatric aspects of child welfare social work until a later chapter, where it will be combined with that of work with adults, and to describe, first, the social work carried on in schools and recreational organizations, and, next, that which is carried on with delinquents and other children who do not conform to social regulations.

### *Case Work in Schools*

Social workers in schools are usually known as visiting teachers, a term that calls to attention the fact that social work in this setting is not an independent enterprise (as is the work of a family welfare agency) but is a part of the educational system and related to its purposes. This is true even if, as in some cities, visiting teacher service is privately financed and administered by its own board of directors. The significance of this observation lies in the fact that, for this reason, visiting teacher work must center around school problems and find its reason for being in the help it can offer to teachers and pupils in that area. The visiting teacher is not a family welfare worker, a child placement agent, or a mental hygienist who maintains an office in a school building because a school is a likely source of clients, nor is he somebody put into the school system to insure that teachers will carry on their work with due regard to their pupils' idiosyncrasies. Rather, he is an integral part of the educational system, with the same sort of responsibility as the school doctor, school nurse, and school psychologist for contributing his skills to the fulfillment of the school's purposes.

This observation is in keeping with our conception of the function of social work. When a family or foster family is the social institution around which social work centers, it necessarily follows that social work is conducted through independent organizations. When the social institution is a relief agency, social workers, if employed at all, themselves dispense the institution's prime service, so that the distinction between social work and the relief agency's own function is seldom noted. When social work is carried on in a day nursery or a childcaring institution, the distinction becomes more apparent, for washing and dressing children, preparing food for them, supervising their education and play are obviously not social work tasks. Nevertheless, since day nurseries and childcaring institutions serve largely the children of the poor, the distinction between these institutions' own activities and those that social workers carry on in connection with them is often disregarded. It is otherwise when social work in schools, courts, and hospitals is under consideration. Here all can see clearly that the social work services are distinct from those of the social institutions in question. What is usually overlooked, however, is the exact nature of their interrelationship.

There are two aspects to that question, themselves interrelated: the services that social workers render to teachers and other school authorities, and those that they render to pupils. The help that teachers seek from social workers is not that of general rehabilitation of those in their charge. They do not say, even by implication, as they might to a psychiatrist or other physician, "Take this child away and fix him up and when he is cured return him to me." Instead, they bring a child to a social worker's attention because they want help in understanding his behavior in school and in planning what they can do about it.

Pupils and their parents, insofar as they are vocal about the matter at all, are likely to agree with this conception of the visiting teacher's task. It seems proper to them that somebody connected with a school should attempt to give help with problems that arise in school. They may, of course, not always want this help, may not agree that a problem exists or that they are the ones to take action in regard to it; but insofar as they are interested in using the social worker's services, the basis for the interest is their concern about difficulties encountered in the school situation.

In consequence of this common-sense recognition of social work's function, the social worker can give help effectively only within the institutional setting; otherwise he is apt to be led astray by the multifarious aspects of each case and to be rejected by both teachers and pupils for overstepping his proper limits. The implications of this statement may become clearer later. We must review first why social work in schools was originally thought necessary and what specific kind of services social workers are called upon to render.

## Objectives of various visiting teacher programs

A diversity of opinion about the chief purpose of visiting teacher work has characterized the movement from the beginning. About 1905 a visiting teacher type of service was independently proposed in several cities. In New York and Boston, settlement houses and private organizations interested in public education were the first to make this suggestion, and they jointly provided social workers for several schools. The chief objective of the New York plan was to bring the educational needs of slum children to the schools' attention, while in Boston the need for promoting better understanding between home and school was stressed. In Hartford, Connecticut, the purpose was very different, the first visiting teacher there being engaged by the school authorities themselves to secure social data and carry on social treatment for the Psychological Clinic, a part of the school system. A fourth aim of visiting teacher work is seen in the statement of purpose made by the Rochester, New York, public school authorities when they initiated this service in 1913 :

> It is an undisputed fact that in the environment of the child outside of school are to be found forces which will oftentimes thwart the school in its endeavors. While this has long been recognized, yet the effort to remedy such counteracting conditions, as far as possible, has not come to be regarded as an established function of the public school. The appointment of a visiting teacher is an attempt on the part of the school to meet its responsibility for the whole welfare of the child. There are few of the children in our schools who are suffering through the wilful neglect and abuse of parents. Whatever suffering comes for which the home is responsible, comes largely through ignorance and necessity. It will be the function of the visiting teacher to enlighten and aid in relieving. . . . Her aim will be to secure maximum cooperation between the home and the school.

Without going into detail about the historical development of visiting teacher policies and methods, it is to be noted that although these purposes became more or less fused in some of the later programs, there are still rather divergent conceptions as to the main objectives of visiting teacher work. In some schools visiting teachers have been assigned the duties that usually belong to attendance officers; that is, the enforcement of school attendance laws. In others they handle placements in special classes for the mentally retarded children and those who have physical handicaps. The distinction between child guidance work (which is primarily psychiatric) and that of the visiting teacher is sometimes not clearly drawn, so that–as originally in the Hartford Psychological Clinic–the visiting teachers perform the same function as case workers in a child guidance clinic.

Again, visiting teachers may be used in what is called a general welfare capacity, which is usually taken to mean that it is their task to secure financial assistance and to exercise a protective kind of supervision over the pupils who are most handicapped by poverty and bad home conditions and thus to further the cause of delinquency prevention. Or their task may be chiefly that of collecting evidence, in the form of case studies, on which planning for improvements in school and community conditions may be based. At the other extreme, there is a conception of visiting teacher work that makes it the counterpart of psychotherapy, applicable in cases in which children's psychological maladjustment is not deemed severe enough to warrant psychiatric treatment.

Since there is such a variety of conceptions about the purpose of visiting teacher work and since the number of schools that employ visiting teachers is rather small (about 150 in 1939) it is difficult to generalize about current practices in the field. We may, however, arrive at an understanding of what appears to be the most recent trend, the one that seems to be increasingly winning the support of trained visiting teachers, if we note some of the difficulties encountered by plans that have earlier been tried.

Let us take first the often-stated objective of preventing the development of psychological disorders by the instalment of visiting teacher services in the lower school grades. Proponents of this point of view hold that many incipient disorders can be recognized and checked by early treatment, and that schools offer the most favorable opportunity for finding the cases and instituting remedial measures. Both theory and experience throw doubt on the soundness of this proposal. After years of research psychiatrists are fairly well agreed that the prediction of later mental disorders on the basis of childhood behaviour is usually impossible. In addition they maintain that little of benefit to children is to be anticipated from telling teachers and parents that certain types of behavior (excessive shyness, for instance, or reticence in social contact, or tempestuous mood fluctuations) portend future mental disease, for such an expectation on the part of the lay public is itself likely to handicap a child who is having trouble in adjusting to social situations.

This is not to say that children who display these sorts of behavior do not need special help. They need it, however, because of their present handicaps and discomfort, not because of what may happen to them in the future. In addition, to give fundamental help to children with problems of this nature usually requires the interest and co-operation of their parents; and it has been found that many parents, even when they desire such assistance, do not want it given under a school's auspices. Parents recognize that schools have one function and psychiatrists or psychologists another, and they are likely to think a school is overstepping its rightful limits when it proposes to institute treatment measures in regard to their children's personality difficulties.

With respect to the objective of preventing delinquency, some of the same arguments obtain. At one time visiting teacher work was looked upon as one of the chief hopes of delinquency prevention, for research had shown that many delinquents began their careers as truants from school. Later investigations have revealed, however, that the causes of delinquency vary widely from case to case and that, though many potential delinquents might be recognised in school, schools have no way of exercising control over most of the factors that are associated with delinquency. It is now held that schools can be of greatest help in delinquency prevention by carrying on their own traditional duties in ways that take into account individual children's needs. Curricula and activities that arouse and hold children's interest, teaching methods that take into account their individual ways of responding and developing–these are among the schools' chief contributions to be made toward delinquency prevention.

These, however, are services that school authorities want to render to all children, not only to those who are likely to become delinquent or psychologically maladjusted. They seek the help of visiting teachers when individual children do not seem to be able to make use of the opportunities offered. Insofar as children turn to delinquency because of inability to find satisfaction in school (an inability which may itself be due to factors outside as well as inside the schoolroom), the help which a visiting teacher may render in this area may lead to delinquency prevention. As an immediate objective of visiting teacher work, however, the prevention of delinquency seems untenable, for it directs attention away from the school's main problems and confuses both teachers and pupils as to the visiting teacher's main function. As a writer on the subject has recently pointed out, "One of the first things a case worker must be responsible for, in meeting new children or parents, is explaining clearly why she is in the school, in order that they may be free to ask her for help if they can use it." That children and parents would find it hard to come for help to a person who was known as one who dealt chiefly with had children and those who are "nuts' is too obvious to need elaboration. It is fear that this is the case worker's function which already seriously handicaps visiting teacher work.

Another conception of visiting teacher service is that which would make it a means through which the environmental difficulties under which children live–especially those of poverty and parental neglect–are relieved. This conception of the work takes two forms. It may mean that the visiting teacher shall spend his time searching for the environmental causes of individual pupils' failure to progress well in school or to conduct themselves well there, and, having found the causes, set about trying to alter the conditions. Or it may mean that through his study of individual cases the visiting teacher shall compile material that can be used for promoting reform of both school policies and community conditions.

The objections to the first plan are similar to those that

have been urged against "paternalistic" or "authoritative" case work in general. Actual practice has shown that people–both adults and children–are not likely to benefit greatly from plans that are made for them by others, especially when they have not even requested help. It is one thing to find out why a child does not do well in school, but it is a very different matter–as case workers have frequently found to their dismay–to try, for instance, to "make" parents ambitious for their children's school success, induce them to treat their children fairly and give them the affection they seek, find a job for an alcoholic father and see that he keeps it, get a child to give up playing on the streets late at night and join the Boy Scouts instead.

Not only are such changes difficult to achieve, but they are unlikely to accomplish their purpose unless they spring from decisions on the part of the individuals involved. Besides, parents may rightly question why a person representing a school should try to change their lives and their ways of dealing with their children. It is unlikely that they attribute their children's school misconduct or failure to mismanagement of their home affairs, and so they are not likely to take kindly to what they regard as interference. For these and other reasons, the use of the visiting teacher as an agent of family reform is not apt to meet with much success. In addition, the whole plan of setting up what appears to be a general welfare agency under school auspices is likely to be regarded by school authorities and the taxpaying public as outside the true function of the school and only remotely justified as an expenditure of either time or money.

As to using a visiting teacher service primarily for collecting material on which proposals for the reform of school or community conditions may be based, it would seem that this is overstressing the research and community planning aspects of social work. As by-products, such information is certainly useful, an school systems and communities have profited from it. But one would question whether a case worker can contribute really useful material for these purposes except through the practice of sound case work, for his peculiar contribution lies in the understanding of individual needs that he secures through that practice, and it would seem to be rather a perversion of his skills to make of chief importance the research rather than the service aspect of his work.

## Current methods and illustrative cases

Instead of trying to carry out these various aims, visiting teachers are coming more and more to define their work in terms of offering help to children, parents, and teachers with respect to the problems individual children encounter in adjusting to school or in making use of their school opportunities. The following situations are typical of those that are brought to a visiting teacher's attention by school personnel, who use most frequently the visiting teacher's help:

Bobby, in the kindergarten, loses his breakfast practically every morning. Is this a nutrition or a personality problem ? Will you see his mother ?

Frances refuses to talk. She is intelligent, always prepared, but will not say a word all day.

John, repeating second grade, can read only a few words. He is pretty good in everything else.

Susan has been getting to school from five to ten minutes late every day for the past two weeks. Her reasons are confused and incoherent. Will you see what you can do ?

Tom is restless, defiant, and failing in his work. I know the home situation is bad but really can't tolerate his behaviour any longer.

The assistance that a visiting teacher is able to offer in cases like these, says the writer who described them, always involves "an approach from three different angles. She must consider not only the child, who is the object of her major concern, but she must know what both teacher and parent can contribute in meeting their common problem of helping him. . . . Sometimes she decides on only very casual contact with the child and concentrates on interviews with the parent. In such a case her relation to the teacher is one of interpretation, and support in planning class room changes, and keeping in touch with their effect upon the child. Sometimes she and the teacher are able to work it out together with little contact with the home. And in still other cases she works directly through interviews with the child. Her start, however, is always related directly to the difficulty as the teacher sees it–the evidence that something is interfering with the child's constructive use of the school experience."

The following case illustrates how much may sometimes be accomplished through one interview with a parent, in which he is given an opportunity to state the problem as he sees it, to make his own suggestion as to what the school might do about it, and to see how genuinely interested the school is in the child's progress. In this case the teacher's initiative in thinking up ways to handle the child was stimulated by the description the social worker gave her of the interview with the father, and it was not necessary for the social worker to work directly with the child.

*Case 22*

Michael was a six-year-old boy in the first grade, of superior intelligence and with outstanding ability in reading. In spite of this, the teacher was troubled by his behvior in the classroom, which he constantly upset by his demands for attention and approval, and by the concern of his parents over the fact that he lost his breakfast every morning before coming to school. When the father came for conference, it was with a real feeling of defensiveness for Michael, and a good deal of emphasis upon the boy's superiority to other children. He pictured him as a child who had learned to read without teaching. He spoke with pride of how at the age of six he reads the newspapers and understands and talks freely about the international situation. Gradually as they talked Mr. G began to see that possibly all this was a little too much of a burden to Michael, and that it might be that he had a real need to be protected from too much knowledge, and to be encouraged in more childlike activities. But he suggested too that possibly the boy was bored by first grade and asked if he might not be allowed to skip a grade. The worker reminded him of the value of first grade as the time when children not only get their fundamentals of schoolwork and learn to get along with other children, but find a real support in the routines of school life, once they have fitted into and accepted them. This was particularly important in Michael's case, since he had not had the advantage of kindergarten experience.

Mr. G brought up the matter of Michael's vomiting. The worker recognized with him the depth of his concern, but spoke too of the number of children who use this way of expressing their fear or rejection of school at the beginning and of how much satisfaction they often get from the amount of attention and concern this creates.

There was plenty of problem in this father's relation to the boy and to the mother, as was indicated again and again as he talked. The worker was well aware of this, and of its significance, but she had learned that by confining her activity to that part of the total problem which related to school, where she had a logical and acceptable function, the other troubles might very probably clear up of themselves. Her conviction was strong that if Mr. G could understand and accept the validity of school procedures and the genuineness of her interest and that of the teacher in Michael, the boy could be freed from the pressure of his father's need to live in *him* so that he would have a chance to start growing for *himself*.

In this case, her hope was justified. The teacher, encouraged by the report of the interview, was able to take back the problem and work out a really constructive approach to its solution. She worked with Michael on his handwriting, which he himself had recognized as his weak spot, thus helping him indirectly to admit himself as really one of the group, where all need help in one thing or another. Six weeks later she reported "excellent adjustment to school. Nothing further heard of vomiting." And at the end of her term, on her own initiative, she recommended double promotion, feeling that he was now socially as well as scholastically ready to work with a more advanced group.

A case at the opposite extreme–in that neither parents nor teacher had much interest in the child, and in that the child himself probably needed psychiatric treatment–is briefly described in the following illustration of a visiting teacher's work.

### *Case 23*

Albert was a seven-year-old boy of good ability, in the second grade. He irritated the teacher by his indifferent, don't-care attitude, his daydreaming and masturbation, his poor posture, and careless, untidy homework. An interview with him in the counselor's office centered around a normal small boy's interests but revealed the fact that he felt that his parents didn't care much about him and were devoted to his little brother. This was corroborated in a long interview later with his mother, who frankly–even insistently–admitted that she and her husband had never liked Albert. . . . He got even with her by a kind of passive refusal to show signs of being upset by her treatment, and by just not doing the things she wanted him to do–like washing his face, and doing his homework neatly. A suggestion of the possibility of child guidance clinic treatment brought a reiteration of her statement that she knew it was her fault–and an anxious question as to whether the clinic would try to change her, indicating clearly that she had no wish to be changed. At one point in a later interview she said that she would like to have Albert placed in a foster home, but her husband would not listen to it, though he was absolutely indifferent to the boy and never responded to him in any way.

The case worker sensed that the mother might have some latent affection and interest in the boy and so she continued to visit her from time to time, but she recognized that she could offer no really constructive help until the mother put up less defense against accepting it.

The teacher, too, was not a person who could be a very strong source of assistance to the boy. To sustain her in her day-to-day work with Albert the case worker gave her a chance to "blow off stream" whenever the boy's conduct outraged her, thus leaving her each time with enough sympathy and understanding for Albert to carry her on for a time.

The case worker's chief efforts were concentrated on Albert himself. With him she did not attempt to carry on the psychiatric sort of treatment which she thought he needed and which a child guidance clinic would have provided if his parents had been willing to accept it for him. She did, however, see him frequently, identify herself with and support his efforts to improve in school work, and let him get a degree of satisfaction from his friendly relationship with her, directed as it was by appreciation of his objective interests and achievements.

The case worker recognized that the support which she was able to give Albert and the teacher might help the boy but that it could not make-up to him for what he had all his life missed. He would have to learn to live and grow without that if he must, but he would need help in the endeavor. It was the case worker's belief that by consciously using the experiences. Albert was having in one area of his life–the school–as the basis for their relationship to each other, she might be able to give him a justified faith in his ability to handle that part of his life and so make the pain of his family relationships a source of developing strength rather than of frustration and conflict.

Two brief cases are not sufficient to illustrate the variety of problems that are brought to a visiting teacher's attention or to show the exact methods he uses in carrying on his work. Our aim, however, is not to describe the technical aspects of social work but to make clear why it is needed and what function it serves. In spite of the diversity of present-day conceptions and practices in visiting teacher work, there appears to be general agreement that its primary concern is the child's effective utilization of the school's facilities. In this relationship to a primary social institution the social work character of the visiting teacher's activities is made clear, and the validity of our definition of social work itself is reinforced.

### *Some Current Concepts about Social Group Work*

Before describing current trends in social work in connection with recreational programs, we must consider, in more detail than in Chapter V, some of the questions that are involved in drawing a line between recreation and informal education, on the one hand, and social work, on the other. The popular conception that the provision of recreational facilities (playgrounds, baseball equipment and leadership, club quarters) is social work if the participants' economic need is sufficiently great would seem to be already definitely disproved–without in the least implying that such facilities are not needed or do not accomplish very important social purposes. The distinction between certain aspects of informal education and social group work is less clear, partly because of the fact that social group work itself has not yet been very clearly defined. Before describing the part that social work may play in connection with the recreational and informal educational aspects of child welfare activities, it seems necessary, therefore, to elaborate somewhat further upon present concepts about group work.

In traditional social work parlance, group work is classified as one of the fields of social work, and most social work organizations are classified as either case work or group work agencies. Authorities on the subject of group work are now maintaining, however, that their activities constitute a process or a method and cannot be appropriately described in terms of agencies or a field. They point out, on the one hand, that group work is only one of the activities engaged in by even leisure-time agencies and that, on the other hand, the group work method can be used wherever the purpose of the organization is to develop personality and evolve character.

Current group work theory puts much stress on the need of individuals for group association in order to further their personality development and the utilization of their latent capacities. This, it will be noted, is the psychological aspect of the need for social organization in general. Such association is provided in all cultures through organization along family, educational, and recreational lines, and in various forms of spontaneously organized clubs, as well as through numerous unorganized activities. Many modern conditions, especially in urban industrial communities, militate against the securing of adequate or psychologically beneficial association along recreational lines. Similarly schools, under conditions of crowding and impersonality, tend to lose much of the psychological value that the "little red schoolhouse," for all its shortcomings, had for teacher and pupils. Neighborhood, too, has lost much of its meaning, and even the family frequently does not provide the amount and variety of human association that it once did. It was these among other conditions that led in the middle of the nine-teenth century to the formation of the Y's, the Boys' Clubs, and settlement houses, and, later, playgrounds, community centers, and numerous youth organizations, and to reforms in educational and recreational methods.

Group work does more, however, than merely provide opportunities for people to secure association with others outside their family and work relationships. Its emphasis is upon supervised activities and upon professional leadership to the end that the group experience shall be adapted to the peculiar needs of the individual group members. In this it is distinguished from mass measures, such as community festivities or formalized education, that are directed toward interests which large groups have in common. Methods currently advocated for use by group workers stress both psychological understanding of individual members' needs and democratic procedures. Emphasis is put, for instance, upon the need of individuals for acceptance and approval by the leader and the other group members, for opportunities for creative self-expression, for mutual planning as opposed to programs dictated by the leader, for the development of the ability to work co-operatively toward ends democratically agreed upon.

It will be readily seen that group work so conceived has much in common with progressive education. In fact, as a process or method it is a characteristic feature of modern educational work. Similarly, its appropriateness to many recreational activities is clear. This has been recognized professionally by the formation of the National Educational-Recreational Council and by the fact that the recently constituted National Association for the Study of Group Work holds sessions with the Progressive Education Association as well as with the National Conference of Social Work.

Instead of the term "group work" it has been suggested that the term "informal education" be applied to those many activities of leisure-time or "character-building" organizations, such as the Scouts, Y's, and community centers, that are carried on not only for the immediate pleasure of the participants but for the values of be derived from group association. Such activities are usually carried on through clubs, while in classes instruction of a more formal kind is generally offered. Progressive or group work methods may, however, be used in classes as well. They are believed to be particularly suitable for groups composed of children or adults that are organized to discuss social and economic questions and those designed to further the education of parents in matters pertaining to child rearing and parent-child relationships. Leaders of the former kinds of groups often regard their purpose as one of contributing to the skills and understanding essential for responsible participation in democratic society (the group itself being a democratic society in miniature), while the latter expect improved family relationships to follow from the emotionally satisfying experiences that a skillfully directed group situation supplies.

It will be seen, then, that the group work process aims to contribute both to the personality development and to the social adjustment of the group members. One writer sees in it a means of "resolving personal strain through satisfying activities and security of relationships"; another says it gives children "zestful play and a sense of security and belonging with their fellows"; a third calls it "practice in and preparation for democratic living." These are among the aims of progressive education and recreation. If they are shared by social work, it is at least clear that they are not peculiar to it or sufficiently characteristic of it to justify including in the social work category all activities that have such objectives.

Closer study shows that the group work process is used in four different fields: education, recreation, psychotherapy, and social work. With regard to the first two uses, probably enough has already been said to make clear what we mean. The third use–to aid in psychological treatment–is seen in various procedures devised by psychotherapists to treat patients in groups rather than individually. As to the use of group work methods to carry out the social work function, we have already given an illustration in connection with family welfare work and noted that settlement house and other organizations endeavor to give help with difficulties of neighborhood and nationality origin through the formation of discussion groups.

Social group work may also be carried on in institutions for delinquent or emotionally maladjusted children. The ideal of most of these institutions is to provide for the children in their day-to-day living the nearest approximation to satisfying family life, and to that end a "cottage plan" is set up and an attempt made to secure "cottage parents" who will provide the affection and discipline which so many of the children are found to have missed. The activities of these cottage parents would not be a part of social work as we are defining it. A few institutional directors, however, attempt to use the cottage situation in a more controlled manner, putting in charge of the cottages people who can utilize the little events of daily life and the influence of the cottage group for specific treatment of individual children's social difficulties. Much the same kind of work is carried on in a few summer camps for "problem" children. In its use of leader (counselor, or cottage parent, or whatever name he goes under) and group it would seem that the process here attempted has much in common with social group work under less continuous circumstances.

Social group work is also used to prepare individuals for participation in the activities of normally constituted groups, and so has a particularly important part to play in furthering the work of recreational or leisure-time organizations. Group work of this social treatment type is still in an early stage of development, and its theory and methods are the subject of much dispute. An illustration of this type of group work will be given below (Case 25). Here we would emphasize that in our opinion *social* group work is neither an educational nor a recreational process, but one of the means of furthering the social work function.

### Social Work in the Field of Recreation

With the distinction between social group work and certain aspects of recreational activities thus drawn, we are in a position to consider, in more detail than the analysis in Chapter V permitted, the peculiar nature of the social work activities that are carried on in connection with recreational enterprises. Both case work and group work methods are used, the aim of both being to promote children's welfare by helping them to utilize the organized recreational facilities that are provided for that purpose.

**Social case work**

The place and function of social case work in connection with recreational activities can be stated fairly easily, in spite of the fact that no very specialized body of practice has yet been developed. The oldest form of service in this field is that afforded in numerous kinds of social agencies when clients are helped to make contact with recreational organizations and given an opportunity to talk about the problems that arise in that connection. Family welfare and child placement agencies, for instance, often secure information about clubs and camps for their clients, help to choose the ones that are likely to meet their clients' needs, and discuss with the clients and the recreational workers some of the questions involved. Child guidance and mental hygiene clinics may provide a similar service for their patients as their needs and desires indicate. This putting of clients in touch with suitable recreational resources is, however, no different from the help in using other resources of the community which social workers commonly offer to their clients as the occasion demands. In addition, close attention to the difficulties that clients encounter in their use of these recreational services is not usually given unless the difficulties are definitely related to the problems about which agency and client are working–as, for instance, in that type of child guidance work in which finding suitable recreational opportunities and helping children to use them is considered one of the important methods of indirect therapy. It is only in a rather remote sense, therefore, that these services can be considered case work in the field of recreation.

Another common form of service is that of helping recreational organizations to select some or all of their clientele and to carry on their work with them. A family welfare organization or a sattlement house may, for instance, operate its own summer camp, and the job of choosing which children shall attend may be given over to staff case workers. Again, camps or clubs or other organizations offering recreational facilities may receive some of their members through social agencies and carry on their work in co-operation with the agencies. In either case the social workers supply the recreational workers with information about the children and maintain contact between the children and their families during the period of absence from home. Work of this nature assumes particular importance when the providing of recreational opportunities is part of a plan for the children's adjustment to family or community life.

The use of case workers in the field of recreation has much in common with early developments in schools, hospitals, and relief agencies, where social work was first regarded chiefly as an aid to the professional workers in the other field (to teachers, doctors, and administrators) and only indirectly as an aid to the individual pupils or patients themselves. In contrast to this use of case workers, some recreational organizations and others that provide recreational facilities along with other services (camps, settlement houses, childcaring institutions, for example) are beginning to employ case workers to help individual children with the difficulties they encounter in using recreational opportunities. This may involve closely co-ordinated activities on the part of recreational group workers and case workers; or the case workers may carry on their work rather independently, only giving the group workers information about their findings and consulting with them about the effects of the case work, in much the manner in which a visiting teacher sometimes operates.

An example of joint work is seen in the following episode from a case in which a case worker and a recreational worker on the staff of a settlement house participated.

***Case 24***

Frances was irregular in her attendance at the settlement, explaining that she had to help her mother with housework. When she did come, she did not seem to enjoy herself wholeheartedly. There were evidences of rivalry with a younger sister who was as blithe and carefree as Frances was worrisome and tense. Frances upset rehearsals for an evening play by her indecision as to whether she would take part, and finally provoked an open quarrel in which she was severely criticized by the other children. In talking with the case worker, she said she could not come because she must help her mother. When asked for other reasons, it developed that she was afraid to be out at night when boys were on the street since people would think that was not nice. Later, when she definitely refused to be in the play, we heard from another child that she thought it was because Frances was just no good with the men.

There were other evidences of conflict in Frances' feeling about boys in the panic in which she ran from a room which they were passing, in her withdrawal from a game watched by a boy, and her later comment when he left that she left "queer."

On the assumption that Frances might be helped by some casual association with boys, plans were discussed for a picnic hike with the possibility suggested of asking two or three boys. In talking with Frances alone after she strongly disapproved this plan, the case worker found her fearful. She refused to sit down and, instead, forcibly punctuated her complaints by banging down chairs which she insisted upon putting away. "I hate boys," she said, and then added, "I didn't mean to say that."

The case worker replied that she could say so, as she seemed to be feeling that way about them just then. When Frances said she couldn't explain how she felt, the case worker replied that girls often had feelings about boys which they did not understand and asked if she knew any nice boys. Her expression softened, and she said she had two brothers and a cousin who were nice. She was uncomfortable the and left hurriedly. The group worker noticed her smiling as she went out. At the next meeting two boys broke in again, and it was interesting to watch Frances first smile at them, and then tell them to leave.

Both workers abandoned the idea of having boys at the picnic since Frances could not accept them at that time, and because mixed groups might be disapproved by her mother. Instead, one of the men students, Mr. B., was asked to come; this was approved by the girls. Frances came, too, although she had declared she wouldn't. On the way, she asked a question of the case worker, who suggested that she call to Mr. B. She did so, and later allowed him to help her across a stream. When he asked for help in gathering branches, she looked up eagerly although she could not ask to go as the other girls did. He included her as if at random, and later reported that Frances always maneuvered so that he would not walk behind her. When songs were begun by Mr. B., Frances sat turned away from him, looked self-conscious and giggled at a popular love song, gradually turned around, and then joined in the singing. Toward the end, she asked him for a song she liked. On the way home, the other girls walking with Mr. B. were joking and laughing, and Frances was noticed struggling with a smile before she made a disapproving remark about them. The case worker suggested that she walk with them, which she started to do, but passed them to join another group ahead. She came back, however, at Mr. B.'s invitation. Several days after the picnic she told the group worker that she had had the best time she had ever had.

In this case both case worker and recreational worker carried out the social work function of helping the child to deal with the problem she encountered in participating in group activities. The group itself was not organized for remedial purposes nor was the carrying on of social work the predominant occupational task of the recreational worker. Nevertheless, the recreational worker had tried to help the child to participate in the group before she called upon the case worker for assistance.

This observation brings to light an interesting point that has not previously been discussed : that social institutions may have social work aspects just as they may have educational or economic aspects without being primarily set up for social work purposes. For instance, teachers in a social or doctors in a hospital give a certain amount of help to their pupils or patients in overcoming the psychological or material difficulties that stand in the way of their getting the most out of the school's or hospital's primary services, and in so doing might be considered to be carrying out a social work function. Similarly, a recreational worker is not concerned only with providing leadership and guidance to the group as a whole but gives a certain amount of attention to helping individual group members fit into the group and profit from what the group activities as a whole have to offer. In fact, this kind of assistance is a part of each profession's duties to its clients. It is only when such assistance entails too great an expenditure of energy or requires knowledge and skill that lie outside the professional person's competence that the assistance of a social worker is sought.

This point is one of particular importance in recreational group work, for recreational, educational, and social work aspects are often closely intertwined. Groups are often organized in settlement houses and community centers, for instance, in order to meet the recreational needs of children in the neighborhood, to teach the children certain skills and modes of democratic bebavior, and to help them to accommodate themselves to the wishes of others and to Act in a way that facilitates their getting the most out of group experience. In spite of this plurality of purposes, the provision of such recreational facilities would not be considered social work according to our criteria, for its primary function is not that of helping the individual group members deal with the peculiar difficulties that stand in the way of their using the services of some other social institution.

### Social group work

The social work function is served, we have seen above, when social case workers help individual children with the problems they encounter in recreational activities. Attempts in the same direction have recently been made by social–as distinguished from recreational or educational–group workers. Their plan is to organize groups specially designed to meet the needs of children who cannot get along in the usual club or recreational activities. In such groups the activities are adapted to the individual children's interests and psychological characteristics. Children who cannot endure the strain of normal competition, for instance, who react to competitive situations either by excessive fighting or timidity may be protected from such experiences; or all the aggressive children may be grouped together and left to fight it out until they develop their own *modus operandi*. In either case much attention is paid by the group leader to building up an emotionally secure relationship with the children, to developing their sense of self-worth, and to giving their native creative capacities an outlet. As the children's ability to participate in group activities increases, situations more nearly approaching those of the usual recreational groups are provided, and the children are thus gradually helped to achieve normal group relationships.

The literature on this subject is scanty and not much case material is available. The following case, however, gives some indication of the method of carrying on social group work aimed at helping individual children with the problems they meet in the usual recreational groups.

#### *Case 25*

Ed is twelve years of age, average in size, usually neat in

appearance, and in the proper grade at school. His mood changes rapidly from one of quietness to a display of temper that often is quite vicious. His home life is made uncertain by an unemployed drinking father who sometimes beats members of the family when he is under the influence of liquor. The mother struggles under these handicaps to raise a family of five children on relief standards. Almost, it would seem, to offset this insecurity at home, Ed strives to gain security in his group relationships by attempting to dominate, causing many discipline problems from that drive. As a result, he is not a very popular member, has few close friends, and is more tolerated than accepted by the groups. A study of his reactions in three different groups sheds light on some of the factors involved in the adjustment of such an individual.

The first was a shop group, where the organization permitted Ed to be rather free as an individual without the demands of too complete group adjustment. As a result, his attempts to dominate were at a minimum, as he was interested in his own work, and if the tools he wanted were available he was not too disrupting. Although he did not hesitate to seize any tool he wanted, regardless of who had it, when these incidents were handled he had to take others into consideration, and a beginning was made in his adjustment experiences. His interest span varied with the activity, and when interest lagged he often amused himself by disturbing others; but for the most part he centered in his own work. The activity of this group met his interests and needs, and when he felt so inclined he more or less ignored the rest.

In the second experience a group of boys organized a cowboy club in preparation for a special event sponsored by the group agency. More unity was necessary here, and Ed found that more concession to the group was essential. He took much initiative in the formation of the group, and because of his interests, past experience, and personality, he assumed the role of captain. The members did not object, as he really did feel much responsibility for the group, but that role carried additional problems for him. Two boys about his own age were individualists in their own right and had minds of their own so were not in the mood to take very many others from Ed. He met this situation by appointing one boy his first lieutenant and the other his second lieutenant, having one of them seated at his right side as he presided over the meetings. If both his lieutenants disagreed with him he allowed himself to be overruled. Dissension in the ranks might mean a break up of the group, and in this instance it was the group itself which was meeting the needs of Ed as an individual. This situation automatically set up an experience that demanded a greater sense of social responsibility than Ed was accustomed to observe, but he had been one of the initiators of the group and had to bow to these self-imposed relationships. Not that there were no struggles, but it was another step in his social education–all within a normal group relationship.

Our third group was presenting a shadow play. Ed could go into the shop group and carry on his own activity whether it was what the others were doing or not, and he had been one of the originators of the cowboy club, but he was entering this group after it had been started and someone else had planned the program. He proceeded immediately to make himself useful to the group on the basis of their interests and plans, assisting in construction work, reading the dialect, and, a general, making himself acceptable to them. This went on for a period of some five weeks before he reverted to his all too frequent behavior. In one evening he turned from an attitude of protection to one cf possession and attempted to dominate the assignment of roles by bringing in two of his friends and overlooking some of the regular members. Being thwarted in this by the group, he flew into a rage, later in the evening, out of all proportion to the provocation and tried in a very vicious manner to kick out two boys who had merely wandered in and asked if they could play a game with them.

The project was a real group experience in that all plans,

selection of play, acceptance of handiwork, and assignment of duties and roles were on a group-decision basis in an informal spontaneous atmosphere. Ed felt a certain security and enjoyment in the group that seemed to be jeopardized by new members or plans he could not introduce or control. He seemed caught between a desire to control absolutely and to follow group planning, and he would give up going home to hear his favourite radio program at one minute and threaten the whole project the next. Group adjustment was a deep struggle for him.

As the time to present the play drew near, personal disputes were more and more placed in the background in favour of the group, Ed agreeing to one of his personal enemies taking a part left open the night before the play was to be given. The first experience was very gratifying to the audience and the players, who immediately embarked upon a second similar adventure. Again the important evening arrived, and for the second time Ed earnestly desired that his mother see the play, but the drunken father could not care for the baby. Hurrying back to the Center only a minute or two before curtain time, his second discouragement was climaxed by a shift in the audience. He had expected to give the play for the mothers' club, but it was raining, and that group was so small that some younger clubs were invited in to enjoy the performance. Ed's "artistic temperament" was keyed for an adult audience; the lights were out, the audience assembled, and the curtain ready to be pulled, when he announced he would not perform for the young group, and to make his decision more effective he hit one of the players because he walked in front of him. Ed was playing one of the lead parts and felt the group could not get along without him. The leader said, "Either get in the play or out of the room," told the stage manager to pull the curtain, and held his breath. Ed picked up is character, sat down behind the screen, and went to work without another word. That experience had real meaning for him. To deliberately stand in front of the group and throw out his challenge, be made to face the responsibility for his decision, and bow to the group within a space of two minutes was a starling experience.

Commenting on the work in this case the writer says, "Here was an individual moving from a rather loosely organized group to one demanding intense cooperation. We see him meeting the demands at one minute and being unable to do so the next; making progress and then slipping; feeling secure and then being challenged; moving out into the group and then withdrawing into himself. Always finding adequate reasons for his own misconduct in someone else's actions, he never faced the responsibility for his deeds, but when the pulling of the curtain left him face to face with his threat, he chose to remain with the group. Each club with its different situations and interplay of personalities added to his education in the give and take of group experience, but without a leader with the ability to turn these incidents into learning situations, either the group would have rejected the child or he would have dominated the group, but opportunity for adjustment would have remained at a minimum."

Such work, in our opinion, is social work rather than either education or recreation, for its aim is to enable the individual to participate in the activities of organized groups, and it achieves that aim by methods that take into account the peculiar nature of the individual's difficulties.

# III

# SOCIAL WORK IN THE FIELD OF CHILD WELFARE: COURTS AND CORRECTIONAL INSTITUTIONS

The analysis in the foregoing chapters has made it clear that the welfare of children is promoted by social work through the help it effords children in making use of certain social institutions. Social work, according to our analysis of its nature, does not duplicate existing institutions or provide substitutes for them (as would be the case were childcaring institutions and educational and recreational programs for the "underprivileged" classified as a part of social work); instead, it facilitates their use by the individuals for whom they were designed. This point is of particular importance when the role of social work with respect to children who are delinquent or likely to become delinquent is under consideration, for it is customary nowadays to regard all activities directed toward such children as being in the field of child welfare and hence, in the opinion of many, a part of social work.

### *The Nature of Social Work with Delinquents*

We have earlier shown why we do not consider all child welfare activities social work. Our position can be summarized by saying that although social work deals with individuals, it deals with them in regard to their relationships to social institutions. The question, then, is what institutional relationship is involved when social work in regard to delinquency is carried on.

It is clearly not satisfactory to group together for separate consideration all social work activities in which delinquents are clients, for there are delinquent children among the clients of family welfare workers; visiting teachers know many of them; child guidance workers recognize them as one particular category of patients. The activities that these social workers carry on with delinquents, however, usually vary with the agencies by which the workers are employed. Family welfare workers, we have seen, are inclined to emphasize the problems that interfere with the adequate functioning of families; visiting teachers are tending to confine their activities to the adjustment of school difficulties, while child guidance workers–it will be shown later–restrict their services to children who are emotionally maladjusted. All of these specialized services may be needed by certain delinquent children, but when such children become the clients of these agencies they are not earmarked for special consideration because of their behaviour.

There are, however, some social agencies whose work is specifically directed toward helping children overcome the difficulties they find in abiding by the rules of community life. In addition, help of this sort is afforded through social work that is carried on by probation officers and by social case workers and social group workers in training schools and correctional institutions. It would appear justifiable, therefore, to consider these activities a special field of social work in child welfare, co-ordinate with those described in the preceding two chapters, for their objective is to enable delinquent children to comply willingly with the rules of conduct prescribed for all who are members of the community.

It should be noted, however, that not all organized

activities that have that objective among their goals are to be regarded as social work. The family, the school, the church, some recreational and informal educational organizations, even courts and police share in the work of securing the social conformity of children. The unique contribution of social work, as has been repeatedly pointed out, lies in its attempt to deal with the difficulties peculiar to each individual client that handicap him in his endeavor to co-operate in some particular form of group life.

Another logical difficulty met with when social work in regard to delinquency is under consideration is that delinquency is a legal term and has never been quite satisfactory to social workers as a means of identifying a certain class of clients, for they and others who work closely with children are well aware that behavior that brings one child to the attention of legal authorities and results in his being pronounced a delinquent occasions the referral of another to a mental hygiene clinic, while in a third case the behavior may go unnoticed or even be approved of as an evidence of juvenile initiative and high spirits.

Social workers know, too, that social and economic factors are very important in determining how a given case of misconduct will be handled. Even though they display the same kind of antisocial behavior, children from well-to-do families are much less likely to come to the attention of police and courts than are those whose parents are poor. Similarly, religious and national groups vary in their attitudes toward resort to the law. Jewish social welfare organizations, for instance, reflect Jewish culture in general in the efforts they expend and the facilities they provide for keeping children out of contact with courts, while Italian and Polish parents are relatively prone to use the court's facilities for settling domestic difficulties, including those of child discipline and management.

Recognizing this situation, social workers in child welfare have been inclined to group together all children who are in need of assistance because their behavior is considered socially undesirable, whether or not they have legally been pronounced delinquent. In addition they usually put neglected children in the same category, their observations having led them to conclude that parental neglect frequently leads to antisocial behavior on the part of the children. In their services to these children social workers are not concerned with protecting the safety, property, or comfort of other members of the community, or with deterring other children from committing similar offenses, for these are among the functions of legal institutions. Rather, they seek to give assistance to children in their efforts to abide by the rules of social conduct that are traditionally or legally formulated to govern their behavior as members of a community.

Among these rules are those that set limits on how children shall eat, dress, and carry on sexual and excretory activities, that regulate the amount of property damage or bodily harm they may inflict, that prescribe how they shall conduct themselves in relation to the adults who are in authority over them. Not all of these rules are specifically defined in the law. Their embodiment in custom is attested to by the fact that children may be judged incorrigible or wayward without having committed specific acts that are legally forbidden. Some of the rules refer to behavior in the family group, some to school conduct, some to relations to other individuals and their property, but all are referable to the fact of co-residence and the rights and duties that social organization on that basis entails. Social work in this sphere, therefore, is again concerned with helping individuals to play their appropriate roles in an organized social group; and whether or not these difficulties have resulted in court conviction is to social workers not the point of chief concern.

### *Causes of Delinquency*

As background for a discussion of social work in this field

one must have at least a passing acquaintance with the theories of the causes of the behavior that may bring children to the attention of the courts, for many of the methods employed for the prevention of delinquency are based upon oversimplified assumptions about its nature. From the point of view of social institutions, delinquency represents the inability or unwillingness of an individual to abide by certain of the rules of behavior prescribed by law–or an ignorance of these rules or of their importance. Behind that are causes–psychological, economic, social, cultural–that often have to be taken into consideration when dealing with the problem on either a mass or an individual basis. Of course the same can be said of other kinds of difficulties that individuals encounter in organized group relationships–in the family, in school, in industry, and so on; but programs for the prevention of such difficulties do not arouse so much public interest nor is there so much confusion as to the relation of social work to them. The following resume of some of the factors involved in juvenile delinquency may, however, throw light on the nature of other forms of social maladjustment as well, such as those displayed by some children who do not get along well in school or in recreational groups and by some adults who find family life or co-operation on a job difficult.

Basic to an understanding of the causes of juvenile delinquency is the theory of how children in general come to accept the restraints that group life imposes upon everybody. There are two ways of looking at that question–the collective and the psychological. The first shows the external means by which the restraints are imposed and the nature of the restraints themselves. The second shows the internal processes, the ways by which self-control is developed so that the need for external compulsions is lessened. Neither of these sets of theories can be developed adequately here, but it may serve our purpose to note the points of chief importance.

**Cultural aspects of delinquency**

On the collective (or sociological or cultural) side it must again be emphasized that the group and the individual are not entities in opposition to each other, the former being the bearer of culture and the latter its unhappy recipient. Rather, all individuals are members of numerous groups, and the groups themselves come into being in response to biological needs and other needs derived from them, as has been shown in an earlier chapter. Culture itself is the sum total of man-made devices for satisfying these needs and includes not only material equipment and goods but language, values, customs, laws, and group activities as well. All human behavior is culturally determined, and not even our simplest or most primitive acts are spontaneous responses to physiological stimuli.

It is incorrect, therefore, to maintain–as is sometimes done–that delinquency is a reaction against the restraints of culture *per se*. It may appear to be so under certain conditions of psychopathology, but even then the casual relationship is more complex. By and large, however, the cultural explanation of delinquency is to be found in the conflicting values within and among various cultural groups and in the fact that individuals belong not to one group alone but to many.

Cultural conflict is a situation often described by sociologists, some of whom are inclined to limit the term to the divergencies between American and foreign ways of life, as found especially in segregated sections of large cities. It is an old story that native-born children of foreign-born parents find difficulty in reconciling what they are taught at home and at school or on the street, often become ashamed of their parents and their foreign ways, and in their attempt to be American may take on the less desirable features of contemporary life. Doubtless this frequently does happen, but it is a phenomenon not restricted to immigrants and their children. The broader fact which this explanation somewhat obscures is that complex, modern civilization–even within the boundaries of one town or city–consists not of one culture, one set of values and customs, but of many. This is particularly true in the United States, not only because numerous national groups live here but because the relatively flexible, non-stratified social system fosters economic ambition and does not define clearly the rights and duties of social classes. There is conflict between cultures and conflict within cultures, and both may be influential factors in any given individual's behavior.

Take first the question of divergencies in customs and standards among groups within the population. This is a relatively unexplored field, but enough is known to indicate clearly that differences are much greater than might at fist be thought. It is well known, for instance, that the sexual standards of certain groups of people are different from those embodied in law. Similarly, there are submarginal economic groups in which certain kinds of stealing are regarded as normal means of getting a livelihood. (Nor must it be overlooked that stealing on a larger scale, frequently with legal assistance, is not unknown in higher economic circles.) Among certain small-scale business groups cheating in weights and measures is taken for granted, even as gambling, prostitution, illegal manufacture and sale of liquor, and selling and buying "protection" characterize the accepted modes of life of other groups. Of the same nature are the activities of the boys' gangs in which playing truant from school, stealing automobiles, damaging property, riding freight trains, and the like, are modes of behavior to which all members are supposed to conform. It is not that most of the people who engage in these activities do not know that they are legally forbidden. To many of them the law and their personal and group ethics are in conflict, and being caught by the police is a misfortune but not a disgrace.

It is important to realize that these groups do not disagree with the total scheme of dominant American values. In fact, in many ways they are strict conformists and are shocked at lapses which they see in the behavior of other groups. Their lack, in other words, is not that of conscience but of adherence to certain tenets of the legalized scheme of values and customs. Nor should this description be taken to mean that all behavior of the types here described is due to divergencies among cultural groups. The point we would make is that delinquency may be due to such causes and, more important, if such is its origin, the modes of reformation must be adapted to take this into account.

In addition to his antagonism between the standards of various groups in a community, there is a possibility of conflict among the values within the predominating culture itself. Karen Horney, a psychoanalyst, has pointed this out and given a few examples, although the problem is primarily a sociological one and has not yet been adequately explored. The most frequently discussed issue is that of humanitarianism versus individual achievement. Dr. Horney shows that children are taught, on one hand, to be kind to others and regardful of their feelings while, on the other, they are urged to excel in all manner of competitive activities. Praise and rewards go to the winners, sometimes without much regard for how they won. In the normal process of psychological development most children achieve a balance between these conflicting demands, especially if they have the intellectual and economic equipment to be successful and to have pleasure in at least some areas of activity. If, however, they are thwarted on all sides, if no compensations are offered for relinquishing what they are told by movies and stories, if not by parents and teachers, are their rights, then some of the brightest and most virile, as well as some of the dullest, may take the legally forbidden routes to that personal success which the culture rates so highly.

It is clear that the problems involved in helping such children are different from those set by the previous group. Offhand one would say that they consist of helping these children to find ways of achievement and satisfaction that do not infringe upon the rights of others. But this is much more easily said than done–especially when the legally forbidden pleasures are so exciting and fruitful. In addition, there is more to be taken into account than the overt fact of lack of satisfaction. It is beyond the scope of this book to go into all of these questions. We would note here, however, that the problems presented to social workers by children who become delinquent because of inability to reconcile conflicting values within the culture are different from the problems presented by children whose values are in conflict with the law.

## How children acquire a culture's standards

So much for the question of culture as an influence making for juvenile delinquency. The next question is how children acquire these cultural standards. The answer-from the sociological standpoint–is simple : they learn them slowly, day by day, through directions and implication, from parents, teachers, and companions, and through books, movies, radio, pictures–all the means by which ideas and ideals are passed along.

In this process the family is the primary socializing agency. Instruction there begins at birth; and even the most neglectful parents teach much, and the most recalcitrant children learn much, about the ways of life in the community and nation in which they live. It is obvious, however, that insofar as family life is disorganized, the parents neglectful, careless, disinterested, or occupied with other matters, the children's instruction will suffer. More important, perhaps, is the fact that without the satisfactions which emotionally comfortable family life affords, children may find their chief source of values in their own age groups of similarly neglected boys and girls. These groups have a culture of their own, also transmitted from generation to generation; but the generations are of smaller age span than those of family life and their ideals are more labile, ephemeral, not subject to the test of life-long experience nor deeply rooted in the ethics of the total civilization.

In this connection it is noteworthy that it is the quality rather than the mere presence or absence of family life that is important. Sociologists at one time put great stress upon "broken homes" as a cause of delinquency, but carefully controlled studies have indicated that divorce, separation, and death are not valid indices of the breakdown of parental hold on children which so often precedes delinquency. The quality of family life as a factor promoting delinquency is important in several ways. There is, first of all, that kind of family in which children are loved and trained but the training is in some respects not in keeping with the ethics of the majority of the community. An example is seen in a recently told story of a father who met his son in a police court line-up. He dashed out of line to greet the boy, took him affectionately by the shoulder, and said that they were now real pals and he'd see him in jail. Such children are probably particularly difficult to reform, since many of them have little basis for dissatisfaction with their ways of life.

Another kind of family is that in which there is absence of control–parents busy, immature, preoccupied, neglectful, careless, or more or less disinterested. Not all children in this situation (or any other) become delinquents, of course; but this kind of family life does make it easier for children to seek from outside sources the values by which to guide their conduct. If, in this process, they find them among antisocial groups and take to delinquency, those who would retrain them must take into account the quality of the emotional relationships that existed in the family, for on these probably depend the children's ability to be influenced by normal family standards.

The third general type of family which is likely to transmit the prevailing standards poorly is the one in which there is a disturbance of the relationships which normally exist between parents and children. Such disturbances are of various kinds (ranging from excessive protection and control on the part of parents to overt dislike or neglect), and the implications for the retraining of children who become delinquent vary accordingly.

## Psychological aspects of delinquency

The explanation of why adverse emotional situations may interfere with children's ability to accept the standards of their parents is found in psychological rather than sociological theory. Psychologists are in agreement with cultural sociologists that children are not born with a sense of moral values but acquire them through association with other people. They also agree that values become an actual part of the personality and so are not wholly dependent upon external sanctions. To these theories they add those that account for the process by which children make the teachings of their cultural group a part of themselves, and they describe the situations that may adversely affect that process.

There are, of course, several schools of opinion on this subject among psychologists. Psychologists with physiological leanings, for instance, would probably stress conditioned reflexes as basic, while followers of Otto Rank would pay chief attention to growth processes and the child's striving to achieve his separate individuality while at the same time retaining the advantages of group life. Freudian theory, on the other hand, emphasizes the child's emotional dependency upon his parents, and shows explicitly why their behaviour and attitudes toward him are the most important elements in the environment in which his basic adjustments are worked out. In spite of their differences, there seems to be common core of agreement among these investigators, which may be stated somewhat as follows.

From birth children find pleasure in the satisfaction of their desires and feel angry when they are thwarted. Frustrating situations, however, arise almost from the start– infants cannot have food at exactly the moment at which they want it, and slightly older children have to learn to control their excretory processes, to refrain from tasting, touching, smelling many things, to share their toys, and so on. The precepts of the culture in which children are to live intrude themselves from the very beginning, and the basis of the ability to accept these limitations on activity and to utilize them for personal development is early laid. In addition to feeling angry and aggressive about being kept from having or doing what they want, even very young children feel fearful and insecure in such situations–perhaps because they sense their dependency upon their parents' good will, perhaps because they fear the parents will feel as angry as they do and punish them. It may be too that this attempt to assert their own wills and to be aggressive–that is, to be independent of their parents in some small way–is in itself a rather terrifying experience.

However that may be, it is held that little children submit at first not so much to their parents' actual commands as to their own phantasies of what will happen to them if they do not obey. This gives them a breathing space, as it were, a calmer period in which to observe more accurately what the parents' attitudes toward their behaviour really are. If this observation shows that the parents are kind instead of hostile, and yet firm in the limitations they set, the children gradually become relieved of their apprehension, their anger becomes less disruptive, and they find it possible to modify their conduct along culturally acceptable lines. Soon, in their affection, they try to be like their parents, and in this way make the parents' standards of behaviour a part of themselves.

If, on the other hand, children find, time after time, that the parents are really almost as angry as their own phantasies about them had at first suggested, their fears, anger, anxiety–the whole complex of confused feelings that the frustrating experience had aroused–are reinforced. In this uncomfortable emotional state it is impossible for children to learn to reason clearly and to understand what is expected of them and why? Some will submit quickly to their parents' orders and withdraw into some kind of phantasy world of their own. Others will fight. Many will show both kinds of reactions and be even more upset–especially as the parents will probably not be consistently antagonistic but will mingle affection with anger and so confuse them still further. Few, however, will develop that kind of strength and ability to be themselves which apparently result when they find that rules of conduct are not expressions of humanity's hostility toward them.

According to this theory, then, the original basis for control of behaviour is phantasy and its accompanying emotions of fear and insecurity. These yield to reason and knowledge only as the child finds love and kindliness accompanying the necessary limitations that are set upon his desires. Whether this explanation is strictly correct chronologically is perhaps not very important. What is important is the observation that children cannot accept and incorporate society's rules and follow them rationally unless they feel secure in the affection of those with whom they live? Lacking this assurance, they are torn by conflicting emotions–suspicious of people's intentions, angry at having to obey rules, fearful of the consequences if they give vent to their real feelings, fighting, withdrawing, or otherwise irrationally reacting to both real and fancied demands. If they are deprived of affection from the very start, it may be that they will not be able to develop consistent self-control at all but will acquire what psychiatrists call psychopathic personalities.

This is the extreme case, of course, but even less unfavourable attitudes on the part of parents may have adverse consequences. Overindulgence, domina‘ion, too great solicitude and protectiveness may be as disastrous as lack of affection, especially if they are accompanied by general friction and unhappiness in the family. It might be thought that a spoiled child is spared some of the anxiety-producing experiences that children usually meet. But the theory has it that there are benefits as well as hazards in such experiences.

When not too beset by fear, a child can use frustrating situations to advance his awareness of his separateness from the rest of the world, to scatter his feelings of love and hate among various persons and objects, and thus to further the process of disentangling his emotions about his parents from the rules of conduct which they try to impress upon him. Consequently, if he is too much shielded, he is handicapped in the growth of both his relationships with other people and his knowledge and control of himself.

There is, of course, much more that the "dynamic" psychologists have to say about the way a child's personality normally develops and the way he makes the customs of society a part of himself. Much attention is paid to the child's attempts to be like his parents and also to his growing sense of difference, and to the part which the parents' healthy balance of affection and discipline play in making this a constructive experience, so that the child takes on their ideals and ways of life without undue anxiety and resentment. Under such conditions the child does not become a duplicate of his parents (as overpossessive parents would like him to be), but he achieves a sense of his own individuality because he is free from fear and able to accept or reject his parents' standards and work out his own pattern of life on a rational basis.

## Implications for treatment of delinquents

The exact relationship between the various types of unfavourable personality development and delinquency cannot be summarily described, but perhaps enough has been said to indicate the main lines of connection. We have earlier suggested that delinquency is a refusal to conform to those customs of society that are sanctioned by law, while we have here indicated that customs cannot be taken oven from parents and made a constructive part of a child's personality if the emotional conditions for their transmission are not favourable. This is not to say that all rejected, spoiled, or inconsistently handled children are overt rebels against society. Some may find sources of strength and security outside their homes. (In this, of course, lies the hope of using teachers, ministers, recreation leaders, foster parents, and others as aides in a retraining program.) Many will express their emotional conflicts in ways that are not legally forbidden.

The Important fact for those who are working with delinquents is that delinquency may represent a child's emotional inability to accept society's rules, his lack of capacity to guide his conduct rationally, and that these conditions, in turn, are often the consequence of the child's unfavourable relationships with his parents. The task of rehabilitation in such cases varies with the nature and severity of the parent-child maladjustment, but it is clear that further punishment cannot be the answer (for such children are overfearful to start with), nor will instruction in how to behave suffice, for such children's difficulties are not the result of ignorance. Somehow or other, if these children are to gain the kind of control over their behaviour that is satisfying to both themselves and society, treatment must be related to the causes of their difficulty, and their basic fears and insecurities must be relieved.

In this brief survey of the causes of delinquency little attention has been paid to those factors which, though often important, appear to us to be secondary and supplementary to the basic ones associated with the transmission of culture and its incorporation into the personality. Under this heading could be listed poverty, adverse school conditions, lack of proper recreational facilities, poor health and handicapping physical conditions, lack of adequate intelligence. To call these secondary may seem unwarranted, since so many delinquents do suffer from these handicaps. Certainly poverty may create or enhance family friction, bring about the situation in which parents do not have time or energy to supervise their children properly, necessitate the privations which are not in accord with the scheme of values which children see portrayed in movies and magazines, and so on. Schools, ill-equipped to meet the intellectual and emotional needs of all children, may provide unnecessarily thwarting experiences for some, from which they may seek to escape by persistent misconduct and truancy. Similarly, poor health, physical disabilities, low intelligence may put a child in an unfavourable competitive condition, and he may search for compensation in delinquent acts. It seems doubtful, however, that these conditions, in and of themselves, produce the kind of persistent, deep-rooted delinquency that arouses the public's chief concern and leads of programs for delinquency prevention and the provision of social work services in this field.

### *Types of Social Work Services*

To return to our original question, we must next sort out from the various measures undertaken to cope with problems of delinquency those that belong to social work. The criteria for judging whether activities should be classified as social work are (1) that they are individualized on the basis of difficulties encountered in some social relationship, and (2) that they are directed toward helping an individual to play his part in a social institution or to make use of its services. Both of these criteria must be met if activities aimed at delinquency prevention are to be considered social work.

Tested by these criteria, several types of work with delinquents or "predelinquents"–children whose behaviour suggests that they are likely to run afoul of the law–are not social work. There is, for instance, the psychiatric and psychological treatment afforded delinquents, among others, in child guidance clinics. It has been shown above that delinquency may be symptomatic of general personality maladjustment, that it may represent a child's more or less irrational attempt to find satisfaction for inner strivings of which he may not be clearly aware. Not all delinquents whose behaviour has such a basis need, want, or can make use of psychiatric treatment, but if such treatment is instituted it will not be confined to or necessarily center around the delinquent acts and the social factors related to them. It will, instead, aim at general personality adjustment, either through direct treatment of emotional difficulties or through the building up of compensatory devices that may enable the individual to operate in a more socially acceptable manner. Without going further into the question of what is involved in psychiatric treatment, it will be seen that, although it is highly individualized, psychiatric treatment of delinquents is not a part of organized social work because it is not limited to helping children meet the difficulties that stand in the way of their participating in particular social relationships.

This is not to say that psychiatrists do not have important contributions to make toward social work with delinquents. Their diagnostic skill may be needed in planning social work efforts; their assistance may be required in understanding the meaning of individual delinquents' response to social treatment. When employed in this way psychiatrists play the same kind of part in a social agency's work as do other specialists–psychologists, home economists, physicians, and so on–but their own activities do not thereby become those of social work.

Application of the criteria of social work to the work of organizations offering recreational and informal educational opportunities and various reconstructive measures in delinquency areas reveals that these, too, are not social work. The measures that such organizations or programs use in the hope of lessening delinquency are numerous. They include, first, large-scale activities that are neither individualized around problems of delinquency nor specifically related to the promotion of law-abiding behaviour. Under this heading may be grouped, as examples, the enlargement of recreational facilities in areas in which delinquency is frequent, the promotion of athletics by the police or other bodies interested in delinquency prevention, the maintenance of day and residential camps for children who live in crowded areas. Second, and further afield, are the broadly preventive efforts of organizations interested in slum clearance, improvement of public health conditions, development of civic pride through festivals and other congregate efforts, and so on.

Third, there are programs that are specifically directed toward delinquency prevention but that assume one of another cause of delinquency to be generally operating and that base their efforts upon it, without paying attention to the needs of individual delinquents. Among activities of this type are the attempts at eliminating "cellar clubs" by providing meeting places and supervision for spontaneously organized groups of delinquents and near-delinquents; the provision of library facilities and reading lists so that delinquents may better participate in the cultural heritage; the setting up of classes in "citizenship training" in which delinquents are taught to be law-abiding.

In pointing out that they are not social work, we do not in the least intend to decry these efforts. Much in the way of delinquency prevention can be accomplished through them, since they supply children with the goods and services, the lack of which may lead to delinquent behaviour. Close examination of the chief function of these activities will show, however, that they are a part of organized recreation or education and that they do not provide for the adjustment to another social institution in the individualized manner that characterizes social work.

In spite of these limitations to the concept of social work, various agencies to provide social work services aimed at helping not only delinquents but other children whose behaviour is considered antisocial to become law-abiding. Both case work and group work methods are used. First, work of this nature is carried on by some protective agencies, such as "girls' service leagues" and "juvenile protective associations," by some family welfare agencies, by child guidance organizations in which social rather than psychiatric treatment is carried on, by rural child welfare agencies and by other organizations that are not part of the legal system. Second, case work with children judged delinquent is sometimes carried on by probation and parole officers in connection with other duties. Third, training schools and correctional institutions may either provide social work services or may conduct their whole program as social work.

In view of the complicated character of the causes of delinquency it is not to be expected that any one approach will achieve a very high proportion of favourable results. Some delinquents need psychiatric treatment. Many are unlikely to become or remain law-abiding unless widespread improvements are made in the educational and recreational opportunities available to them, their family life becomes more satisfying in both economic and affectional aspects, or changes are effected in the scheme of values by which large groups of the population, urban and rural, live. Others (and some of these as well) can probably be helped by having an opportunity to consider with a professional person what they can do about their difficulties, to secure assistance in their personal efforts or to participate in group experiences designed to foster social co-operation. This situation is, of course, not peculiar to delinquents. The causes of social maladjustment of all sorts are equally complicated. It has seemed worthwhile, however, to describe the delinquency situation in some detail because it is fairly typical of various forms of social maladjustment and because it throws into high-light the role of social work in relation to other social institutions.

### *Social Work with Delinquents and "Predelinquents" under Other than Legal Auspices*

As has been said above, social work with delinquents and with children displaying behaviour that may later bring them into conflict with the law is carried on by various kinds of social agencies. Children judged delinquent by juvenile courts may be given into the care of family welfare societies, child placement agencies, rural child welfare or visiting teacher organizations, or other types of social agencies. To some extent the selection of an agency is based upon the supposed needs of the individual child. This would necessarily be the case, for example, when the help of a child placement agency is requested by a court. Frequently, however, agencies do not strictly limit their intake to cases involving difficulties in one or another particular area of social life (family agencies in small cities, in particular, are prone to offer service to any socially maladjusted person regardless of the chief area of his problems), so that there may not be this close correspondence between the usual services of an agency and the need of a delinquent child for help with the difficulties that precipitated his illegal behaviour.

There are, however, certain types of agencies or divisions within agencies that are specially set up for social work with children who are delinquent or in danger of becoming so. The Girl's Service Leagues do some work of this nature with adolescent girls. Juvenile Protective Associations and Societies for the Prevention of Cruelty to Children frequently provide for such case work service. Big Brother and Big Sister organizations are beginning to engage in professional social work, although most of them still use volunteers and provide a less specialized from the assistance to the children in their care. In rural areas the federal plan for the development of child welfare services specifically designates "children in danger of becoming delinquent" as one of the groups for whose assistance the federal subsidy is to be expended.

## Social case work

A survey of the social case work activities carried on under these various auspices would involve us in too much detail, but before a description of the work of one particular type of agency is given, it must be pointed out that the same dichotomy in method that runs throughout the rest of social case work is found in this field as well. This is the division of opinion and practice that ranges on one side case workers who conceive their task chiefly as one of diagnosing the nature of a client's difficulties and setting in motion plans for their elimination and, on the other side, those who are chiefly concerned with engaging the individual in the solution of his problems. Both groups do a good deal of work with families, teachers, recreational workers, and others in order to help their clients to become law-abiding. The one group, however, would keep the planning about how to meet the client's problems largely in their own hands and would take into consideration all aspects of the delinquent's life. The other group would give more attention to the difficulties as the client himself sees them and would do more work *with* the child and less *about* him. These latter social workers would not think it necessary that all aspects of a delinquent's life be set straight (that his personality problems be resolved, his health needs attended to, his school and recreational difficulties met) before he could be expected to become a co-operative member of the community. Rather, they would concentrate their efforts on discovering why it was that he found conforming to legal requirements to difficult and would attempt to give him assistance in dealing with those problems.

The following case is cited in illustration of the kind of social case work that aims to help delinquents to find their way to abiding by the community's laws. The agency was one that includes among its numerous facilities a training school for delinquents and other socially maladjusted children. Some children are committed to the school by a court; others come at their parents' or guardians' request. On parole from the school most children are assigned to case workers from the agency's child guidance staff of otherwise kept under the agency's supervision. The boy in this particular case was placed in a residential clubhouse that the agency maintains and was supervised by one of its case workers.

***Case 26***

George, age 18, was a boy who had had an unfortunate family life. His mother had been committed to a mental hospital when he was nine years old, and his father shortly afterward received a prison sentence. George spent most of the rest of his childhood in an orphan asylum and in several foster homes. His adjustment in the homes was said to be satisfactory and his school work fair, but he became involved in several thefts and was finally taken into court for burglarizing a store in company with another boy. He was committed to a training school maintained by a private social agency. There he was found to have normal intelligence and unusually good mechanical ability. At the school he had interviews with a case worker, but he never responded well to them, for he was highly suspicious of anyone connected with the institution. He did, however, make considerable progress in developing his mechanical abilities, and after some time he was allowed to leave the training school on parole and was placed in a residential club that the agency maintained.

During the first month of his stay in this residence George was friendly only with other boys from the training school and was very outspoken in his suspicion and distrust of the staff. In his relationship to the case worker to whom he was assigned he was overtly hostile and freely said that he considered him a policeman who was going to keep a check on him. The case worker's first opportunity to discuss this attitude with George came when he lost his job and could not pay for his room and board. George was immediately concerned about where he was going to get money for recreation, clothes, etc. In the interview about these matters he started the discussion by listing his grievances against society and the agency and the injustices that he felt had been accorded him in his short life. When the case worker agreed that he had had many deprivations, emotional and material, George was at first taken back but did become less insistent on being given financial aid. When the case worker pointed out that his comments really meant that he expected to have his request refused, George responded by citing many incidents to show that he was doomed to be distrusted, rejected, and dominated by people in authority.

For two months the case worker devoted the interviews to helping George to elaborate upon his intense feelings of deprivation and to giving him sympathy and explanations in terms of his original family difficulties. His demands for clothing, for instance, called forth the comment that he must feel uncomfortable because he had no family to help him secure the things and give him the advice that would help him get along in the community. At the end of this part of the treatment George expressed his wish to see his mother. It seemed to the case worker that in making this request George was trying both to see whether the case worker would make the necessary arrangements for him and also to learn whether the case worker thought that he too was insane. In this interview George was led into a discussion of his reactions to life in the city, especially as it pertained to his adjustment to his job and his relationships with other boys and with girls. He gradually brought out that he was feeling much handicapped by not having a family (girls' parents, for instances, would inquire about that) and by having been in an institution as a delinquent.

From these discussions about his day-to-day living and his experiences in relation to other people, the worker was able to show George that part of the difficulty lay in his low estimate of his own worthiness. For example, George was constantly complaining about his low wages and the employers' indifference to his own and the other employees' welfare. In these talks George revealed a strong need to be respected by his employer; he would describe almost uncontrollable outbursts of rage against the employer when he made some derogatory remarks about his work. After George had told about a number of incidents, the worker was able to show him that he wanted to get unconditional praise and favour from the employer. The implication that he was trying to be the favoured child made George angry; but when the worker pointed out that George had every reason to want to be in a such a position because he had never had such love from any adult, George revealed even more how much he desired to be admired, loved, and understood. He said, however, that the could never expect to be in that position, for his physical make-up was unattractive and he had been damaged by his experience in the various institutions.

These comments and complaints called forth more sympathy from the case worker, but he also turned George's attention to his successes along mechanical lines. The case worker was also able to discuss the situation with George's employer and to secure his agreement to "give the kid a pat on the back." This the employer was willing to do, for George really did good work. As the boss's attitude changed, George became less suspicious of his motives and entered into bantering discussions with him. He also began to have more confidence in his own ability and so was able to accept the case worker's explanation that much of his difficulty lay in his distorted estimate of his own worth.

In the meantime George was invited to join in various activities carried on under the club's group work program. There he found in the group leaders the same attitude of sympathy and understanding he had experienced with the case worker, with the result that he was soon able to branch out and be friendly with all members of the clubhouse staff. As George himself put it, he found that "these fellows are not trying to tear me down because of what I was. They are trying to build me up." By the time that he left the clubhouse it was clear that George was no longer thinking of himself as inferior because of being like his mentally sick mother and his undependable father. Consequently, he did not have to fight everybody because of his oversensitiveness but could accept the rules of the game as he met them in everyday life.

The worker attributed this boy's delinquency to psychological maladjustment. His aim, however, was not to resolve the basic emotional conflict but to help the boy with his problems in social relationships (family, job, and associates) in order that he would not have to rebel against society.

## Social group work

Attempts are frequently made to deal with delinquency by group work methods. Such work is often carried on in settlement houses or through boys' and girls' clubs, and in a few cities agencies specially organized for this purpose have been set up. To qualify as social work according to our criteria such group work would have to be specifically designed to help the individual group members to overcome the obstacles that stand in the way of their being law-abiding. Not that this would consist of a "head-on" attack on the problem; what we mean is that social group work would not aim only at providing recreational or informal educational opportunities for the children but would use these and other means to meet the individual children's specific difficulties.

Some indication as to how such group work may aid a delinquent child is given in the following case. Unfortunately, the case record did not make clear just what part the group leader took in the process. Notwithstanding the paucity of technical data, however, the case is of interest because it shows how group standards and group loyalties may be utilized to strengthen an individual club member's desire to be law-abiding. The case illustrates various other social work principles as well–notably, the influence of personal relationship on behaviour; the ability of children to make a good social adjustment even though they are severely handicapped intellectually, physically, and economically; and the variety of resources that may be utilized in helping individuals to make an adjustment.

***Case 27***

Joe was a white boy, eleven years old, I.Q. 71, in the second grade in school. He was the sixth of nine children in a family that was known to many social agencies. The father was frequently drunk and seldom employed. The mother seemed to be incapable of giving the children adequate care. Joe's unkempt and ragged appearance was accepted by the teachers as inevitable. All the siblings had poor academic records, but some had attended school regularly and were now at work, while others had continually been truants, had juvenile court records, and seldom held a job long. The family's social inadequacy was of long standing.

Few as were the privileges that any of the children in the family received from their parents, Joe felt particularly discriminated against. "I don't get nuttin'," he told the psychiatrist when he was brought to a child guidance clinic for examination. "My sister, she gets it all. She makes her communion. I don't get no communion. They are all down on me."

About Joe's behaviour there were many complaints. In school, in a room for subnormal children, he was said to be very quarrelsome, in need of constant supervision, easily discouraged by failure, and given to rapid changes of mood. Outside school he belonged to a gang of boys who frequently engaged in stealing and other antisocial conduct.

There were, however, certain positive factors in Joe's equipment, though they were not the sort that would usually be recognized as such. He was very small for his age, and he spoke indistinctly. As the psychiatrist put it, "He was very unattractive but made a very pathetic appearance." Apparently there was something in the pathos of his appearance that appealed to adults, for the teacher, a capable person, was said to be particularly interested in him, the principal was "very optimistic" about him, and the leader of a settlement house club to which he belonged was "enthusiastic about the boy's work." In addition he was an influential member of his gang, much liked by the members. Nevertheless, the school authorities often despaired about working with him. As the principal put it when the case was referred to the child guidance clinic, "I have known this boy for four years. He has been tried with several teachers, all of whom have said they could do nothing with him. My conclusion is that almost any monkey in the zoo could be more depended upon than Joe."

Although Joe became a patient of the child guidance clinic, most of the work with him was carried on by a club leader in the settlement house. The clinic's activities were confined to consulting with the schoolteacher about the boy's behaviour, and neither psychiatric nor case work treatment of the boy was attempted. The club leader had "enticed" Joe's gang into the settlement house, where they had been holding club meetings for a year or more before the incidents to be described here took place. During that time the gang had developed much affection for the club leader, and he had been able to teach them to use democratic, self-governing processes in conducting their club activities and had made some progress toward developing their interest in being socially conforming.

The gang, or club, was composed of "expert little shoplifters and beggars," but most of them had "kept straight" ever since the club had come under the settlement house's auspices. Joe, however, had been the most difficult child to handle. He attended meetings regularly but was a "disrupting influence" and continued his delinquencies on the outside. The club members wavered between accepting his leadership and abiding by the club leader's standards. They apparently compromised by always being amused by Joe's antics.

One day a crisis arose, centering around a particularly flagrant department store theft which Joe had committed. Action was taken by the club at the monthly "truth meeting," and there followed a rapid social transformation on Joe's part. At this truth meeting the club decided to make itself a court and try Joe. In that capacity they decided that Joe should go to the Juvenile Court Detention Home because of his offense and because he had a cold and needed a clean bed in which to sleep. After the decision, the club members lined up and shook hands with Joe, some of them weeping over his plight. The club leader took him to the home that evening, and he stayed there for six weeks. The club members frequently inquired about him, visited him, and were very enthusiastic in greeting him on his return.

As to how Joe felt about this treatment it was difficult to determine. His replies to questioning varied from "The settlement house sent me there for nuttin'" to "I had to go there to get straightened out." He did admit, however, that he did not like the Detention Home and said solemnly, "I almost cried everyday."

Whatever the inner working of the change in Joe, it is a fact that his improvement dated from that time–both in school, in the settlement house, and in the neighbourhood. At school the teacher reported that he was friendly, well liked, and no problem at all. In the settlement house he become so reliable that he was given a leading part in a play, and at an annual dinner in a large hotel he led the singing and "surprised every-body by being neatly dressed." Only once during the ensuing period of a year or more did he engage in delinquency. At that time several club members joined him, and he and they were temporarily suspended from the club by the others. Joe visited the settlement house regularly and begged to be reinstated in the club. After he was finally taken back, his behaviour became–as the group leader put it–"unimpeachable," and continued so from that time on, as far as is known.

## *Social Work in Juvenile Courts*

On of the most disputed areas of social work activity is that which has to do with juvenile courts and probation. Some authorities view the juvenile or domestic relations court and the probation office as almost the equivalent of a family welfare agency. Others say that courts should be restricted to the carrying out of the judicial function, and that the childcare aspects of work with delinquents should be left to public and private child welfare agencies. Our own survey of the functions of social institutions in general and of social work in particular leads to the conclusion that a juvenile court is not in itself a social work agency, but that social work has a function to perform with respect to courts and their charges just as it does with respect to schools and hospitals. It seems to us, however, that the supervision of delinquents who are on probation is an activity distinct from that of juvenile courts; hence in this survey of social work with delinquents we shall consider juvenile court and probation work separately.

### Nature and function of juvenile courts

To enter into a detailed analysis of the place and function of courts in the general social structure of society would take us too far afield, for this is a subject which has occasioned much discussion and on which there is far from complete agreement. The popular conception of a court's function as that of determining disputes between individuals or groups may be noted, however, and with it one authority's point of view that while the "members of a court may perform many other functions they are a court only if and when they try an issue."

Juvenile courts are sometimes regarded as being of a different nature. "The fundamental idea of the juvenile court law," wrote the committee of the Chicago Bar Association that in 1899 prepared the first Juvenile Court Act, "is that the State must step in and exercise guardianship over a child found under such adverse social or individual conditions as develop crime... [so that the child] may be treated, not as a criminal or one legally charged with crime, but as a ward of the state, to receive practically the care, custody and discipline that are accorded the neglected and dependent child, and which... shall approximate as nearly as may be that which should be given by its parents."

Juvenile courts were set up to take children out of the jurisdiction of the criminal law, with its jury trials, limitations on types of data admissible as evidence, and fixed penalties, and to permit the adapting of the sentence to the needs of the case. Accordingly, hearings in juvenile courts are usually informal, there are no attorneys and no jury, and social evidence in addition to that immediately related to the offense is admitted for the judge's consideration. That the child has been delinquent, according to the meaning of the law, must, of course, be determined; but since the term delinquency covers such behaviour as waywardness, incorrigibility, and habitual disobedience, it is often not so much specific offenses as general conduct that is the point at issue.

To justify this departure from established legal procedure the common-law doctrines concerning the young child's incapacity for criminal intent and the court's function of *parens patriae* were adduced, for otherwise it might be held that juvenile courts do not proceed in accordance with due process of law. Concentration of attention on the social and psychological factors associated with delinquency and the kind of measures needed to alleviate them has led in theory, however, to a disregard and almost denial of the whole legal situation. Rather than affix penalties, judges are said to prescribe treatment, and all that is ordered is held to be for the child's own good.

This emphasis on the diagnostic and prescription-of-treatment aspect of the juvenile court's work has led some authorities to conclude that the juvenile court is a social work agency. In fact, as the complicated character of the factors involved in delinquency and the need for careful adaptation of treatment measures to individual needs have become increasingly evident, there has been take of substituting social workers or psychiatrists for judges and giving the supervision of delinquent children over to child guidance clinics, child welfare workers, or other nonlegal agencies.

The conclusion that in carrying out its legally prescribed duties the juvenile court functions as a social agency rather than a court seems to be erroneous for several reasons. It overlooks the element of compulsion that attaches to all court activities; it glosses over the community's insistence that children be restrained from engaging in certain forms of behaviour, and in general it mistakes the methods of the court for its function. Actually, regardless of whether the procedure of a court is "socialized" or not, the fact remains that a court is an instrument of government among whose duties are, first, to determine whether the conduct complained about in a given case is the kind that is forbidden by law, and, second, to institute measures looking to the prevention of its repetition. That this latter objective is best accomplished by the court's finding out why a child engages in the forbidden behaviour and basing its decisions on such evidence does not so alter the nature of the juvenile court as to make it a social work rather than a judicial agency.

With respect to social work, the conclusion that the juvenile court is a social agency seems also to be in error, for it equates social work with social diagnosis. This is a rather prevalent conception among social workers themselves, but consideration of the multiple causes of juvenile delinquency will indicate that no one profession can take to itself the task of determining whether a given child's conduct stems from neurological disabilities, defective intelligence, cultural conditioning, or adverse parent-child relationships–to mention but a few of the possible reasons for a child's committing delinquent acts. In performing such a diagnostic task and instituting appropriate measures for the correction of the difficulties the court has need of the help of numerous specialists, among them social workers. But it does not become a social agency thereby.

### Casework in connection with court activities

Even through this point of view is accepted (that the court is carrying out a judicial rather than a social work function in determining whether a child's acts are such as are legally forbidden and in setting in motion activities designed to forestall the likelihood of the continuance of such behaviour), it does not follow that social work cannot be profitably carried on in connection with a court's activities.

The element of compulsion that is inherent in the court's relationship to its charges somewhat alters the character of the social work that is carried on under court auspices, even as social work under school or hospital auspices has its specific elements arising out of the nature of the problems to be solved. This, however, would seem to make it more rather than less necessary that social work with delinquents not be wholly dissociated from court connections.

There are two fairly distinct aspects of a court's work in connection with which social case work may be carried on. One is that of "intake"–the receiving of complaints against children and the making of arrangements through which charges may be preferred against them. The other is that of gathering and compiling information about the children's social situations for the judge's use. Both of these activities may be carried on in a routine manner or without reference to the individual peculiarities of the problems involved, and such a way of carrying them on is very common. On the other hand, both afford opportunity for that individualization of service and that attention of the difficulties attendant upon the utilization of a social institution that are the essence of social work.

These two categories of activities are usually entrusted to probation officers, although in some courts representatives of social agencies are given semiofficial status to assist in intake work. The historical basis of this practice is clear. As early as the middle of the last century prisoners' aid and children's aid societies and societies for the prevention of cruelty to children sent representatives to courts to investigate children's cases and to arrange for foster home placement, and in 1869 a Massachusetts law designated an agent of the Board of State Charities to do this work. A paid probation officer attached to a court was first provided for by a Massachusetts Act of 1878. This officer, on the staff of the criminal courts of Suffolk County (Boston), was used to investigate persons charged with or convicted of crimes or misdemeanors and to "recommend to the court the placing on probation of such persons as may reasonably be expected to be reformed without punishment."

This use of probation officers to investigate cases, compile information, and make recommendations to the judge dates back, it will be seen, to those pre-social-work days when it was thought that a dependent or neglected child's problems were solved when a new home was found for him. Supervision of delinquents who were placed on probation–like supervision of children in foster homes–was limited to routine check-up of their behaviour, and the probation officer's main task was considered that of determining who should be put on probation rather than that of working with the children who were assigned to that status. This conception of the duties of probation officers is still widely held and accounts for the apparent inconsistency in procedure by which services to children placed on probation are under the court's administration while services to children committed to institutions or whose cases are otherwise disposed of are separately administered. With the entrance of social work into the field of probation it has seemed to some that the probation office should be separated from the court. However that maybe, to designate as a probation officer the person who receives complaints against allegedly delinquent children and investigates their social situations is confusing, to say the least. Under whatever title he operates, however, it is this person who can function as the court's social worker, for in this area of activity opportunities are presented both for helping individuals to make effective use of the court and for helping the court itself to individualize its services.

Let us consider first the activities centering around the court's intake. Social work skills can be utilized there in several ways. In the first place, there are many cases in which the individuals who are preferring charges against children are not wholly certain that this is a course of action they want to pursue. This is particularly likely to be the case when the complainants are the children's parents, but others may also feel dubious about instituting court action. To give such individuals an opportunity to discuss their doubts and indecisions as well as their reasons for wanting to take the case to court is clearly case work, not only because it calls for the use of the kinds of skills in which case workers are trained but, more important, because its purpose is to help individuals to make effective use of a social institution's services. The aim of these interviews is not (as might be thought) that of discouraging complainants from taking the cases into court; rather it is to help the individuals to act with a surety of conviction, for it is believed that even a parent's decision to institute court action against his child can often be mutually beneficial if the parent can proceed without too many unresolved doubts about the wisdom of his action.

Social work in the court's intake office is also called for by the fact that the other possible sources of assistance to both children and complainants must be known, their services described, and, sometimes, their co-operation solicited. Then, too, there are interviews to be held with the children themselves, not only to secure information on which decisions about the course of action to be pursued shall be partially based but to help them, if possible, to relate themselves to the court in a manner that is socially beneficial. All of these activities call for that attention to the idiosyncrasies of individual clients' problems in relation to the use of social institutions which is the prime characteristic of social work.

The other aspect of social work in a juvenile court is that of collecting and compiling information about the cases for the judge's use, and, presumably, the children's benefit. In order that the judge shall know what kind of treatment to prescribe, it is commonly held necessary that a complete record of the child's capacities and environmental situation be compiled. Among the data said to be needed are those regarding his behaviour at home, at school, and in the neighbourhood, his previous contacts with the police and courts, his living conditions, his relationships with and attitudes toward parents and siblings and theirs toward him, his religious and recreational affiliations, the character of his associates, as well as his physical and psychological assets and liabilities. On the basis of this material the probation officer's duty is to make on "analytic diagnosis of the factors involved" with a view to aiding the judge to determine what kind of disposition of the case is most likely to secure the delinquent's social readjustment. Our earlier discussions about the nature of case work will have made it clear that much of this material will be valid and useful only if due attention is paid to the meaning the facts have to the children and their families. In addition, this social investigation aspect of probation work calls for the use of case work skills because in the process of collecting data many opportunities are presented for helping the children and their parents put the court's services to effective use.

In these various ways, therefore, social work has contributions to make to the juvenile court and its clients. It would be misleading, however, to imply that these social work services are available in most juvenile courts as presently constituted. Actually, most of the work of intake and social investigation is given over to untrained probation officers or other court officials who carry it on without any particular attention to the individual peculiarities of the persons concerned. In some few courts, however, social workers (either as representatives of social agencies or on the staff of the court itself) operate in more or less the manner here described and demonstrate that social work has a contribution to make to courts as to various other social institutions.

**Is the supervision of delinquents on probation social work ?**

Among the chief duties of probation officers is that of supervising delinquents who are placed on probation by the court. It has already been pointed out that this part of the work could be conducted independently of the court, paralleling the training schools or other correctional institutions as means of dealing with juvenile offenders. This separation of the probation system from the juvenile court has been recommended in order to limit the court to the exercise of judicial functions and to place the discharge of social work functions in independent agencies. Our analysis would suggest, however, that there are social work services to be performed in connection with a court's judicial work also. These differ functionally, however, from the services to be offered in connection with the supervision of delinquents on probation, for the social institution with which they are concerned is the court, while social work with delinquents on probation centers around the community and its laws.

Regardless of whether the supervisory aspects of probation work are administered by the court or independently, the question of the relation of social work to them remains to be answered. The work of probation officers with children on probation may be simply supervisory or, in a sense, custodial; or it may aim, in addition, to give assistance to the children in overcoming the difficulties that stand in the way of their being law-abiding members of the community. In the latter case probation work would clearly entail social work activities; and it is here that the chief dispute about the proper scope of probation work centers. Some authorities say that probation work is social work; others recommend that all of the childcare aspects of probation be given over to already established public and private social agencies. Numerous arguments pro and con are adduced, but no conclusion has been arrived at that is satisfactory to all concerned.

One of the arguments for separating the supervisory functions with respect to juvenile delinquents from those of social work is put forward as "realistic." It points out that in most courts neither judges nor probation officers are equipped to deal with questions of social relationships. In spite of the fact that by 1939 all states except Maine and Wyoming had made express provision for separate juvenile courts or for specialized jurisdiction and procedure in other courts in the case of juvenile offenders, and practically all juvenile court laws authorized the appointment of paid probation officers, very few judges were specially trained for work with juvenile offenders, and the laws required only that probation officers be "discreet" or "suitable persons" or "of good moral character." In this situation it is held by some to be futile to urge the carrying out of social work procedures; rather than work for the raising of probation officer standards, they recommend the entrusting of all social work with delinquents to already established agencies.

Against this seemingly reasonable position two arguments may be urged. On the one hand, most social work agencies are loath to accept many delinquents as clients, not so much because of the numbers involved but because the services of the agencies are specialised (centering, as we have seen around difficulties in particular institutional relationships) and, in addition, are not likely to be profitably used by persons who became clients involuntarily. On the other hand, the choice of the proper social agency for each delinquent and the working with the agency is regard to the case would usually itself require knowledge of social work. It would seem, therefore, that whether or not the services of other social agencies are utilized, the social adjustment of delinquents (in contrast to the mere checking up on their behaviour) requires that probation officers be trained in social case work.

Another argument maintains that the probation officer's position of authority over a delinquent makes it almost impossible for him to carry on social casework with the child. It is undoubtedly true that individuals cannot be forced to accept help with their problems of social relationships, nor can the authoritative element in the relation of probation officer to offender be denied. These are reasons for concluding that not all of a probation officer's supervisory duties can be classified as social work. But they are likewise reasons militating against the delegation of the probation officer's social work functions to some other agency, for delinquents who are averse to discussing their social difficulties are probably no more likely to accept help from one source than from another.

A third argument refers to the confusion in attitudes and emotions that is entailed for the child and his family when the same person collects information upon which the disposition of the case is based, enforces the court's orders, and attempts to give assistance in adjusting to the community's regulations. This argument could be met by separating the work of social investigation from that of probation supervision–a separation that, we have seen, could be justified for other reasons as well.

Analysis of the actual work of problem officers leads to two conclusions with respect to its relationship to social work. First, not all of any probation officer's activities are social work, for in addition to being a social worker he must always function as a representative of the state entrusted with seeing that its rules for individuals on probation are enforced. Second, not all probation officers attempt to carry out the social work function, and those that to attempt it vary in the methods they use and their conception of the purpose to be served.

## Methods of casework employed by probation officers

The probation officer's social work task is frequently carried on in the way recommended in Mary Richmond's *Social Diagnosis*. Much attention is given to producing what is considered a favourable environment for the child, and foster home care is quite frequently used. Attempts are made to remedy the child's physical disorders and defects. Affiliation with organized recreational groups is secured and church contacts are encouraged. School changes are made if thought necessary; vocational guidance is offered. The objective is to bring about the child's "reintegration into society as a self-sufficient and permanently useful member," and that end is thought to be frequently obtainable if the probation officer will put enough energy and wisdom into working out his plan.

Of course the child's part in the program is not overlooked, but it is conceived as one of co-operation. Even Hans Weiss, one of the most skilled of probation officers and most understanding of children, said: "The probation officer is the executive of the plan. He organizes the helpers–teachers, club leaders, agencies, judges, clinics, parents, older brothers and sisters. The central link in the chain is naturally the child. Unless he is won over to the realization that he is on the team and not playing against it, our efforts are bound to be futile."

That in its individualization of treatment and attention to social aspects of the problem this kind of probation work is social case work cannot be denied. But it lacks the sharpness of focus and precision of method which perception of specific function has given to casework in some other fields. Recent developments in case work make it increasingly clear that it is not the task of the social case worker to attempt to effect the total readjustment of an individual but rather to offer help in regard to difficulties that he is encountering in some particular group relationship. Likewise, since the sources of dissatisfaction, the reasons for the inability to operate well in relation to the organized group are known only to the person concerned (even though he may not be able to analyze them logically), and it is only through his efforts that changes can be made, modern casework works with the client rather than on his behalf. According to this conception, the casework of a probation officer should start with a frank recognition of the fact that the child has had restrictions imposed upon him and that the reason for this lies in certain of his deeds. Nor, under this theory, should the probation officer dissociate himself from the authority of the state. It is his job–both he and the child must recognize–to find out whether the probation conditions are observed, as well as to institute measures that may lessen the likelihood of the repetition of the illegal behaviour.

The centering of the probation officer's attention around the delinquent acts is what differentiates this kind of probation work from that which is generally recommended. According to the plan usually proposed, the delinquency tends to be forgotten or pushed aside, emphasis is put on the probation officer's being the delinquent's "friend", and efforts are made (theoretically) to deal with all aspects of the delinquent's life which seem to the probation officer to be unsatisfactory. The new approach is more firmly based on reality. The right of the probation officer to be in the case at all is based on the child's delinquency. Both he and the child know that. They also know that to be subjected to the restrictions laid down by the court is usually unpleasant and is a kind of punishment, a fact which is evidenced by the imposition of greater penalties if the child's behaviour does not change. The question then before them (and the fact that it is a matter between them and not one that primarily involves other people is one of the distinguishing characteristics of the new point of view) is what to do about it. Within this framework of restrictions, the probation system offers the delinquent an opportunity to work out the reasons why he has gotten into trouble and to receive help in removing the obstacles that stand in the way of his being law-abiding.

It is held, therefore, that the center of probation work should be the child and his disapproved behaviour. Investigation of the environment surrounding him–both physical and personal–may be called for, and the probation officer may need to have the advice of physicians, psychologists, and psychiatrists if the child's physical and mental capacities seem to be conducive to his delinquency. The help of parents and foster parents, teachers, recreation workers, and other may have to be enlisted; but through all the work–motivating it and giving it direction–is the fact of delinquency and the objective of its elimination? Since ultimate control over that rests with the child, both his and the state's purpose is best served by planning with him rather than about him. The probation officer, as a caseworker, officer his help to the child in overcoming and preventing a repetition of the situation in which the child finds himself, but he cannot by his own efforts force such changes to take place. The help may include many of the same activities as those used by probation officers under the other system–enlisting the parent's and teachers' interests, finding a suitable foster home, arranging for work or recreation. These activities, however, are carried on not primarily to forward the child's general welfare and so indirectly to prevent further delinquency but to remedy situations that are specifically productive of the child's misbehaviour and usually so recognized by the child.

The causes of delinquency are many and complicated, and we do not mean to imply by these statements that a child can be a good diagnostician of all of them. What is meant is that insight into causes can seldom be obtained when the child's feelings about the numerous aspects of his situation are left out of account? Nor are plans in which the child has no part and which do not engage him actively in improving his situation likely to be effective in developing his desire and ability to avoid further delinquency.

When probation is viewed in this light (as being a situation in which a child has ben placed by the duly constituted authority of the state because of his misdeeds) and the probation officer accepts his part as representative of the state in both an authoritative and service capacity, it seems doubtful whether the proposal to delegate the treatment of delinquents to other social agencies is valid. This might profitably be done, of course, if the kind of assistance the other agency affords is what is found to be needed to overcome the delinquent tendencies. For instance, the treatment services of a child guidance clinic may be required for children whose delinquency is traceable to a psychiatric disability; those of a child placing agency if the problem revolves around the child's adjustment to a foster home. But even such cases would probably entail a joint decision with the child–so that he would know why he was using the services of the other agency–and joint work on the part of the probation officer and the other agency as well. In such cases the probation officer would retain his responsibility for finding out whether the child was abiding by the probation rules as well as for consulting with the child about the progress of the treatment measures.

Under such a conception of probation work the old problem of how to carry on casework within an authoritative setting disappears. In probation work it is authority that creates the situation in the first place and that determines its conditions and limits. The help that the probation officer offers the delinquent concerns the difficulties that brought him into that situation, and the help is offered in the hope that through it a way will be found to prevent their recurrence. The probation officer cannot be helpful to his client by denying these facts, for the delinquent knows them full well. He cannot play the role of a "friend," for, as all delinquents maintain, a friend would not report one's misdeeds to the judge. He cannot play the role of a therapist, for the essence of therapy lies in its non-judgemental character. He can be only what he is–a representative of the state, employed to give aid and counsel to each delinquent with regard to eliminating or avoiding the situations productive of delinquency and to keep the court informed about the delinquent's progress in this endeavor.

The work of the probation officer so conceived, it will be seen, carried out the general social work function of helping individuals with the difficulties they encounter in a group relationship, rather than attempting to remodel them and all their environment. Emphasis is put not so much on what caused the maladjustment in the first place as on the dynamics of the present situation. As these are revealed, largely through conversations with the children themselves, aid can be offered in overcoming the obstacles to law-abiding behaviour. This assistance will often include attempts to improve home, school, or neighbourhood situations if it is in them that the present basis of the difficulties seems to be; but the central focus of treatment remains the child, and upon the probation officer's ability to arouse the child's interest in change and his assumption of responsibility for change the outcome usually depends.

### *Social Work in Correctional Institutions*

Much that has been said about casework in the field of probation applies to casework in correctional institutions as well, but the institutional setting creates special problems that give this work a distinctive character. Children are presumably sent to training schools instead of being put on probation because the seriousness or the long-continued character of their offenses suggests that they can be helped to become law-abiding only if they are removed from the community and given the special training that the institution provides.

It is frequently held that commitment to a training school is not punishment but a means of furthering a child's welfare. The fact is, however, that institutions are often used for taking out of the community the children who are the most annoying, most difficult to handle, and most deprived, and those for whom no other provisions can easily be found. The result is that the training schools receive very divergent types of children, ranging from extremely feeble-minded to psychopathic misfits and including many who suffer chiefly from poor home and neighbourhood conditions. The character of training schools' intake is changing, however, for with the enlargement of child welfare services courts are beginning to reserve institutional commitment largely for children who appear to be amenable to treatment only under restraint, and they are making much greater use of foster home placement.

As with the probation system, the equipment of training schools in terms of personnel and policies tends to lag for behind theory. As described by leaders in the field, the aim of such schools is to effect the adjustment of delinquents to community life on the basis of a careful study of individual needs and the provision of remedies. A desire to punish is disavowed, and attempts are made to dissociate the whole system from that of crime and correction and to ally it with social work instead. This is in line with many child welfare developments, though, for some of the reasons noted above, the legal aspects of the work must not be overlooked. As Grace Abbott has pointed out in regard to juvenile courts, however, the "task [of curing rather than punishing], regarded as not difficult twenty-five years ago, is one for which, as experience showed, our knowledge of human conduct and our traditional methods of treatment were quite inadequate." Even the knowledge that is available is seldom wholly put into practice. There are a few training schools with excellent equipment and programs in one sphere or another, but it is difficult to find one that has the proper staff and facilities to provide all the kinds of assistance needed by the children in their charge.

It is not surprising, therefore, to find that social work in correctional institutions is seldom highly developed. Social work activities in this sphere have, however, a rather long history. They originated in the latter half of the nineteenth century in the prisoners' aid societies, organizations which were chiefly interested in finding jobs for individuals on release from prison and giving them counsel and guidance in their after-prison adjustment. Later the development of parole created a body of officials very similar to probation officers, who gradually came to regard their duties as in the field of social work. Finally, caseworkers were added to the staffs of some correctional institutions, particularly those to which young people were committed.

As they are now operating there are two general plans for the use of caseworkers by correctional institutions. The usual one is that with confines the caseworker largely to work outside the institution. He collects data–much in the manner of a probation officer–concerning the child's life in family, school, and neighbourhood, on the basis of which he draws up a report about the social factors accounting for the delinquent conduct. Together with reports of physical, psychological, and, perhaps, psychiatric examinations, this material is used in drawing up a plan for the child's treatment in the institution. Then, during the period of the child's commitment, the caseworker may keep in contact with the members of the family, attempting to enlist their interest in the child if it is lacking, giving them information about his progress, and making arrangements for his return to the community. Under this plan the caseworker is not likely to have very much to do with the child himself, except perhaps to give him some information about his family.

By law, training schools and other correctional institutions for minors may retain authority over their charges until they come of age, and consequently "aftercare" work is considered especially important. Some institutions have their own parole officers, frequently using the staff workers in the capacity, while in others children on parole are given into the probation officers' charge. Whichever system is in effect, the work at this time is fairly similar to that of probation (except that more emphasis may be placed on job finding the home adjustment), and the methods and quality of the work show the same kind of variation as has been described above.

It will be noted that this general plan for the use of caseworkers by training schools is of the information-gathering, environment-manipulation type that tends to disregard the part which the child himself has to play in his readjustment. The alternative plan, as yet well developed in only a few institutions, is more in line with modern casework theory. There the caseworkers have the double duty of helping the children to use the resources of the institution and to deal with the social situations that led to their delinquency. Under this plan caseworkers are resident members of the training school staff and are available to the children either by appointment or whenever the children feel the need for their services. These caseworkers are not so much concerned with making social investigations as with affording the children an opportunity to discuss their difficulties both in and out of the institution and to formulate and put into effect plans for the alleviation of these problems.

From information obtained through these interviews, as well as from discussions with the children's relatives, the caseworkers provide the rest of the institutional staff with data that may help them in their work with the children, even as they receive from other staff members information that will be useful in casework. For under this conception of training school work, the whole staff is engaged in a mutual enterprise for child welfare. Each staff member–administrator, teacher, recreation worker, "cottage parent," doctor, and so on–has his clearly defined part to play, and all work is directed to the end of putting the children in a position, psychologically, physically, and educationally, in which they can function adequately within the framework of legal restrictions which membership in a community imposes upon everybody.

Such combined efforts might be regarded as a special form of social group work. The following case illustrates how it was carried on with one delinquent boy whose problems were so extreme that he was at one time considered severely neurotic.

***Case 28***

Marvin, an eleven-year-old boy, was committed by the court to the Hawthorne School as a neglected child. He was extremely antagonistic to his mother, fought with her, had attacked her with scissors, and refused to go to school. He had had trouble getting along with people ever since he entered school. The other children teased him about his very large, protruding ears, and he retaliated by fighting with them and being generally aggressive.

Marvin's home situation was extremely bad. His father, who had deserted six years earlier, was a cripple, paralyzed on one side. His mother was an eccentric neighbourhood character, who had been diagnosed a paranoid psychotic but not judged committable to a mental hospital. She owned and operated a surgical appliance shop, the income from which was unknown but seemed sufficient to cover living expenses. She and Marvin lived in the back of the shop and shared a bedroom. Toward Marvin the mother was extremely dominating and possessive, not being willing to let him out of her sight. She had ideas of grandeur and persecution regarding both herself and Marvin, and Marvin had taken on some of her delusional ideas.

Marvin had been under psychiatric treatment in the out-patient clinic of a psychiatric hospital, where it had been recommended that he be placed in a foster home. His mother refused to consider this plan, but Marvin had been placed for a time in a institution on court order, the school authorities having taken him to court on a truancy charge. The mother interfered with his adjustment in the institution by her constant visiting and her complaints. Marvin's present placement in the Hawthorne School, an institution for socially maladjusted children, had resulted from the failure of this first placement.

Psychiatric study at the School led to the conclusion that Marvin was in need of socialization and of being given an opportunity to develop some feeling of being a child. Some of his difficulties were thought to be due to his not having a father with whom he could identify himself, but more important was his relationship with his mother. It was recommended that a woman caseworker help him solve this problem and that the "cottage mother" make a special effort to win his affection. His intelligence quotient was found to be 83.

On admission to the School Marvin was very quiet and kept to himself. He conformed to routine but made no effort to play with the other children. He had a furtive, suspicious way of looking at people and spoke either under his breath or in a very loud tone of voice. The children immediately began teasing him about his ears, to which he reacted by crying.

The caseworker and both cottage parents worked together in trying to help Marvin. The caseworker had regular weekly appointments with him in her office. He was uncomfortable in that situation at first–would squirm in the chair, respond in monosyllables to direct questioning, and was never spontaneous, this behaviour being in marked contrast to his relationship with her outside the office. Slowly, however, Marvin began to take with the caseworker about some of his problems. His chief concern was about home visits: why couldn't he go home and why couldn't his mother visit him ? (His mother was allowed to visit only once a month for half an hour and then under supervision, this plan having been deliberately made because of her personality and her relationship with Marvin.) The caseworker got Marvin to discuss why he thought these restrictions had been put upon him, and she explained that because of the trouble he had with his mother the School thought separation from her might help him.

At first Marvin insisted that he loved his mother, missed her, and was homesick. Later he said the real reason he wanted to go home and have visitors was that he wanted to be like the other boys. This revelation of what Marvin was thinking led the caseworker and the cottage parents to devise a plan for giving Marvin some special privileges to compensate for the restriction on his visits. These consisted of trips to the city, special assignments, and the like. Marvin was told that these arrangements were deliberately planned for him : that he was on the "special privilege list" because he deserved it for his good behaviour (his behaviour in the group really had improved greatly) and that in this he was like some other boys was adjusted well in the School in spite of being restricted in their home visits. Fortunately, the two boys to whom this applied were among the most popular in the School, so Marvin accepted the explanation cheerfully and went around saying "Me, Sunny, and Jim are on 'special privileges.' "

In the meantime the cottage parents were making a special effort to secure Marvin's interest and affection. In the beginning he was very shy, would stay on the edge of the group of children, and cry when he was teased. Gradually he became attached to the cottage mother and looked unhappy when she paid attention to the other children. Then he began to try to get close to the cottage father, but was rather pushed aside by the more aggressive boys. The father, however, engaged him in as many activities as he could without pressing him too much. The friendly response of the cottage parents and their willingness to let him go his own pace gradually broke down Marvin's shyness, and his next step was to find a boy in the group to be his "partner"; that is, his "buddy" or special friend. With that much achieved Marvin progressed rapidly. He began defending himself in a normal boy manner when teased about his ears–gave one boy a bloody nose in a fight about the matter and was very proud of the back eye he himself suffered from the combat. He accepted his share in household chores willingly and became a real participant in the cottage activities.

A concrete sign of Marvin's improved emotional adjustment was given by his realistic acceptance of the physical handicap his ears presented and his attempts to do something about it. He asked the cottage mother whether it would help to put adhesive tape on them at night. This request led the cottage mother to discuss with the caseworker the possibility of securing a plastic surgery operation for Marvin, a plan with which he joyfully concurred. Carrying out the plan involved securing both the medical facilities and Marvin's mother's permission, the latter being a specially difficult task because of her persecutory ideas. The mother objected at first but Marvin told her, "They'll see that it gets done. They know how much I want it." The caseworker was able to allay the mother's suspicions and to show her how much the operation meant to Marvin, with the result that she agreed and the operation was successfully performed. After this, Marvin's socialization continued apace, and he participated in school plays, enjoyed parties, and joined in the pranks and mischief of the other children. His attitude was summed up in a statement he made spontaneously to the caseworker: "Before I came here I never played with boys. I never was to a party. Gee, what I've been missing!"

# IV

# CONSIDERING SOCIAL DIFFERENCE

## Introduction

The practice of child protection is beset by many difficulties. This chapter considers child protection theory and practice in situations where what is conventionally described as cross-cultural and cross-national issues predominate (Boushel, 1994; Korbin, 1991); that is, where there are differences in perceptions about what constitutes satisfactory and unsatisfactory childcare. Situations where there is some perceptible difference between the formal agents of child protection and the clients raise fundamental questions about how we understand and cope with social difference. They problematize our definitions of abuse, our justifications for intervention and our conceptions of 'good' practice. This chapter proposes that conceptualizing difference solely in terms of culture and ethnicity is unnecessarily restrictive, because it ignores other aspects of difference and, most crucially, delimits the consideration of broader issues of power and social structure. This chapter considers how we think about social difference, how child abuse is defined; where child protection workers stand, and finally how such workers might begin to understand and intervene in situations of social difference. It therefore represents an attempt to use the concept of difference to link thinking about child protection more firmly into the constantly developing anti-discriminatory approach to theory and practice.

**Understanding oppression**

The importance of factors such as gender, race and class has been extensively acknowledged within the general literature of social work (Cheetham, 1986; Dominelli and McLeod, 1989). Within child protection literature there has been a particular focus upon the impact of child protection services upon black children and their families (Phillips, 1995). Unfortunately, some writers, in their desire to establish the harmful consequences of some forms of discrimination, have produced analyses which tend to oversimplify events. This oversimplification is most apparent in the tendency to adopt a monodimensional framework. For example, one writer might discuss racism without mention of gender or class, while another might analyse the destructive effects of partriarchal societies without recognizing that their impact may differ according to a woman's colour or class.

While each approach contributes to an appreciation of what is distinctive about racism or sexism, in their haste to reject the negative constructions of inferiority attached to particular groups the authors tend to portray all black people or all women as if they were a universal category–that is, as if they were all the same (Sibeon, 1992). Unfortunately, in rejecting the negative assumptions which derogate particular groups of people, the writers do not ultimately reject the essentialist nature of the constructs which underpin such prejudices. Paradoxically, in resisting negative attributions by attempting to replace them with positive ones, they may unwittingly reiterate the assumption of universality by claiming an homogeneity of experience and social situation for all group members. There is a fundamental problem with this approach: despite the deprecations of racist or sexist commentators, neither women nor black people are necessarily, or intrinsically, coherent, homogeneous social groups. Apart from their gender or race they may have little in common, for there may be as many differences within these categories as there are between them. Brah, in discussing the question "Is sisterhood global ?", illustrates this problem in her statement that 'we do not exist simply as women but as differentiated categories such as working class women, peasant women, migrant women' (1992).

Arising from the problem of monodimensionality is a tendency, often unwitting, to establish 'pecking orders' of oppression (Hudson, 1989): that is, to assert the primacy of, say, race or class in the overall analysis, while other factors such as gender or disability are relegated to secondary status. This is an understandable consequence of people writing about child protection practice from their own particular social locations. After all, who else is better placed to describe the consequences of oppressive actions than those who suffer from them ? However, this grounded knowledge can have problematic consequences, especially when, as Brah has noted, some writers seem to believe that:

> The mere act of naming oneself as a member of an oppressed group was assumed to vest one with moral authority. Multiple oppressions came to be regarded not in terms of their patterns of articulation/ interconnections but rather as separate elements that could be added in a linear fashion, so that the more oppressions a woman could list the greater her claim to the higher moral ground. (1992).

The problem with constructing hierarchies of oppression is that it oversimplifies the realities of social life and leads to a simplistic analysis of how oppressive ideas and actions actually impact upon the lives of those subjected to them. While the violence of racist thugs or rapists leaves little room for doubt about their perceptions of black people or women– in the sense that they may perceive either type of 'victim' as undifferentiated categories–much of what is oppressive in people's lives is often less dramatic and more subtly enacted. While oppression may be marked by the trauma of violence and aggression, its harmful effects are frequently more complex, both in their impact and in their implications. These negative effects, which may encompass social and material deprivation, the internalization of negative imagery and ideas, poor self-esteem and so on, are by no means inevitable. Therefore, while being black or disabled in British society may be highly predictive of group experiences, it is not inevitably so for individual members of such groups. While we can be reasonably accurate in predicting the general consequences of racism or disability, the particular experience of individuals is less certain. They may be protected by other factors or resources such as family life and social supports, political beliefs, religions and ideologies, wealth, class and occupation. For example, while white feminists have generally pointed out the negative consequences of the family, some black feminists have been more appreciative of its capacity to act as a safe place and a power base from which to engage with a predominantly white racist society. Oversimplified approaches to anti-oppressive practice carry other risk too. They may focus responsibility inappropriately. After all: 'Anti-discrimination is neither the preserve nor the responsibility of those who are discriminated against' (ILPS, 1993. Furthermore, such approach may allow some practitioners to avoid recognizing that, unusually, they are not the agents of change but are instead the subjects for action (Campbell, 1994).

The anti-discriminatory perspective which has been developing over the past few years has established a broader analysis which recognizes the specificity of particular forms of discrimination such as racism, while emphasizing general features which contribute to injustice and inequality, such as ideology, power, stigmatization and derogation, and at the same time pointing out the similarity of some of the consequences of discrimination in terms of marginalization, poverty and poor life-chances (Dominelli, 1988; Thompson,

1993). The application of an anti-discriminatory perspective to the issue of child protection has immediate relevance in two ways; first, it raises the question of cultural difference in conceptions of what constitutes abuse. Secondly, it highlights the differences in power between workers and clients, and thus problematizes the relationship between them.

### Social difference

In the past, accounts of injustice and inequality in respect of child protection matters tended to be presented along a single dimension of social difference, such as culture, race or class. While this was helpful in spotlinghting unjust and unfair practice, it led to a rather fragmented analysis of oppression within society. The more inclusive concept of social difference has a greater utility because it:

- broadens the scope of the analysis to include many forms of difference, and thus can incorporate recognition and analysis of sexism, racism and so on;
- can enhance the analysis of the means by which difference is constructed and maintained? In this way, questions about power, social structure and location, and social definition become central to the discussion.

British society is sometimes assumed to be an homogeneous entity in which white, English-speaking, heterosexual culture is the norm, and thus all other variants are perceived as either abnormal or subcultural–in the sense that they are viewed as minority features which are pathologically different–or simply as irrelevant to the dominant mainstream. Not only are such ethnocentric representations inaccurate, but they are also self-serving devices for those people who express them. They are convenient justifications of their advocates' position, not simply because social difference can be represented as inferiority, but because it allows social problems to be seen as essentially marginal concerns which, tragic and deserving of sympathy though they maybe, are not regarded as intrinsically connected with the social mainstream.

This representation of social homogeneity has, however, been extensively challenged by anti-racists, feminists and others, who have sought to point out the social differentiation which exists and who have also attempted to show how these 'problems' are inherently bound up with the social structure of contemporary British society. Therefore, adopting an approach to child protection work which recognizes the range of social variation and acknowledges that social difference will accompany many of the contacts between workers and their clients not only allows us to begin to understand what may be problematic when, for example, educated white workers with poor, black clients, it can also encompass other variations which exist, such as differences of class and education between black workers and black clients. Thinking in this way does not deny what is specific about such situations, but it does subsume them within a more wide-ranging analysis. Adopting this higher level of generality improves the likelihood of a theory of anti-discriminatory practice which has more widespread application, but it has the accompanying disadvantage that, in doing so, we may lose sight of the important features of particular forms of oppression. Furthermore, it carries the risk that it may be misused as a sophisticated way of avoiding confronting racism or sexism within particular circumstances, by allowing unscrupulous practitioners to make an overly abstract appeal to higher-level theory.

Nevertheless, despite these risks, I believe that such an approach has considerable potential for developing child protection practice in a socially differentiated society. For example, while it recognizes that unfair recruitment practices have led to an under-representation of minorities in employment, it does not inevitably presume that a child protection worker will necessarily be a white person who somehow represents the 'normal mainstream'. Most significantly, it allows practice to be conceptualized in a manner which explicitly acknowledges the power difference between workers and clients and recognizes the reality that, however much we may attempt to 'match' clients and staff, this can never fully address the issue of difference. For, while the experiences of, for example, a black female worker and a black female client maybe similar – particularly in respect of their experiences of racism – other dimensions of difference may distinguish their lived experience.

It is my contention that social difference is an inevitable aspect of any professional practice with people and that we should not seek to diminish or deny it, but should accept that such a contingency may have to be navigated and negotiated in every encounter (Thompson, 1996). This overt recognition of social difference between workers and clients opens up the possibility of more honest and direct acknowledgement of how interventions in child protection may proceed. Most crucially, it avoids any double agendas, or feelings of betrayal by clients, when workers are sometimes forced to become more authoritative in their intervention.

## Social location and situated knowledge

Phenomenologists have long argued that all knowledge is partial, that it is related to the social position of the person. Anthropologists and ethnomethodologists have also developed epistemological positions which are essentially appreciative in the way they approach the question of what it is possible to know. Similarly, a central theme in the literature of emancipation, and especially in feminist accounts, is that those who wield power or seek to change things should have an appreciative understanding of the experiences of the outsider, the underdog, the excluded and marginalized. Narayan has called this insider knowledge 'epistemic privilege', by which she means that 'members of an oppressed group have a more immediate, subtle and critical knowledge about the nature of their oppression than people who are non-members' (1989). This does not mean that non-members cannot develop an appreciation of the oppressed person's position, but that this appreciation is not easily achieved, nor will it always be complete or directly felt. Acknowledgement of the epistemic privilege of insiders does not, however, imply that they necessarily 'have a clearer or better knowledge of the *causes* of their oppression' (Narayan, 1989). Otherwise, the result, as Brah notes, it that 'Assertions about authenticity of personal experience could be presented as if they were an unproblematic guide to an understanding of the processes of subordination and domination' (1992).

The implications for child protection practice are twofold. First, it is vital that workers make some attempt to listen to the narrative offered by the people they work with. This applies to possible abusers as well as to the victims of their alleged actions. Secondly, child protection workers should not accept these accounts uncritically. If we pay no attention to the accounts of the alleged abusers, then we will certainly fail to understand what meanings, if any, abusers attach to their behaviour. This could be a crucial omission given the importance attached in UK law, and Western thought generally, to the *mens rea* –that is, the intentions that existed in the person's mind when they acted. Similarly, as Chapter 11 in this volume illustrates, if we do not appreciate the child's reality, then we may fail to understand not only what has happened to them but also, more importantly, how best to help them. Nevertheless, neither account should be accepted uncritically because, for adults, they may simply be self-serving justifications which are used to deny culpability, and, for children, they may be inaccurate or mistaken stories which arise from confusion and misunderstanding. Our understanding of social location and situated knowledge also has to encompass an awareness of our own position. The recognition of the centrality of social differences thus provides a means by which we may begin to address some of the ideas and assumptions which inform our practice.

## How is child abuse defined ?

Child abuse may be defined in terms of the behaviour of the carer(s) towards a child, and / or in terms of the consequences for the child. There is no doubt that defining and intervening in child abuse is a normative enterprise, in that it relies upon some notions of desired, preferred or acceptable levels of child welfare, risk and outcome. The crucial question is: what, and whose, norms are being used ? Workers who unwittingly and uncritically use as their point of reference norms derived from an idealized and stereotypical white middle-class family, or from other personal experience of childhood and family life, are more likely to make unfavourable assessments of those who differ from these norms. This is most apparent in situations when workers are working with poorer working-class or black families, where they may apply deficit models of child welfare which may bear no relationship to relevant criteria or actual risk. Such models are culturally biased in an ethnocentric fashion which almost inevitably leads to discriminatory and negative assessments of those families who do not conform to the supposed norm. A cross-cultural comparison of different societies quickly establishes that, while all societies have expectations and norms about what constitutes acceptable childrearing, there is considerable variation in terms of what is defined as abuse. For example, Emelie Olson (1981), an anthropologist who undertook fieldwork in Turkey, reported that local women expressed concern about her practice of allowing her 18-month-old daughter to play outdoors in a tub of water in warm weather, because of their belief that small children could easily catch a chill and die. Yet they saw nothing unusual in their advice to her to praise and kiss her daughter's genitals when bathing her, as an appropriate expression of 'positive motherly action' (Korbin, 1991). To what extent would an explicit consideration of meaning enter into our response to Olson's example ? Would we automatically regard the act of a mother kissing her daughter's genitals as 'dirty', obscene, invasive or, alternatively, in a slightly more 'enlightened' fashion, would we think that this was an inappropriate but understandable attempt to value and appreciate her daughter's body ? To what extent would we consider the mother's account of her behaviour ?

Korbin, in a review of cross-cultural perspectives on child abuse, states that:

> Cross-cultural variability in childrearing beliefs and behaviours makes it clear that there is not a universal standard for optimal childcare nor for child abuse and neglect. This presents a dilemma. Failure to allow for a cultural perspective in defining child abuse and neglect promotes an ethnocentric position in which one's own set of cultural beliefs and practices are presumed to be preferable and superior to all others. On the other hand, a stance of extreme cultural relativism, in which all judgements of humane treatment of children are suspended in the name of cultural rights, may be used to justify a lesser standard of care for some children. (Korbin, 1991).

Korbin begins to address the complexities of this question by suggesting that there are three ways in which we can define child abuse. Thus, abuse may be said to occur when:

- people do not follow the culturally acceptable behaviour expected within their own culture;
- practices deemed acceptable in one culture are rejected as being abusive or harmful in another;
- social conditions 'such as poverty, inadequate housing, poor maternal and child health care, and lack of nutritional resources either contribute powerfully to child
- maltreatment or are considered maltreatment in and of themselves' (Korbin, 1991).

Child protection intervention in British society is primarily conceptualized as being about the first category of definition, while the second category only becomes recognized as an issue when the perception of social difference is signalled by language, race or some other distinctive indicator of ethnicity and culture. Consequently, much of what may be significant is ignored when the markers of difference are not recognized or are overlooked–for example, when a client's first language is not English but he or she is, none the less, perceived to be competent in it as a second language. The third category of abuse is not usually seen as the preserve of personal social services and is typically perceived as being about general social welfare, since good conditions for parents and carers equate with good conditions for their children. Of course, as writers like Parton (1985) and Gil (1976) have noted, there may be telling reasons why governments and welfare agencies do not espouse the conceptions of child welfare and protection implicit in this third category.

Parton, reviewing the social context of child protection, succinctly notes that: 'Ideologically the way that the problem has been constructed blames the parents and social workers and absolves society and the state from issues of social distribution' (1985). While any further consideration of children's life-chances and general welfare is beyond the scope of this chapter, we should not ignore this aspect, and should note that, when pursued, it may lead to some surprising observations. For example, given the greater number of child deaths caused by road traffic accidents, why do we feel more moral outrage about abuse by parents and carers than about the injuries or deaths that are directly or indirectly caused by the actions of poor drivers or by the omissions of traffic planners and the police ? Boushel has noted that within a European context, the British approach to child abuse can be characterized as an overly punitive one which pays little regard to the 'amelioration of the personal and social factors underlying it' (1994).

## Taking difference into account in assessments

The perils of ethnocentric assessment were made plain in the death of Tyra Henry (see Chapter 3 in this volume) and continue to be a problematic area of practice (Phillips, 1995). In the absence of grounded knowledge, too many workers seem prepared to fill the gaps with stereotypical assumptions and inaccurate 'knowledge'. Even when they obtain accurate information, they may still be uncertain of how to use it, and what sense to make of it. Boushel has noted that, while the Department of Health has instructed workers to 'incorporate a cultural perspective' into their assessments, they have not provided much 'guidance on how "cultural variations" might be relevant to the assessment process' (1994). Fortunately, Korbin, proceeding from her review of the research into different cultural patterns of childrearing, has made constructive suggestions as to how child protection workers might amend their assessments about people who are different from them (Korbin, 1991). She proposes three dimensions which should be examined when making such risk assessments, namely:

- the value attached to children in general within a specific culture, and the ideas held about specific categories of children which may increase vulnerability;
- the embeddedness of childrearing in wider social networks;
- the pace and extent of social change.

### Vulnerability

Korbin suggests that child abuse is less prevalent 'in cultures where children are highly valued for their economic utility, for perpetuating family lines and cultural heritage, and as sources of emotional pleasure and satisfaction' (1991). However, in all societies, including these, some categories of children are more vulnerable than others. Children with health problems, those who are 'deformed' or 'handicapped', those who are unwanted, or those who are 'born under unusual, stigmatised, or difficult circumstances' are more vulnerable to neglect and abuse. Additionally, in industrialized nations particular stages of 'normal' development, such as 'toilet training' and adolescence, where oppositional behaviour or non-compliance with carers' wishes is more likely to occur, are also risky. Gender, too, is also associated with risk, typically where preferences are for male rather than female children – but not exclusively so, as sometimes there may be higher expectations of boys, which leads to harsher punishment if such requirements are not met. Behavioural expectations and particular personality characteristics may increase the level of vulnerability according to how these are perceived within specific societies.

Finally, diminished social support appears to increase the risk of abuse in many cultures. Thus, children born outside marriage, stepchildren and orphans are generally more vulnerable. It should be noted that any judgement about the likelihood of increased vulnerability can only be made with some 'insider' knowledge of how these categories are perceived within a particular culture. For example, economic utility alone can lead to the exploitation of children as workers by exposing them to high levels of health risk and by depriving them of opportunities to develop their formal educational skills.

**Embeddedness**

The potential for risk in any situation can be reduced by the extent to which childrearing is embedded within wider social networks. At its simplest this is evident when people other than the parents either assists or take a direct hand in looking after the child, since this tends to mitigate 'the consequences for children of having an inadequate or aggressive parent' (Korbin). Somewhat surprisingly culturally acceptable patterns of childcare which appear to enhance children's safety are child-lending, fostering and informal adoption, although these measures need to be understood within their cultural context, since children who are redistributed for economic reasons are more likely to be at risk if they 'fail to be useful'.

Korbin suggests that urbanized industrial societies with smaller living units are less safe for children because of the relative social isolation, and particularly when there is less consensus about what constitutes acceptable childcare. Hartz (1995), in a study of conflict resolution patterns in Hawaii, notes that, while Polynesians as a rule cherished their children, in the traditional village children who faced the prospect of being physically punished by their parents could escape their fate by simply moving around to another house in the village, where a friend or relative would shelter them. If they actually succumbed to the physical punishment they would shout out loudly so that neighbours and relatives could hear what was happening to them. In such circumstances it was considered acceptable for other people to intervene. Korbin similarly notes that, amongst rural Hawaiians, 'relatives do not hesitate to yell from one house to another if a spanking has gone on long enough or is too severe for the child's misbehaviour' (1991). The point is than urban life, with its smaller family units and less tightly knit societies, offers fewer opportunities for informal intervention, support and assistance. These aspects of urban life, when coupled with the view that childrearing is a private and not a public responsibility, increase the risk of abuse.

### Rapid social change

Korbin suggests that rapid social change itself increases the risk of abuse. This increased risk is believed to arise from the breakdown of traditional structures and values. The social networks and patterns of obligation noted in the previous section are diminished or destroyed at the very time that carers are subject to greater stresses. Korbin does not uncritically accept this position and suggests that such change is often unfavourably contrasted against an idealized backcloth, distinguished by the 'assumption of a lack of deviance in small societies' (1991). Nevertheless, social change may well reduce the value attached to children. For example, when people move from agrarian to industrial societies, children change from being a productive asset, in terms of their potential as labour, to being a drain upon family resources in societies where schooling is compulsory until well into their middle teens; that is, they are potentially devalued by the change in circumstances.

We should be wary of romanticizing the 'old ways', for while it is all too easy to see how societies undergoing rapid change may begin to 'discover' their own child abuse, there is little doubt that such discoveries are linked to changing perceptions of what is considered acceptable childcare. Mejiuni, writing of Nigeria, explicitly makes this point: 'Many adults appear to have warped notions and wrong perceptions both of their duties to their children/wards and the children's responsibilities to them' (1991). Interestingly, Mejiuni's justification for intervention derives not from an explicit acknowledgement of civil rights, but is expressed in terms of the greater good of the society: 'The extent to which children will be able to partake in nation building either as leaders or followers when they become adults will depend upon the type of nurturing they have received' (1991).

Korbin's work usefully points child protection workers towards a much wider assessment of their social situation, but in my view her dimensions for risk assessment are probably most usefully employed not to replace the more traditional methods of assessment used by workers and agencies, but to extend or amend them. Boushel's work (1994) provides one example of how this might be accomplished. Specifically she has developed the dimensions into a framework which has four factors.

- the value attached to children;
- the status of women and carers;
- the social interconnectedness of children and carers;
- the extent and quality of the safety nets available.

This approach develops the socially situated analysis of child abuse even further away from narrow perspectives on child protection which conceptualize abuse solely as the result of individual pathology. From this position Boushel argues that not only will workers make more accurate assessments of risk, but that they will make better plans for intervention because they can recognize other protective factors and strategies involving more collective and community-based actions. However, as Simpkin (1979) has noted, we should not be naive as to the potential political implications of developing our notions of assessment and intervention in this manner–it will very likely lead to conflicts with our 'political masters' and with critics who disapprove of any moves which appear to politicize what they presume, or prefer of pretend, are non-political problems.

## Where do we stand?

Korbin does not address the issue of cultural dominance and the question of which culture is promoted and policed within a particular society, nor does she address the question of cultural difference within a given society. But it is precisely these questions which may cause difficulty in situations of social difference within contemporary practice. For example, while it may be generally accepted within UK society that committing actions which kill children is unacceptable and is thus reflected in the use of the criminal law to prosecute offenders, there is less agreement about acts of Omission such as withholding life-saving treatment on religious grounds. However, child protection practice does not revolve solely around immediate life-or-death issues but also involves less clear-cut issues of neglect, physical punishment and emotional abuse, and while there may be widespread agreement about the extremes of behaviour, it is likely that many cases are far more ambiguous. What would we think if we directly encountered the practice recommended to Olson by her Turkish counterparts ? Why do we forbid the genital mutilation of girls but permit it – albeit in a much less severe form–in circumcision of boys ?

To some extent we may choose to dodge these difficult issues by seeking refuse in an 'apparatchik' stance: that is, by claiming, as Davies (1981) did, that it is our job to enforce the laws, not make them. Unfortunately, it is not that simple. This is a naive and disingenuous stance because it suggests that all behaviours are neatly defined into discrete categories of permitted and prohibited actions, whereas in the multiple processes of law enforcement there is considerable space for idiosyncratic interpretation, selective application and personal and institutional bias (Cicourel, 1968; Heidensohn, 1985). Furthermore, the uncertainty of interpretation and response in child protection practice is additionally complicated by the fact that such practice is conducted within an ever-changing society, one which is continuously creating and recreating itself and its ideas of what constitutes acceptable practice by parents and workers. While statute law, case law precedents and formal policies do establish 'rules' by which we may judge adult behaviour towards children, this is, in part constructed by our own practice. So, while some ambiguities and uncertainties may be 'tested' formally by the court, or informally by the media and wider professional opinion, much of our practice is effectively shrouded from the wider public gaze by the restrictions of confidentiality, and by the covert assumptions and invisible processes of thought which precede and accompany our actions. Davies' stance simply fails to acknowledge these sociological aspects of practice and barely recognizes the extent to which workers themselves may be important actors for changes in policy and statute.

Whether we like it or not, our knowledge is situated: that is, it is related to our specific social location along the various dimensions of difference–our position in terms of occupation, gender, language, race and so on. What, therefore, is the justification which allows us to sift, screen and ultimately accept or reject different narratives ? In part, it probably derives from our own moral and social perspectives, which in turn arise from our acceptance of social norms regarding acceptable childrearing practices. Potentially, the most powerful justification might derive from our professionally privileged knowledge about the harmful effects of child abuse upon its victims (see Chapter 4 in this volume).

The crucial question for the development of an anti-discriminatory practice is: how do we acknowledge the reality of cultural variation without adopting an extreme cultural relativism in which anything goes ? A conventional response is to make reference to notions of civil rights: thus documents like the UN Charter on the Rights of the Child are cited in support of our duty to intervene. This of course begs the question of whether these legitimizing devices are themselves simply social constructions which reflect particular discourses about human society. In my view, proponents of the anti-discriminatory perspective should be quite adamant in rejecting the kind of simplistic multiculturalism which leads to a stance of uncritical relativism – a position which effectively neutralizes the possibility of intervention. Instead of proposing a more-or-less explicit rights-based approach to social action, we should accept that at the heart of the anti-discriminatory perspective is a moral choice, namely a fundamental commitment to the core value of human equality. Therefore, as I have argued elsewhere (Pugh, 1996), despite accepting the socially constructed nature of all knowledge, the anti-discriminatory approach ultimately derives its legitimacy from an examination of the consequences of human actions. It is our knowledge of the damaging consequences of child abuse within Western societies that provides our most secure justification for intervention, and we should not allow the sophistries of postmodernism to deflect us from this 'common-sense' appreciation of actions and consequences (O'Neill, 1995). This is a complex area which warrants a more extensive discussion. However, for those readers who wish to venture further, Malik (1996) has provided an interesting exploration of this aspect of social action, and he too, while accepting the constructed nature of human thought, argues that amongst the multiple accounts of the social world, there are both more and less accurate renditions of it.

**Approaching social difference**

The preceding discussion has been rather analytical, and the implications for practice may not be readily apparent. This section attempts to pick up some of the relevant points which workers should consider in their practice.

When a worker and client clearly perceive difference between each other, the recognition may trigger other underlying assumptions and expectations of each other's behaviour, attitudes, beliefs and competence. Conversely, when they do not jointly perceive difference, they may presume a similarity of shared ideas and attitudes. Problems are likely to arise when the perception of similarity is mistaken, and a sense of confusion or betrayal is not an uncommon response amongst clients who thought that they were 'getting on well' with their workers. Davis and Proctor (1989) suggest that clients who perceive that they differ from their worker are likely to have three concerns.

- Can I trust this person ? (Does this person like/dislike or respect me, or people like me ? The client's perception of the likely response to these questions will determine the extent to which they, in turn, are prepared to trust the worker.)

- Is this worker competent ? (Does he or she have the knowledge and skills to help me, or deal with me fairly ?)
- Does this worker understand my social world ? (Does he or she know about people like me ? Is this person a credible person whose advice and suggestions may be valid ?)

Research undertaken in the USA has shown that perceived trust, competency and validity are socially structured (Davis and Proctor, 1989). For example, male workers are often perceived by clients as being more competent than women. Black workers may be thought by black clients to have more goodwill and to be more trustworthy and white workers. However, we should be wary of assuming that this will hold for all similar situations. For example, Jaffe (1995), in a study of the influence of ethnic stereotypes upon clients' preference for workers amongst Sephardi (Israelis of Middle Eastern origin), and Ashkenazi (Israelis of Western origin), found a clear preference amongst both groups for Ashkenazi workers. This initially seems surprising given that the Sephardi are, in many respects, marginalized within Israeli life and might therefore be expected to express a preference for workers from their own ethnic group, but it clearly raises complex questions about employment opportunities, social contact, socialization, and perceived social and professional status within an unequal society. Unfortunately, little research has been done into the perceptions and expectations held by ethnic minorities within British society.

In view of this, an open and explicit acknowledgement of difference is probably best made early in the initial encounter. For example, when a white worker meets a black client, questions or comments such as 'Do you think my being white will affect our working together ?', or 'If you think at any time that I don't understand what you mean because or backgrounds are different, I hope you will tell me', signal the willingness of the worker to consider the relevance of what is different between them. The message conveyed is: I will work hard to understand your situation and I recognize that the difference between us may raise sensitive and difficult issues. Most importantly, the worker is signalling that he or she realizes that the client may well have valid reasons for doubt or suspicion. Professional courtesies are very important. Proper introductions, titles and handshakes (where appropriate) should be used to convey respect. An authentic professional demeanour which is based upon the worker's personality but conveys a professional seriousness of purpose can be undermined by superficial attempts to relate to clients using inappropriate argot, slang or dialect. Culturally appropriate attending skills and knowledge relating to expectations about eye contact, interruptions and turn-taking in conversation and other non-verbal behaviours, should be acquired and used. There are considerable cultural differences in the extent to which different groups respond to aspects of practice such as directness, self-disclosure, empathetic understanding and disagreement. For example, workers with little experience of non-European cultures should be aware that some of the 'traditional' Western principles for practice such as confidentiality and individualization may simply be regarded as irrelevant or obstructive by some clients from African cultures (Silavwe, 1995).

## Conclusion

From the preceding discussion it is clear that an anti-discriminatory practice encompasses many of the general rules for good practice, where careful listening, accurate feedback, consultation, reflection and reliability demonstrate the worker's understanding and commitment, but it goes further in embedding these rules within a broader appreciation of the demographics and biographies of both workers and their clients. Thus, workers should strive to:

- inform themselves about the complexity of social location and social diversity for both themselves and their clients;
- have some understanding of, and sensitivity to, the oppressive experiences of particular groups without being overly deterministic in their expectations in respect of any given individual;
- be aware that their own position is not neutral, either in terms of their own location within service agencies, or in terms of an explicit commitment to anti-discriminatory practice;
- understand the importance of hearing the narrative of the other person, but not accept these accounts uncritically.

We should acknowledge that our existing formal knowledge base is in many respects inadequate.

There are a number of areas where existing knowledge is limited, in particular in the British context, where there is very little published material on how different ethnic communities conceptualize abuse. This is rather different from the USA, where there is much more information and interest in how abuse might impact upon children of different backgrounds. This difference could relate to the circumstances of abuse as well as the child's reactions to it. Sanders-Phillips, in her research in Los Angeles, found that there appeared to be significant differences in the susceptibility to and level of depression between black and Latino girls who had been abused. She suggests, for example, that: 'Cultural sanctions against premarital sex may also decrease self-worth in Latino girls who were forced into premarital sex' (1995). Ho (1990) has suggested that, because Asian women in the USA have been socialized into placing family harmony above their own personal well-being, they put up with higher levels of made violence in their homes before seeking help and protection for their children.

Similarly Boushel suggests that the position and experience of abuse victims within Irish travelling communities is related to the internal norms of the group. Thus, where there is a 'high value on marriage' and few opportunities for women to sustain themselves outside the group, 'the options facing vulnerable women and children within the travelling community are limited' (1994) and the experience of abuse may differ accordingly. The point is not to 'discover' differences in abuse rates amongst different ethnic groups – in fact, when adjusted for socioeconomic circumstances, US studies appear to show little variation - but to sensitize ourselves as workers in a British context to the possibility that children who have been abused may respond differently according to their particular ethnic background, and to begin to develop responses and strategies for intervention which take account to these difference. However, with all of this recognition on difference it is vital to remember the point made earlier, that there may well be very important commonalities amongst clients. Similar experiences of oppression, of poverty and of situation may prove highly significant in terms of problem analysis, intervention, advocacy and self-help.

Finally, the recognition that the pursuance and development of an anti-discriminatory child protection practice is both a political and a moral enterprise requires that a worker's personal commitment to equality should be more than a superficial statement of adherence. As Archard (1993) has indicated, it requires a rethinking of our notions of what childhood itself is, for no longer can we sustain romanticized constructions of it as a state of innocence and incompetence. Good practice therefore implies that we do not simply to things *to* and *for* children, but that as far as possible we attempt to work *with* them.

# V

# GENDER EXPECTATIONS AND CHILD PROTECTION PRACTICE

## Introduction

Different gender expectations for boys and girls are widely recognized, particularly in terms of such things as patterns of dress and behaviour. Powerful social pressures operate which influence the ways in which adults think about children and which also influence children's expectations of themselves. I have found that young children quickly conform to gender expectations, so that even when parents make a special effort to address this problem, by offering their children a variety of toys, employing different role models and using non-sexist language, children are often inhibited or discouraged by other adults or children from pursuing activities outside the gender norms.

This short chapter examines some of the consequences of gender expectations upon the ways in which adults and children respond to sexual abuse. It is intended to increase awareness of the ways in which these socially structured ideas may be reproduced and reinforced, and it attempts to link abuse of, and by, children into broader issues of power and powerlessness. In this context, childhood can be understood as a powerless phase in the human life course during which we are dependent on others for our physical and emotional have little or no control over life decisions. When the powerlessness of childhood is exacerbated by the oppression of abuse, then correspondingly the degree of helplessness is greatly increased. A damaged sense of self, a lack of personal autonomy, and a sense of uncertainty and confusion about adult roles and responsibilities are common amongst victims of abuse.

**What do adults think?**

There is little doubt that many adults who accept conventional gender expectations of adult male female and sexuality attempt to make sense of the sexual abuse of children in these terms. Consequently, in a society in which boys learn expectations of aggression and predatory sexuality, while girls are taught a more passive role, adults may trivialize, dismiss or deny sexually abusive behaviour by young males as simply 'boys being boys'. For example, the behaviour of one 13-year-old boy who attempted to bugger a 7-year-old boy was described and assessed by the police and by the parents of both children as 'a childhood prank', 'a game that got out of hand', and as 'a misunderstanding' ! This response may, of course, derive from a more widespread denial of children's sexuality in our society, although arguably each of the parties involved may have had rather different reasons for characterizing this attempted rape as child's play. The behaviour of boys who sexually abuse girls is also frequently interpreted by means of the conventional gender expectations. It is perceived as a 'normal' urge, wrongly expressed or inadequately controlled, a misguided extension of supposedly 'normal' behaviour.

Conventional gender expectations, when applied to girls who are victims of sexual abuse, result in considerable sympathy for those who fit the preconceptions of passivity and weakness, and who are therefore viewed as understandably tearful victims. However, abused girls who breach conventional expectations, and who are perceived as being in some way either sexually provocative or precocious, may be blamed in much the same way as some adult victims of rape are, being described as 'slags' or as having 'asked for it'. I once overheard a male colleague say to another male colleague: 'No wonder she has been abused, did you see the way she was dressed?' In a similar fashion, the out-of-role behaviour of girls who victimize others is either dismissed as 'play' or treated with total disgust or bewilderment.

**How do children respond?**

If the abuse suffered is that of sexual abuse, then the child's feelings may be independent of their gender, but the way they express these emotions will be shaped by it. Boys seem to be more likely to express their distress through externally directed, more active behaviour, which may include aggression and violence towards other people. In contrast, girls' responses appear to be more passive and internally directed: their distress may be expressed tearfully, by running away or, in severe cases, by self-mutilation. Additionally, children's perceptions of why the abuse happened, and its consequences, may also be gender-based. For example, some boys who have been abused by men have subsequently asked: 'Does it mean I'm a "poof"?'

Victims of sexual abuse will look for situations which help them regain some feelings of control. New behaviours may be tried out by the child, and they will experiment with such behaviour until they understand its processes, variations, what it feels like, whether it is enjoyable, fun, satisfying or painful, and so on. It is likely that any behaviour which gives an abused child power or allows the expression of powerful emotions will be reinforced in that child. The child's experience of the behaviour and its consequences will determine whether the behaviour is reinforced or abandoned by the child. For a child who has been abused and who has not had help to come to terms with and make sense of the experience, there are, in both the long and the short term, two negative possibilities.

- to enact sexual behaviour by continuing in the role of victim;
- to become a victimizer themselves.

While these potential outcomes exist for girls and boys alike, it is my belief that the gender expectations prevalent within our society tend to steer boys towards an abusive victimizing role and girls into a perpetuation of the victim role. There are serious implications for the safety of the victims and of other children whenever either of these two possibilities occurs. Children who have been sexually abused may re-enact some of the behaviours they have seen or been subjected to. These re-enactments may include both victim and aggressor behaviours. As noted in the previous section, adult social reactions to boys and girls when they re-enact elements of their experiences will often be quite different. However, in the absence of any decisive adult censure, control and support, a victimizing child of either sex may be perceived by their less powerful peers as being powerful, and he or she may continue to abuse younger children, physically and sexually with virtual impunity.

## Some consequences of abuse

When a child exhibits sexually victimizing behaviour they have power over the victim. If adults ignore this behaviour or minimize it by calling it sexual experimentation and thus unwittingly allow it to continue, then the victim becomes powerless. Alternatively, if adults react in a shocked, angry, anxious or horrified manner, the victimizing child may understand that the adults are unable to cope with his or her behaviour. This realization can thus reinforce a potentially powerful pattern of behaviour.

It is especially difficult for children who live in families where there is an expectation that boys will grow up to abuse others, and that women and girls will always be powerless victims. If a boy remains in such a family, then he is likely to reproduce such expectations, and if his mother escapes from such a household with him, then the behaviours which he has already learned may act as unwelcome reminders of what has gone before. The boy's unwanted behaviour may consequently be perceived as deliberately abusive and somehow inevitable.

The consequences of failing to realize or respond effectively to abused children may continue into those children's adult lives. Undetected and uncontrolled, boys may continue into adulthood as abusive men, men who remain a risk to all children with whom they come into contact. Such men may deny their own abusive behaviour, and may also apply the same denial to abusive behaviour by other males and thereby fail to protect children from the depredations of other men. In fact, involving other men may even provide some sort of comforting rationale, a means of avoiding labelling their own behaviour as illegal or abusive.

Similarly, if girls are not taught that they have a right to assert their wishes, or at the very least that they have a right to say 'no', if they never experience non-abusive relationships or realize that such relationships exist, then they too may carry the consequences of abuse into adult life. Abused girls who are not helped to come to terms with their experiences may, as mothers, be afraid to touch or hug their own children because they fear that the child may interpret this as abuse. Some mothers may remain afraid that they may actually abuse their own children. In contrast, other women who have suppressed their abusive experiences may, as adults, miss or deny the symptoms of abuse in their own family or household. Those who have continued in a passive victim role may, in their adult life, replicate risky relationships based on submission to more dominant men. Their capacity to recognize and resist both their own continuing experiences of oppression, as well as that of their children, is thus severely impaired.

## Conclusion

While it is by no means inevitable that children who are subject to abuse will themselves become involved in abuse in their adult lives, there is a higher risk of this being the case than with children who did not suffer abuse. Therefore, apart from the obvious therapeutic benefits to the children, there is a clear case, in terms of prevention, for providing post-abuse therapy for children, therapy which incorporates work on the issue of re-enactment of behaviour. Children need to have boundaries set for their own behaviour which are realistic in terms of their age and gender. Such therapy should facilitate the safe expression of anger and teach the child non-abusive ways to exercise control over things: that is, to learn appropriate ways of feeling powerful. This work must include an assessment of how gender roles are affecting the child, and should help them challenge the gender expectations which may have shaped or reinforced their particular patterns of thought and behaviour.

While girls are more likely to need help in the overt expression of anger and boys in expressing their sorrow, the eventual goal is to reach a point in therapy where they can place responsibility for their experience of abuse on their abuser whilst taking responsibility for their own re-enactment of behaviours. From this point they have choices about what they will do in the future. All victims, male and female, have the potential to make the transition from victim or victim/abuser to survivor, but this is made more likely with skilled help.

# VI

# RETHINKING PRACTICE: LEARNING FROM A BLACK FEMINIST PERSPECTIVE

## Introduction

Major developments in child protection, such as the Children Act 1989 and the numerous official inquiries into cases of abuse, have stimulated many child protection professionals, especially those working with children and families from diverse backgrounds, to rethink their approach to their work. However, some agencies and professionals seem unable and unwilling to develop holistic, integrated approaches to assessment of such individuals and families - approaches which incorporate an understanding of the nature and operation of power and oppression. In such instances, those working in this arena need to reassess their own values and methods, and attempt to understand the important relationship between them.

This chapter advocates an approach to assessing and working with children and families that incorporate some of the core themes presented in the auto/biographical and theoretical writings of black feminists. Some of these writes, such as Barh (1992), Collins (1990) and hooks (1981, 1984, 1989), have written extensively about the relationship between their values and their methods for understanding social science and social relationships. Their analysis focus upon the personal and political dimensions of lived experience relating to race, class, gender, sexuality and social difference. A common feature of their work has been the desire to view these social divisions not as additive systems but as interlocking systems of oppression, a standpoint which promotes a more thorough analysis of difference and of the social reactions to it. Thus, an appreciation of black feminist perspectives is more likely to sensitize workers to the lived experience of their clients and to encourage a more developed understanding of the complex factors which interact with and act upon their clients' lives.

**Learning from our mistakes**

The 1980s witnessed several major child abuse inquiries; it was a volatile time for those involved in child protection. These inquiries highlighted important concerns about how agencies and workers were investigating child abuse, and about how they sought to protect children who came from backgrounds different from those of the workers involved. These inquiries alerted us to the existence of stereotyping within the assessment process and to the problems which have been arisen when professionals have assumed universal categories of race, culture, class and gender. In such instances, workers have assumed rather than assessed (Thompson, 1993). Sometimes this has resulted in a failure to protect black children in abusive situations because workers have based their assessments upon cultural assumptions made about particular 'racial' groups. Such assumptions may be punitive or liberal in their perspective, but both are likely to prove dangerous in practice.

Ahmed et al. (1986) have noted the tendency to base assessment on such assumptions and have highlighted severe discrepancies in the way black families and individuals have been dealt with. Ahmed (1989) has also noted the prevalence of punitive and coercive approaches to black families. In some cases, black children have been unnecessarily moved from their families when workers, and not just white workers, have used their own assumptions about family life as a baseline in their assessment, and have thus failed to recognize the strengths of black families. This may partly account for the notably higher proportion of black children in care than white children (ABSWAP, 1983). Such misguided and mistaken assumptions may operate in different and apparently less punitive directions, as, for example, in the case of Tyra Henry. Here the black grandmother was not seen as an individual but as a stereotype, albeit a positive one in this instance - as the 'all-coping indestructible African Caribbean matriarch' - an assumption which, as events sadly demonstrated, contributed to a failure to recognize the dangerousness of Tyra's situation, because of the overestimation of the protective influence of the grandmother (Lambeth, 1987).

## Relevant themes from black feminist perspectives

This section outlines some of the relevant ideas found in the auto/biographical and theoretical writings of black women – women who have advocated that 'Understanding does have to be founded on an analysis of real interconnecting, systematic, material oppressions as well as the personal experiences of their effects' (Clifford and Cropper, 1994). The following subheadings are used simply as a device for identifying some of these core ideas found within the literature and are not intended to represent the entirety of the perspectives, nor to imply that each idea is somehow a separate entity. They are clearly interlinked, both theoretically and in their implications for practice.

## Non-universal categories and the interconnection of oppression

Black feminists have been prominent in emphasizing the various ways in which oppressions interconnect and overlap, and they have criticized feminist and anti-racist theories which have excluded dimensions of race, class, disability and sexual orientation from their analyses (Collins, 1990; hooks, 1981, 1984; 1991; Lorde, 1984). What has also been critiqued are perspectives which advocate a hierarchy of oppressions in which racism comes first, while some of the others, if mentioned at all, trail far behind (Kershaw and Logan, 1994). Thus, what is most significant is the recognition that the category of 'woman' is not universal, and that an analysis of women's position must look at how a woman's situation is affected by interconnecting issues of race, class, disability, sexual orientation, age, and so on. For example, a woman's experience of living in poverty maybe further compounded by race and disability (Glendenning and Millar, 1987). Black feminist literature was examined the effects of racism on black people's lives and raised awareness that, for example, being black in Britain is different from individual to individual and community to community. It is vital for workers to connect biography, culture, structure and history when working which clients, as it is evident that black people are not a homogeneous group - the common dimension is that, while all black people are subject to racism in its various forms, the personal experience of individuals will differ according to other factors in their lives. Cosis-Brown (1992) has cautioned against any stereotyping that assumes certain individuals as a type.

## Identity and difference

Analysing difference and concerns with issues of identity have been at the forefront of black feminist literature. Approaching and working with social difference is made more complex by the reality of shifting identities and cultures, where individuals' identities and positions are not static but are fluid and can change over time (Lorde, 1984). This can best be seen in the case of black women who have multiple identities and who may align themselves with different groups such as black groups, women's groups, lesbian groups or disabled groups at different times. Workers who perceive individuals simply as members of a single social category will inevitably limit the scope of their assessments. There are obvious issues here around identity in terms of children in care. The care process can have profound implications for a child's self-image and identity. Research on black children has suggested that many of them have an early awareness of the negative images of their blackness (Maxime, 1986; Milner, 1983; Varma, 1993). In addition to whatever other problems they may face, these children have the pervasive effects of racist stereotyping and negative and derogatory imagery to contend with. Workers should therefore acknowledge the lived experience of black children and be aware of the impact this may have upon the children's development and upon their perceptions of adults and authority figures.

**Mother-blaming**

While feminist writers have raised professional awareness and challenged sexist assumptions and stereotypical notions about women's roles, the incorporation of such ideas into practice is often quite superficial. Braines and Gordon (1983) have pointed out that much of the literature on child protection is preoccupied with the mother's responsibility for abuse and protection. Apart from the obvious fact that this attribution of culpability is inherently problematic, it tends to devalue the role of other significant people and agencies by pathologizing women as 'poor mothers' who have apparently 'failed' to protect their children from men. Women abusers who do not fit into the stereotypical notions of 'woman' and 'mother' are generally treated differently and more harshly, as though they are doubly at fault by being abusers and by not conforming to the conventional stereotypes of women. Furthermore, mother-blaming is problematic because, at one level, issues of poverty, isolation, racism and stress are conveniently ignored while, at another, it downplays the potential contribution of other individuals, especially within 'non-Western' family structures.

**Narrative and standpoint**

Black feminists have advocated that the narrative form is crucial to their ways of understanding, assessing and communicating (Collins, 1990). Black women, being at the 'sharp end' of discrimination, can speak with some authority about their lives and the experience of marginalization and disadvantage. Their accounts of their lives have produced a triangulation of knowledge, experiences and perspectives that can be used by others to understand the problems they face. Thus, the special knowledge gained by oppressed individuals who occupy what has been termed as the 'outsider within' position in society (Collins, 1990; hooks, 1981, 1984) allows other more powerful people to appreciate the underside of oppression. Being the 'outsider' brings with it a certain kind of knowledge concerning those who are in dominant positions as well as the different knowledge of the dominated. Collins (1990) argues that this ontological knowledge and experience should be used as a valid viewpoint on the social world. She also puts forward the need to develop an interlinking of theory and lived experiences which can acknowledge and respect differences without fixing them outside history of contemporary social relations.

Narratives need to be viewed in both personal and political contexts. Accurate assessment and informed intervention are dependent upon hearing the voice of the other person and require an appreciation of the wider context in which that voice is speaking. It is imperative to give people a voice - to hear what they are saying and how they are saying it. Historically, it has been difficult for many clients to tell their stories, especially those people who have been perceived as different, deviant and 'difficult'. In the case of children who have been abused, the formal guidelines for interviewing still impede these young victims' narrative and make it difficult for their voice to be heard through the constraints of gathering formal evidence. In working with children, adults should be aware of their relatively powerful position and should thus seek ways of enabling children to communicate, as well as reflecting upon the language they use and the pace of conversation. One example from my own practice involved a black girl who was showing me her life-story book. Towards the end of the book, there were some typed notes which described how her mother had schizophrenia, and in a welter of social work jargon recorded the reasons for the girl's admission into care. When I asked the child what this page was, she told me that she did not want to look at that page because it was boring and she could not read some of the words, nor understand them. Clearly, this child was not being allowed to tell her story and record it in her own voice.

## Reflexivity and power

Linked to the analysis of difference and social divisions are issues concerning reflexivity and power. The concept of reflexivity is not a new one, and although it was developed by feminist writers (Stanley, 1990; Williams, 1989; Bhavnani, 1993) other writers have included issues of reflexivity and power within their perspectives (Freire, 1972). Reflexivity refers to the process by which individuals need to acknowledge their own role and position in any social interaction, and the effects that this has upon the interaction itself, upon themselves, and upon the people with whom they are interacting. It is important for workers consciously to locate themselves within the intervention and interaction - that is, to become aware and take cognizance of their own position, perspective and values, and to appreciate the other person's perceptions of them. Thus, in any client/worker relationship it is necessary for us to be aware of the influence we have as workers - workers who occupy specific positions in terms of profession and other social differences - upon the individuals and situations we are assessing. This is important because these perspectives and values will determine which 'facts' we select from our interactions and how we subsequently choose to interpret them. My own research into fostering and adoption assessments highlights the complexity and fluidity of such power issues. I was a black woman interviewing mainly white, female, working-class applicants for fostering and adoption, but unusually perhaps, I was the one who had power by virtue of my formal role of practitioner / researcher.

## The personal as political

Black feminists have highlighted how black women's lives and oral narratives interconnect and cannot be separated from the social, political and economic aspects of the society they live in. In most cases black women do not have a choice about whether to separate their personal lives from wider, external societal issues. Again, this was a feature of my research in which black, disabled and gay interviewees appeared to have some understanding of this concept and spoke about how being black, disabled or gay had implications in both their personal and outside lives. For example, black women's experiences are shared with, and are part of the lives of, others, particularly when they live within black communities.

## Contemporary policy and practice

Much of the literature of the 1980s failed to make reference to black children and families and those from various other ethnic minority groups whose diverse life experiences will be compounded by racism and who may encounter such racism from the agencies which strive to maintain their care and welfare. This literature therefore made little attempt to develop an analysis of oppression and power in both personal and structural terms. For example, the Department of Health (1988) booklet *Protecting Children* made only very limited reference to race and, while the Children Act 1989 requires 'due consideration' to be given to a child's race, religion and culture, some have interpreted these requirements in minimalist terms. Within the formal knowledge base of social work, explicitly anti-racist and feminist approaches to theory and practice have attempted to challenge race - and gender - oppressive theories and practice at both personal and institutional levels (Dominelli, 1988; Dominelli and McLeod, 1989; Thompson, 1993). One major theme within this literature is that the categories of race, gender, class, disability, age and sexual orientation are not viewed as single-factor issues in isolation from each other. Other writers have also highlighted the strengths of various individuals and communities who had previously been portrayed as problematic and pathological (Ahmed, 1990), and this has encouraged workers to reassess some of the more common stereotypical assumptions. For example, Asian women have provided analyses on roles and relationships within their cultures which present quite a different picture from the simplistic portrayals of them as quiet, passive women, repressed by arranged marriages (Bhavnani and Coulson, 1986).

Some social work agencies have dealt with difference by trying to match workers and families, particularly in terms of race and gender divisions. While it is useful for children and families, particularly in the sensitive area of child abuse, to be matched with individuals who can share and understand experiences of racism, sexism and other oppressions, it is essential for *all* workers to have an understanding of how oppression operates. It should not be a foregone conclusion that all black people and all women are able to recognize race and gender oppression, particularly given that we are all subject to the internalizing of racist, sexist and other oppressive stereotypes. Black workers alone cannot solve all problems, some of which have been created by the oppressive practices of such agencies. Thus, black workers may be isolated, marginalized and exploited within some agencies, having difficult cases to attend to and advise upon, and receiving limited support.

## Making assessments

While official policy on child protection advocates a comprehensive assessment in order to 'understand the child's and family's situation in order to provide a sound basis for future assessments' (Department of Health, 1988) and thus acknowledge the importance of workers understanding the cultural context, workers should be wary of cultural relativism and an overreliance on cultural explanations (Channer and Parton, 1990). If not, such analyses may 'detract attention both from significant emotional factors as well as structural factors, such as class and race' (Ahmed, 1981, cited in Gambe et al., 1992). Despite efforts to incorporate issues of race and culture when working with black families, there is an unfortunate tendency to omit other dimensions of social difference. Such reductionist approaches isolate and marginalize race from the other dimensions of class and gender. However, race and racism can only be fully understood if analysed in the context of these other dimensions to the lives of individuals and families (Gilroy, 1992). Furthermore, there is a tendency to construct a hierarchy of oppressions in which racism comes first and the others follow on afterwards, whereas, as noted in the previous section, factors such as gender also affect how women experience racism and being black.

The danger of these stereotyped assumptions has been that individual families and their norms, values and functioning have often not been assessed in a holistic sense, by attempting to put families and individuals into convenient 'boxes' it has had the effect of limiting workers' understanding of such clients and their situations. In the case of black families, black communities vary enormously in terms of social and cultural traditions, so that there is no single style of black family functioning. The same applies to white families, who are not homogeneous in terms of values, norms, culture and traditions? Although 'white family' is not a term that is used in the same way as 'black family' is used, it should be noted that most people would be hard-pressed to define white family norms in the way that black family norms have often been unquestionably defined. Indeed, we are usually never alerted to the fact that an assessment or report is actually about a white family, as whiteness is assumed as the norm. With both white and black families it would be equally wrong to impose middle-class, heterosexual stereotypical norms and values. It is difficult for social workers to make 'clear, comprehensive and expert judgements' (Department of Health, 1988) if they persist in using such limited references and analyses of difference.

## Taking power into account and locating the worker within the assessment

While it is important to look at individuals' life experiences, where it is possible to locate individuals within their particular, personal experiences and thus avoid stereotyping, care should also be taken to encompass a much broader framework which includes issues of power and oppression and some reflection upon the worker's own position. This points to 'a need to look at ways in which our [workers'] membership of different social categories has affected our perceptions and others' perceptions of us' (Clifford and Cropper, 1994).

Difficulties can occur whenever there is a difference in power between client and worker. Indeed, black families themselves do feel that class is often an issue with any worker – black or white (Rhodes, 1993). The fact is that *all* workers have power over their clients by virtue of their professional and their class position. These factors potentially influence all worker/client relationships and so impinge upon all aspects of intervention. Reflexivity is a two-way process, and thus it is necessary to be aware of the influence workers will have on clients' lives and the effect clients and their situations will have on the workers'. This is particularly so within the area of child protection where the very nature of such work can lead to intense stress and sometimes burn-out. Workers need to recognize their professional status, whoever they are - their race, gender, age or other social division does not take this dimension away.

Issues of reflexivity and power are of prime importance when workers are engaged in comprehensive assessments involving family members' life histories, or are helping individuals in making sense of their own lives and actions. It is imperative that individuals are allowed to speak their narrative – that is, talk about their own lives in their own words. This avoids the immediate perils of unwittingly superimposing meaning upon the actions and motivations of other people. Listening carefully to the narratives of clients may help workers to gain insight into the individual's experiences in a way that can guard against their being influenced by assumptions and stereotypes.

## Conclusion

It is my view that the broad themes I have identified as central to black feminist perspectives can be used to assist social workers and other professionals to achieve more comprehensive assessments - assessments that are nor reductionist in nature. Thus an appreciation of the ideas of non-universal categories and interconnection of oppression; identity; mother-blaming; narrative and standpoint; reflexivity and power, and the personal as political should serve to raise personal awareness of these issues and potentially can be developed into a more thoroughgoing analysis for child protection practice and process - analysis which is able to acknowledge the diversity of individuals' experiences, grounded in the very different social conditions of their lives (hooks, 1981; Lorde, 1984). Furthermore, such knowledge generated from black feminist perspectives can be used to assist an understanding of the position of all individuals, whether they are black or white, female or male. This is possible because black women have been concerned about promoting multiple standpoints and have allowed for difference in a way that others have rejected or analysed in narrow terms. Incorporating some of these themes in theoretical and practical terms may pave the way for a more holistic and thorough approach to assessing children and families in the arena of child protection. Therefore, all workers are recommended to attempt to:

- make connections between individual lives and the wider social political structures and history;
- listen carefully to personal narratives, and to situate these within the broader context;
- explore areas of misunderstanding and personal ignorance by asking for explanation and clarification, and thus avoid making ethnocentric assumptions.

# VII

# RESEARCHING THE EFFECTS OF CHILD ABUSE

## Introduction

Much research time and effort have rightly been directed to the detection and investigation of child abuse. However, for practitioners working with those who have been abused, there is a relative dearth of information about its effects, both long - and short-term, upon which to base appropriate intervention (Oates and Bross, 1995; Reder et al., 1993). In the absence of such information, many practitioners may develop their knowledge of such effects from their personal experience of practice and from the acquisition of the 'common sense' stock of knowledge about child abuse. This 'common sense' is likely to presume as a 'fact' that child abuse is damaging in its consequences, and that it can so damage children that they, in turn, may become abusers of others. It is not the intention of this chapter to reject that assumption, but it is my aim to attempt to clarify which effects are well established by research and to point up some of the limitations of that research. For example, in Chapter 7 in this volume, Bannister and Gallagher, in describing work undertaken with children who sexually abuse other children and noting the effects of previous abuse as an important factor to be considered in the causation of abuse, are careful to acknowledge the limitations of our 'knowledge'. This caution is well founded for, as research by Dobash et al. (1993) has shown, 77 per cent of the perpetrators studied had not been abused themselves.

While there is a growing body of research in the USA, in the UK, as the report *Child Protection : Messages from Research* (Department of Health, 1995) has identified, there remains a shortage of information that can be used to guide child protection practice after the initial stages of investigation and detection. It is the purpose of this chapter to provide a review of recent research into the effects of child abuse, with a view to highlighting issues which will be of use for practitioners in working with the effects of abuse on children. These effects, which may be manifested in childhood or later in adult life, can usefully be categorized as being of the three types – that is, the consequences for the victims in respect of:

- sexual and criminal behaviour;
- mental health;
- parenting behaviour.

These divisions are made in order to make the studies easier to understand. They are not intended to oversimplify or misrepresent the reality of abuse, nor are they seen as being mutually exclusive consequences - clearly, the effects may be complex and interwoven.

There is no discussion of possible development delays resulting from traumatic experiences in childhood, but suffice to say that much of the literature is relatively limited in terms of the timespan of recording and observation. However, Gibbons et al., who undertook a study which examined the effects of physical abuse on children nine to ten years after the abusive events were discovered, found that their data:

> pointed away from the conclusion that physical abuse in early life had a direct [or long-lasting] effect on

> children's development. It seemed rather that physical abuse was in some cases an important sign of a number of other generally damaging circumstances, in particular of a harshly punitive, less reliable and less warmly involved from of parenting. (1995)

Of course, there are some events, such as severe injuries, which are so traumatic that their effects cannot but be found in later childhood or adult life, and it should be noted that this study did not attempt to investigate the more subtle, but perhaps more pervasive, effects of emotional abuse upon personal esteem and identity. What follows, then, is a review of the research material divided into the three broad categories of the consequences of abuse, as listed above. In each of these areas the results of research will be discussed and the veracity of their findings will be described as the researchers assess them. This is followed by a brief review of some of the methodological problems involved in this area of research, and a summary of the main implications for practice.

**Sexual and criminal behaviour**

Much research has attempted to describe possible links between the experience of childhood sexual abuse (CSA) and the victim's subsequent involvement in abusive or inappropriate behaviour. In Friedrich's (1993) review of the literature, he outlines a range of studies which use diverse methodologies based on empirical assessments of sexual behaviour in relation to children. These include reviews of personal records; parent reports; the relationship of abuse variables to sexual behaviour; psychological assessment of the child, and direct observation of the child's behaviour. Friedrich concludes that there is an increasing body of research which has demonstrated that sexual abuse is linked to increased sexual behaviour in the victim following the abuse. In particular, increases in this behaviour appear to be related to specific abuse factors such as the number of perpetrators, and to more general behaviour disruption.

However, one problem is that the type of assessment method used relates to whether or nor sexual behaviour is observed in the first place. Some methods are less reliable than others. Commenting on the use of children's drawings to infer experiences of abuse, Friedrich noted that mixed results were obtained and were less significant than direct observation of children. As he remarked:

> Direct observation of children led to relatively consistent findings on increased sexual behaviour. It appears that drawings, for example, are one more step removed from the child than the more proximate behaviour observed either by parents or other observers. (1993)

The limitations of this method are obvious: the subjective interpretations of these drawings may say more about the viewer than about the artist. We should be wary of inferring abuse from what may be quite benign representations of family life or general life experiences. Similar difficulties have also been highlighted in observing the play of children with 'anatomically correct' dolls and then interpreting its significance as a sign of abuse. Everson and Boat (1994) found a wide range of interpretations between professionals as to what forms of play constituted evidence of sexual abuse. Howitt (1992) describes this research and highlights some of the differences. For example, while 'Half of the social workers saw the laying of the dolls on top of each other as abnormal - only one fifteenth of law enforcement officers did'

In concluding his review, Friedrich notes that increased sexual behaviour by sexually abused children is consistently recognized and that more research needs to be devoted to assessment and intervention and the longer-term implications for the children. This conclusion mirrors that of Hallett and Birchall (1992) for a UK context: 'sound empirical evaluations of outcomes of treatment options are lacking'.

Adams et al. (1995) studied a group of 499 'seriously

mentally ill' children receiving treatment at a psychiatric hospital. The subjects were categorized as follows :

| | |
|---|---|
| no inappropriate sexual behaviour | (n=296) |
| inappropriate sexual behaviour | (hypersexual, n = 82) |
| | (exposing, n = 39) |
| | (victimizing, n = 82) |

Information was taken from hospital records in the form of chart reviews. Although there are obvious methodological problems arising from the nature of the sample (thereby prompting caution about the extent to which it is possible to make any wider inferences), the study had the benefit of using a comparison group (no inappropriate sexual behaviour) to highlight which clinical features were specific risk factors for the inappropriate behaviour group, rather than those more broadly associated with mental disorder. Overall, 82 per cent of those with inappropriate sexual behaviour had some history of being sexually abused, but in the comparison group only 36 per cent had similar histories. Within the inappropriate sexual behaviour group with more severe problems (exposing and victimizing) there was a clear association with a number of factors, such as development delays, lower IQ scores, other behavioural difficulties, and also having been abused. It was clear that there was a stronger association between having been sexually abused and displaying inappropriate sexual behaviour than other factors. The researches found that the greater the severity of the history of abuse, for example in terms of the number of perpetrators involved, then the greater the chance of envolvement in the more serious forms of inappropriate sexual behaviour.

Widom and Ashley Ames (1994), using analysis taken from criminal records in Indiana, attempted to assess the long-term criminal consequences of childhood sexual abuse. They compared cases of validated childhood sexual abuse with a group consisting of physically abused and neglected children, and with a control group who were matched for age, race, sex and class. They concluded that, compared with other types of child abuse and neglect, childhood sexual abuse does not uniquely increase an individual's risk for later delinquent or criminal behaviour. However, when compared with the control group, both groups of children who had been abused were significantly more likely to commit a sexual offence. Where these three characteristics were found together (neglect, and physical and sexual abuse), then victims were more likely to run away than was the case for those experiencing sexual abuse only. It is significant that the majority of both the male and the female sexually abused children in this study did not have an official criminal history. We should therefore recognize, as the authors note, that 'Delinquency and criminality represent only one possible type of outcome associated with childhood sexual abuse' (1994).

This is an important finding, as it suggests the multifaceted nature of the effects of child abuse in later life and directs us to be sceptical of attempting to highlight one consequence as being necessarily more significant than another in the experiences of survivors of abuse. One encouraging finding was that a relationship with a significant and supportive person may act as a buffer for the long-term consequences of abuse. This raises crucial issues for future research, as examining cases where children appear to overcome, or have been protected from, negative consequences of their early childhood experiences may have considerable implications for how social workers attempt to prevent and work with the damaging consequences of abuse. Furthermore, it suggests that the status of 'victim' is not an inevitable nor an irreversible consequence of childhood abuse. Child protection workers should, therefore, more readily consider the potential benefits to be gained by working in the long term with survivors, and also acknowledge the potentially valuable work of survivor groups who have been able to step away from and challenge the status of 'victim' so readily imputed to them by some professionals.

**Mental health**

The traumatizing effects of childhood sexual abuse (CSA) on mental health have been widely noted. It is accepted as axiomatic by many practitioners that it carries a legacy which feeds into long-term psychological harm. This appears to be borne out by the prevalence of CSA amongst those seeking help with psychological problems (Davenport et al., 1994).

The study by Davenport et al. attempted to gauge whether there was a consensus as to what abuse people considered to be most severe in terms of its consequent effects. The authors wished to assess whether these views coincided with wider, more grounded, empirical research and observation. Their simple, which consisted of professionals in the field, students, and patients with eating disorders who themselves had a high incidence of CSA, showed a high level of agreement between respondents as to what factors contributed to CSA. The people in the sample were also asked to identify the relative strength of the relationship between the duration and forms of abuse and the consequences, by distinguishing between those factors which they perceived to be less serious and those which were deemed most serious. The results, as one might expect, showed that the abusive act itself was seen as a highly significant element. Thus, abuse which involved physical contact abuse was rated more serious than non-contact, but the use of force to overcome resistance of CSA was considered to be potentially even more traumatic. Less predictably, the variable which received the most consistent results was the disclosure of CSA and its effects upon the victim. This traumatic effect was not limited simply to the initial response at the time of disclosure. In fact, there was broad agreement that a lack of continuing familial support was the worst post-abusive environment for the CSA victim.

To professionals who are considering what kind of support would be most beneficial for a victim, this finding suggests that interventions such as family therapy and groupwork may be more effective than individual support offered in isolation. This should not diminish the overall importance of disclosure itself as profoundly therapeutic, since, as Davenport at al. indicate, such disclosure can be extremely helpful in reducing feelings of shame, stigma, guilt and personal blame. Speculatively, however, it seems that the broader acknowledgement that abuse has taken place and the social support offered by significant others is most helpful in diminishing the traumatic effects of CSA on a victim.

The existence of a consensus on the relative importance of the different factors associated with abuse should not be taken as evidence of the inevitability of a victim being damaged by even the most traumatic events, nor of the relative inn-ocuousness of seemingly trivial incidents - although, clearly, the possibility of agreement between professionals and their clients about the effects of CSA will be important for the process of helping. For example, such agreement means that the client will have a greater chance that their feelings and expectations will be understood and met by the worker. The importance of this finding is crucial in enabling professionals to distinguish those factors which either contribute to or hopefully mediate against abuse at various stages of the abuse cycle. In developing this line of research, it may be productive to distinguish between the primary and post-abuse situation and therefore identify those interventions which are of most help at the respective stages of abuse and recovery.

Rowan et al. (1994) studied 47 survivors of CSA who had sought help. The authors attempted to examine the relationship between the seriousness of CSA experienced and the subsequent development of post traumatic stress disorder (PTSD). Using a standardized measure of PTSD, they found significant correlations between the intensity of the abuse in both duration and severity and a diagnosis of PTSD and its level of severity. The problem with the study, as the authors note, concerns the influence of other childhood/adult traumas in the subjects' lives which might have affected the development of PTSD. As the authors remarked: 'Given the report of these other traumas, it might have been expected that these other traumas would have been significantly related to the PTSD measures'. Therefore, we should be wary of mistakenly attributing cause and effect to incidents which may have had their roots in the past and which may also have been significant in forming the current level of trauma. Davenport et al. (1994) suggest that researchers undertaking studies should, in the future, obtain more extensive measures of other trauma experiences. For practitioners, this observation highlights the importance of obtaining accurate histories of family and client experience, and implies that we should be careful not to oversimplify the possible interlinking of different factors in constructing our understanding of problems, causes and possible therapies. Wind and Silvern (1994) tried to address this issue by studying how difference in the personal experiences of parental warmth and childrearing affected female survivors' psychological difficulties in relation to their childhood physical and sexual abuse. They found a clear differentiation between victims' perceptions of parental warmth - which strongly influenced the relationship between intrafamilial child abuse and levels of self-esteem and depression - and the association of abuse with post traumatic stress syndrome - which was independent of perceived parenting.

Brayden et al. (1995) attempted to study the lasting influence of CSA upon adult mental well-being and feelings of physical self-esteem. They studied the hospital records of women with a history of mental health problems and searched for differences between those reported as having been sexually abused in childhood and those with no recorded history of such abuse. The authors were somewhat surprised to find that childhood sexual abuse was not a good predictor of how sexually abused women felt about their emotional and psychological health after family and other demographic variables were taken into account. However, despite this lack of a direct independent association between this hypothetical concept and CSA, the levels of physical well-being and worth were lower for sexually abused women than for non-abused women when other explanatory variables were controlled.

Interest in the impact of the severity of CSA experienced by its victims has been stimulated by the controversies about the existence of ritualized forms of abuse. Lowrence et al. (1995) attempted to assess the impact of such abuse in relation to women who had been sexually abused in childhood. Their study was an empirically based assessment of the consequences of self-reported CSA which examined whether there were differences between women who in childhood had experienced ritualistic forms of abuse (CRA) and those who had experienced non-ritualized forms only (NRA). The study found that the CRA group exhibited and experienced significantly higher levels of trauma, which related to factors such as the duration of abuse and the number of perpetrators. Although the study made no claim as to the veracity of the CRA group's claims, the symptoms reported were consistent with profiles of individuals who have suffered other, more easily discernible forms of traumatization.

La Fontaine (1995), in her research on ritualized abuse, found that many of the children who reportedly had been subjected to CRA had suffered extreme levels of traumatization as a result of their experiences, but that there was little evidence that CRA, as distinct from NRA, was a significant factor. More pertinently, the levels of trauma appeared to be linked to the seriousness of the abuse, in terms of factors such as the number of perpetrators and the practices involved, rather than to any ritualized components. However, because these cases were rather extreme ones, the impact on the children was in turn intense and, for many workers, highly disturbing. La Fontaine suggests that the effect of this on professionals was for them to 'seek evidence of an event of assault or abuse commensurate with the magnitude of the damage', to the extent that they sought, or were susceptible to, notions of unusual ritualized practices. The practices were, in La Fontaine's view, mostly known forms of sexual deviation, all being behaviours depicted in existing child pornography. Furthermore, these demonized explanations tended to obscure more significant factors, such as the extreme poverty and deprivation in which many of the children lived.

The impact of such evidence of traumatization and its effect on workers is notable in the response of workers to therapeutic issues. Recognizing the scope and scale of the distress felt by the children and the effects this trauma has upon workers themselves requires that workers are clear about their own feelings of abuse, given that some may have experienced abuse themselves. In this context, self-help groups for practitioners and survivors of abuse may well be an important source of support in dealing with this kind of trauma (Lloyd, 1993).

## Parenting behaviour

There are two dimensions to this type of effect. First is the effect of abuse upon the child's parent(s) and their subsequent response to the child and his or her behaviour. Second is the longer-term effect upon the abused individuals in adult life when they themselves become parents - that is, upon their capacity to parent their own children.

Recent work in the UK has focused on the impact of abuse upon the mothers and carers of abused children. Two studies by Monck and colleagues both examined the effects of 'treatment' plans on such children and their carers, and found that, while there was little change in the children's feelings of depression and suicide after intervention, there were significant improvements in the carers' self-esteem and parenting skills. Monck and New (1995), in a study of a group of mothers of children subjected to CSA, attempted to examine the efficacy of groupwork compared with family work alone, but were unable to come to clear conclusions in this respect. Although their evidence was not conclusive, the clinicians involved in assessing the participants' progress did claim improvements for those additionally involved in group therapy. The children were able to share their feelings about their abuse with others, and mothers were said to have made progress with their own feelings regarding their children's abuse. Mothers reported fewer behavioural problems in their children and that their relationship with their children had improved. Differences in the researchers' and the clinicians' findings may not necessarily invalidate the group approach. As Monck et al. (1995) suggest, it is possible that groupwork may well deepen mothers' and children's understanding of whose responsibility the abuse was, yet it may not lessen the feelings of depression which may arise in the short term as a result of this increase in understanding. Thus, if the research was carried out over a longer term, the benefits described above might become more apparent. The positive message from this research is that interventions of whatever kind (group/family or both) could reduce feelings of depression in carers and so enhance their capacity to cope with their children's behaviour, 'normal' or otherwise.

A common concern expressed by parents who were themselves victims of childhood sexual abuse is their fear that they will be unable to parent their own children adequately. This fear in itself can be debilitating and, in turn, may lead to problems in parenting their own children. Cole at al. (1992), in a study of incest survivors, attempted to assess the range of difficulties that such parents experienced. The study compared three groups of women, those:

- whose father was alcoholic (often associated with incest) but not abusive;
- with fathers who were not abusive nor alcoholic;
- with fathers who had involved daughters in incest.

In comparison to the other two groups, the women who had experienced incest felt inadequate as parents. They reported feelings of lack of confidence and lack of control, and felt emotionally overwhelmed by the demands of parenting. This was particularly difficult in relation to the promotion of autonomy and self-control in their children. As Cole at al. noted, parental consistency, organization and a sure but sensitive manner are usually positively associated with the development of self-control and autonomy in children. The difficulties incest survivors reported with their own children suggest the possibility of a vicious circle of feelings of inadequacy which both impairs their capacity to cope and exacerbates the difficulties they have with their children, and which in turn leads the carers to feel move inadequate and less confident in parenting.

Relationship problems with their children also fed through into survivors' relationships with their partners, as the incest victims' experience of their family of origin was significant in corroding the trust that builds between partners in adult life. Finding a positive relationship with their marital partner, as the researchers describe it, predicts feelings of confidence and control which may suggest, as noted above, the importance of supportive relationships in mediating the negative long-term effects of incest.

## Some problems of methodology

For a variety of reasons, as most researchers would concede, researching the effects of child abuse is fraught with methodological difficulties. These might begin, for example, with the question of defining what actually constitutes abuse

(Department of Health, 1995) and extend through to the reliability of self-report and recall studies, encompassing the whole gamut of problems traditionally associated with survey research. This section does not attempt to provide a thorough review of these difficulties but, instead aims to alert the reader to some of the more pressing problems in respect of the studies reviewed here.

### Conceptualizations, design and representativeness

Ghate and Spencer (1995) note that the way in which child sexual abuse is conceptualized and operationally defined influences the overall design of the study, the nature of the questions asked and, crucially, the estimates of the prevalence of such abuse which are produced. A review of the literature shows that a wide variety of different methodologies are used. These range from self-report data (Bagley et al., 1994) or empirical research based on clinical samples using structured interview techniques (Rowan et al., 1994), to questionnaires used with groups outside the identified abused population, such as students (Davenport et al., 1994). Much of the data gathered by these studies is specific to the research design and the nature of the population studied, and so there are obvious limits to the extent to which it is possible to generalize from it. This problem of representativeness means that studies based upon, for example, samples of children and adults undergoing psychiatric treatment may be highly unrepresentative of the wider population of people who have been abused.

### Research instruments, measurement and comparisons

Clearly, such selectivity has benefits in terms of targeting research but it undoubtedly influences the professional 'common sense' assessment of the effects of abuse, particularly the impact of these effects on the future physical and psychological health of those abused. This aspect is raised in a review of the empirical assessment of sexual behaviour in sexually abused children made by Friedrich (1993), who notes that increased sexual behaviour in such children is consistently identified as a consequence of sexual abuse. The problem here is that: 'The type of assessment method [used] seems related to whether or not sexual behaviour problems are observed' in the first place. The potentially self-fulfilling nature of such activity is obvious: the significance is that our knowledge of CSA and its consequences is affected by the ways in which researchers choose to study the problem - that is, the methods they adopt to measure the extent and prevalence of such abuse within their chosen population. Many studies do not allow effective comparisons to be made either between different populations or over the passage of time. It would be useful if researchers attempted some standardization of the research instruments used for the assessments of children both before and after therapy, and if they clearly specified the criteria for successful outcomes.

**Conclusion**

While these important methodological problems must be acknowledged, it should also be recognized that, in view of the low level of knowledge currently obtaining, these studies do provide some important information for practitioners wishing to understand the effects of abuse on victims. What I am arguing for in this review is an informed and critical reading of the literature, which recognizes the limitations of the studies in terms of their absolute validity, but which does not dismiss the information contained in them as having no practical value at all.

The first major point is that while practitioners are extensively engaged in the detection and investigation of child abuse, there has been less focus on more positive aspects of how to work with the consequences of abuse for both carers and children. Following in the wake of the Cleveland Inquiry and the persistent underfunding of social service provision

(Schorr, 1992), part of the problem in the UK in recent years has been this imbalance of effort, where prevention and ameliorative efforts have been overwhelmed by the focus on guidelines for greater sophistication and accuracy at the assessment stage (Farmer and Owen, 1995). Although the intention of the Children Act 1989 was to create a framework for partnership in childcare interventions, as noted in Chapter 11 in this volume, this is not without its own problems. For example, not all families wish to be assisted or are in a position to be treated in the way that some practitioners may want to work with them. Nevertheless, it is probable that the best way to help children who have been abused is not through individual therapy but by supporting their carers.

This review has, for the heuristic reasons noted in its introductory section, separated out different categories of effects of abuse, but perhaps the most significant finding from the research is the multifaceted impact of the effects of abuse, rather than the isolation of single outcomes (Widom and Ashley Ames, 1994). The complex interaction of multiple factors in the abusive actions, in the child's experience and in the carers' responses should compel us to treat with caution any unitary views on the effects of child abuse which isolate that abuse from the social context in which it takes place.

Given the potential benefits of various forms of family work, groupwork and peer support, it remains questionable whether these forms of long-term intervention have any priority in many social services departments in the UK. Although recent government guidelines have indicated that social services departments may be too focused on prioritizing protection work, the problem of resources as well as the operational perspective will continue to impede developments. The dilemma that departments face in this area is acute. While a shift of focus would provide greater opportunities for workers to justify and embark upon long-term supportive work, the resource base for children's services continues to be under threat and at risk of collapse, especially in inner city areas, as successive reports into child abuse failures have documented (Parton, 1991). If government attempts to refocus social service departments on-to issues of prevention are successful, then it is to be hoped that resources will be available to provide the longer-term support and intervention that this review has shown to be so crucial in working with child abuse. However, there remains a more fundamental question about whether it is appropriate to frame intervention solely within the narrow therapy-oriented model which continues to dominate everyday practice (Hallett and Birchall, 1992; Parton, 1985).

# VIII

# AN INTERNATIONAL A REVIEW OF CHILD PROTECTION SERVICES

## Introduction

In the 1960s, while Kempe at al. first reported the 'baby battering syndrome' in 1962 and the NSPCC research unit into 'baby battering' was established by 1968, public and professional awareness and acknowledgement of child abuse were limited. However, this innocence was shattered in 1973 by the death of Maria Colwell, which taught the UK that child abuse could be a killer and that it was a problem our society must address. Since then, a succession of highly publicized inquiries have established a general perception of both the prevalence and consequences of abuse, and the inefficiency of social work services. Subsequently, a key question in the minds of the public and politicians is: how effective are child protection services in reducing the annual toll of that most extreme consequence of child abuse, child death ? Until recently there wee relatively few outcome studies in respect of child protection to offset its poor media image. However, over the past decade or so there has been growing evidence that good social work works (Pritchard, 1986; MacDonald et al., 1992; Raynor et al., 1995; Sheldon, 1995). There have been, of course, a number of very important child protection studies (for example, Parker et al., 1991) and, more recently, broader studies which have explored outcome over time (Thoburn et al., 1994: Gibbons et al., 1995) or analysed variations in rates of children on the Child Protection registers or numbers in care (Little and Gibbons, 1992; Gibbons and Bell, 1994).

Crucially policy issues drive practice, not least because of the high media–and therefore high political - profile child protection has. Given the growing use of audit by the Department of Health (1992), with in increasing emphasis upon prevention, it is expected that similar 'targets' will be demanded of Social Services. Some researchers have used child death rates as outcome measures, though this is not an uncontested practice (Lindsey and Trocme, 1994; MacDonald, 1995). Evidence from such studies in the USA is contradictory. For example, claims of a reduction in child deaths being associated with an improvement and increases in the levels of reporting of abuse (Besharov, 1990) were challenged by Lindsey and Trocme (1994) and Pritchard (1992a).

There are, of course, difficult methodological and ethical problems in child protection research (Gallagher et al., 1995). Obviously one cannot compare non-intervention against intervention, and at best, therefore, it is 'special' versus standard care which can be evaluated. Yet the consequences of ineffective child protection - apart from fatality, which is relatively rare (Greenland 1987; Pritchard, 1994) - cannot be overstated. Adults with a history of abuse or neglect are disproportionately represented amongst a whole range of adult psychosocial pathology (Hawton and Roberts, 1985; Van Egmond and Jonker, 1988; Pritchard et al., 1990; Akhurst et al., 1995; Cox and Pritchard, 1995). Paradoxically, because the problem is so serious, only the most rigorous research is acceptable, but methodologically this is so problematic that it has to be acknowledged that many studies, including this work, have limitations. None the less, child protection outcomes should be reviewed nationally because, self-evidently, if there is no improvement or, indeed, matters have deteriorated, we are morally bound to consider alternative practice and policies. This chapter aims to provide such a review of child protection services by an examination of national and international trends in child homicide.

**Practice outcome studies: an early positive outcome**

In the late 1980s, Hampshire Social Service Department reviewed, via a retrospective analysis of the case records of 60 families on the Child Protection register, the impact of their child protection services. By definition, families on the register would be expected to be especially disturbed, and this was confirmed as the majority experienced multiple psychosocial problems, with half the mothers having experienced neglect or abuse when they were children (Pritchard, 1991). It was important to gain an independent and validated assessment of the degree of risk the children faced, and this was the first study in Europe to use the 'Assessment Scheme' of Baird (1988), which is increasingly being utilized in the USA because of its brevity and ease of use.

In the Hampshire cohort only 5 per cent of the families were assessed as being at 'Moderate Risk'; 85 per cent were 'High Risk', and a further 10 percent were assessed at the 'Very High Risk' level. Considering these scores, and comparing them with work in the USA, it was anticipated that four out of five children would have been subjected to abuse or re-abuse, with at least half the sample being received into care. However, the Hampshire results were considerably more encouraging. In spite of the high levels of psychosocial disruption, some 90 per cent of the children had been successfully reintegrated into their family of origin and remained so for two years after the closure of the case. Nevertheless, because of the impact of the media upon our perceptions, such a positive outcome had not been expected.

A core theme in the direct work by the social workers was

practical help within the essential context of a supportive and, at times, supervisory relationship. It was clear that, in the vast majority of families, despite most of them having a history of long-standing disruption, the social workers were able to engage the families in a constructive, but not sentimental, relationship. One-fifth of the families had had their children taken into temporary care, but in such a manner as was eventually perceived as caring and supportive. Initially, many of the parents needed a degree of dependency upon the social worker(s), until they were sufficiently empowered to meet the needs of their children. These themes were noted in an earlier study from the USA by Burch and Mohr (1980), who contrasted a standard level of provision against an enhanced service described as 'Positive Parenting'. Here, again within the context of an appropriate relationship, the workers utilized 'educational' principles, recognizing that their cohort of families needed to learn parenting skills, because most had never experienced them at first hand themselves.

Families who received the focused 'educational' rapport model did significantly better than clients receiving another standard child protection service, with less abuse/re-abuse, lower in-care rates and better social adjustment. This caring *and* controlling/supervisory relationship was also found in another outcome study by Zimrin (1984), in which success was essentially due to the level and strength of contact, as family aides had intensive contact over a three-month period. Quite literally the families were under daily supervision in every sense of that world, as they were given practical demonstrations of home care and childcare so that, in all cases, positive and sustaining relationships were developed, to the extent that, when the service ceased, there was measurable deterioration. Again, the enhanced service did better than the standard level of care. Of particular interest is the work of Gibbons et al. (1995), who showed that, in relation to both attitudes of the protection services and parenting styles, the quality of relationship was crucial to the long-term development of children who had been abused.

**How good, nationally, is our child protection ?**

The results of the Hampshire study were discussed confidentially with a number of senior practitioners, who expressed the opinion that an evaluation of their own services would have similar results; at least 80 per cent of their children 'at risk' would be successfully reintegrated into their families. If such success was fairly widespread, it seemed logical that there should be some indication of improved child protection at the national level over time. The problem was how to demonstrate an event - abuse - which if prevented would not be visible. The problem was resolved by revering the equation. Instead of attempting to measure success, indicators of failure were analysed, based on the notion that, whilst prevention by its very nature is invisible, failure can be seen amongst a number of possible criteria such as children in care or accommodated, hospital admissions, and so on.

The indicator of failure finally decided upon was not the level of reported neglect, which is fraught with methodological difficulties (Lindsey and Trocme, 1994; Greenland, 1987; Gallagher et al., 1995), but a measure of the extreme end of the abuse continuum, child death. At its harshest, one cannot argue with a 'body count', although it is recognized that there may be debates about how the 'count' is made (Greenland, 1987; Creighton, 1993; Pritchard, 1993; Lindsey and Trocme, 1994; MacDonald, 1995; Pritchard, 1996). This method is in effect epidemiological - that is, measuring mortality rates in relation to environmental factors over time. The approach reflects the Durkheimian thesis that changes in certain types of death mirror changes in society, classically in respect to suicide - a thesis which, a hundred years on, continues to have empirical support (Diekstra, 1989; Lester, 1993). The method has also been used to examine international studies of suicide and unemployment, and the sudden infant death syndrome (cot deaths) since the early 1970s (Pritchard, 1992b, 1994; Pritchard and Hayes, 1993).

Rather than compare death rates *between* countries, an individual country's mortality rate is compared over time, thus avoiding the problems of different recording and legal systems (Gelles and Edfeldt, 1986). An example best illustrates the method. In 1973, Anglo-Welsh 'All Accidental' baby deaths were 502 per million, yet by 1992 this had fallen to 172, an index of 034, equivalent to a 66 per cent reduction. To take another example, Germany had a rate of 1336 in 1973, which fell to 415 baby deaths by 1992, an index of 031. While Germany still has a higher baby accidental death rate than England and Wales, it has actually decreased at an even faster rate.

In Gelles and Edfeldt's study, baby (<1 year), infant (1-4 years) and older child (5-14 years) homicide rates were reviewed annually up to 1992. Because the actual numbers are relatively small, the inevitable annual variations are evened out by taking the average rate for a two-year period, 1973-74, and comparing this with the latest years available, 1991-92. The underlying thesis is simple: if child protection at a national level has made little or no difference, then the rates and index would remain the same - that is, an index of about 100. However, given that this time period encompasses two severe recessions, and that inequality also increased (OPCS, 1995), it is not unreasonable to expect that some forms of child abuse and neglect also might have increased (Holinger, 1987; Judge and Benzeval, 1993), and that this would be reflected in increased number of deaths. This study concentrates upon baby (<1) and infant (1-4) deaths, because these younger children are predominately victims of an assailant from within the family, mainly parent figures, whereas older children (5-14) are more often victims of extrafamilial violence (Bourget and Labelle, 1992; Somander and Rammer, 1991). This latter point needs to be borne in mind when considering the rationality of associating child homicide rates with the extremes of child abuse and neglect.

## Child homicide in England and Wales 1973-92

Table 8.1 is based upon OPCS data (OPCS, 1975-94, 1986-94), and shows the numbers of baby, infant and child deaths between 1973 and 1992. From the index of change it can be seen that there is a decline in baby deaths in particular, although the 'blip' following a recording change after 1979 should be noted (Creighton, 1993). Nevertheless, taking the simplest of statistics, the index for baby deaths is 031, equivalent to a 69 per cent reduction, while 'all children' homicide from the two years 1973/74 to the two years 1991/92 fell from 208 to 70, an index of 034–that is, equivalent to 64 per cent improvement. However, it may be possible that some child abuse deaths may be hidden in the Undetermined Deaths (UDs) category (Creighton, 1993), and therefore the total of UDs are also included in the table. Certainly there was a marked rise in UDs in the early 1980s, followed by a decline with a peak in the later two years. However, even when all homicides and UDs are combined, the index still shows a fall of 070, a 30 per cent overall reduction. None the less, it should be remembered that 'undetermined' means just that, and we should not automatically assume that such deaths are necessarily the extreme consequence of hidden child abuse.

Rather than just look at the index of change, we can compare differences between two decades (Table). Over the twenty years from 1973 to 1992 there had been 1212 homicides, an average of 60.6 deaths per year. In the earlier decade of 1973-82, there were 770 homicides, compared with 442 for 1983-92. Or, in other words, 64 per cent of all homicides occurred in the first decade.

## TABLE 8.1
## Numbers of child deaths in England and Wales, 1973-92

| | *Homicide* | | | *Undetermined deaths (UDs)* | | | *Total deaths* | |
|---|---|---|---|---|---|---|---|---|
| *Year* | *Baby (<1 years)* | *Infant (1-4 years)* | *All (0-14 years)* | *<1* | *1-4* | *5-15* | *Total UDs* | *All Deaths* |
| 1973 | 40 | 22 | 102 | 6 | 11# | 39# | 56 | 158 |
| 1974 | 35 | 40 | 106 | 8 | 10 | 22 | 40 | 146 |
| 1975 | 33 | 30 | 86 | 9 | 12 | 22 | 43 | 129 |
| 1976 | 36 | 26 | 85 | 10 | 11 | 14 | 35 | 120 |
| 1977 | 18 | 33 | 78 | 2 | 11 | 17 | 30 | 108 |
| 1978 | 29 | 38 | 92 | 11 | 3 | 21 | 35 | 127 |
| 1979 | 38 | 28 | 94 | 17 | 21 | 26 | 64 | 158 |
| 1980 | 13 | 17 | 47 | 17 | 13 | 12 | 42 | 89 |
| 1981 | 10 | 7 | 30 | 25 | 24 | 32 | 81 | 111 |
| 1982 | 13 | 17 | 50 | 23 | 15 | 24 | 62 | 112 |
| 1983 | 15 | 22 | 45 | 18 | 19 | 12 | 49 | 94 |
| 1984 | 9 | 23 | 50 | 11 | 22 | 13 | 46 | 96 |
| 1985 | 11 | 28 | 59 | 14 | 16 | 27 | 57 | 116 |
| 1986* | 22 | 9 | 50 | 17* | 10 | 14 | 41 | 91* |
| 1987* | 13 | 15 | 41 | 17* | 17 | 22 | 56 | 97* |
| 1988* | 21 | 19 | 54 | 26* | 19 | 14 | 59 | 113* |
| 1989* | 17 | 11 | 37 | 22* | 17 | 18 | 57 | 94* |
| 1990* | 8 | 17 | 36 | 23* | 17 | 30 | 70 | 106 |
| 1991* | 11 | 16 | 41 | 17* | 28 | 18 | 63 | 104 |
| 1992* | 12 | 13 | 29 | 29* | 21 | 31 | 81 | 110 |
| *Index of change* | | | | | | | | |
| 1973/91 | 067 | | | | | | | |
| 1973/92 | n/a | | 034 | | | | 149 | 070 |

*Sources:* OPCS (1975-94, 1986-94).

*Notes :*

# Corrected in 1973 to include the 15 year age, based upon the average for the age year– thus, the actual total of deaths is for 0-15 years.

*Includes neonatal deaths, that is <28 days (OPCS, 1975-94, 1986-94).

Total Homicides [n = 1212] 1973-82 770 (64%) v. 1983-92 442 (36%)

Total Undetermined Deaths [n = 1067] 1973-82 488 (46%) v. 1983-92 579 (54%)

Combined Deaths [n = 2279] 1973-82 1258 (55%) v. 1983-92 1021 (45%)

Null Hypothesis – no significant difference over the years in relation to Total Homicides 1973-92:

Year-On-Year Total Homicides 1973-92 $x^2$ = 199.62 19d/f P = < 0.0001

Year-On-Year Combined Deaths 1973-92 $x^2$ = 70.67 19d/f P = <0.0001

Therefore the Null Nypothesis is rejected at the 0.1% level of confidence.

**TABLE 8.2**
**Homicides and undetermined deaths, 1973-82 *v.* 1983-92**

| *Year* | *Homicides* *n = 1212* | *Undetermined* *n = 1067* | *Combined* *n = 2279* |
|---|---|---|---|
| 1973-82 | 64% | 46% | 55% |
| 1983-92 | 36% | 54% | 45% |
| *Index of change* | | | |
| 1973/82-1983/92 | 056 | 117 | 082 |

*Notes:* Combined Deaths Decades 1973-82 v. 1983-92
$x^2$ = 69.88 d/f P = < 0.0001

A comparison of the Undetermined Dealths (UDs) between 1973 and 1992 shows that there were 1067 UDs, with 46 per cent (488) occurring in the first decade, and 54 per cent (579) in the second, confirming the increase in this category noted by both Creighton (1993) and MacDonald (1995). The simplest statistic, the index of change, shows that in respect of homicides the index fell to 056, an equivalent fall of 44 per cent, to be set against a rise in UDs of 17 per cent, and a fall of 18 per cent in combined deaths. On comparing the two decades, a Chi Square test yielded a highly statistical significant result (P =<0.0001), showing an unequivocal fall in the number of child deaths between 1973 and 1982 and 1983 and 1993. And, while there were undoubtedly more UDs over the period, there were also significant reductions in the child homicides.

However, to be doubly sure, the year-on-year variations contained in Table 8.1 were tested. The null hypothesis - that is, that there were no significant differences over the years in relation to Total Homicides 1973-92–showed a highly significant Chi Square value of 199.62, which allows us to reject the null hypothesis at the 0.1 per cent level of confidence. In addition, the Combined Deaths 1973-92 yielded a significant Chi Square result of 70.67, which also supports the rejection of the null hypothesis at the 0.1 per cent level. Thus, no matter which way the figures are reviewed, there was a real fall in combined deaths, and especially amongst baby, infant and child homicides, in England and Wales between 1973 and 1992.

## International comparision of child death rates in industrial nations

This section compares the English/Walsh experience with that of other industrial nations. To enable direct comparison of countries with different levels of population, child death rates per million population rather than their actual totals are used. Because this is potentially an unreliable measure in the case of countries with small populations, comparisons are made only of countries with populations of over 14 million.

From the figures in Table 8.3 it can be seen that there was a substantial fall in the proportion of Anglo-Welsh baby deaths between 1973/74 and 1991/92, and index of change of 030, equivalent to a decline of 70 per cent, whilst the total homicide index was down to 033, a fall of 67 per cent. Other countries also had substantial falls: Japan (57 per cent), Australia and Germany (44 per cent), Italy (39 per cent), the Netherlands (24 per cent) and Canada 23 per cent - though only Japan (57 per cent), Germany (51 per cent) and Australia (39 per cent) had significant falls in total homicide. England and Wales thus headed the league table of reductions for both baby and all/total child homicide. Indeed, even if all the smaller nations had been included, the Anglo-Welsh would still have led the field in this respect. However, whilst the Anglo-Welsh reduction is impressive - especially baby deaths, which fell from 114 to 34 per million, Australia, Italy, the Netherlands and Spain have a lower rate. To put this in perspective, in 1992, when both child homicide and road deaths reached record lows, for every child homicide there were nine child road deaths, and in relation to deaths from strangers the road fatalities were 30 times higher, confirming Greenland's (1987) point that, while any child death is undoubtedly a personal tragedy, child deaths are fortunately relatively very rare.

So, despite challenges to this approach (Creighton, 1993; Lindsey and Trocme, 1994; MacDonald, 1995), which admittedly has its limitations (Pritchard, 1996), we can nevertheless be confident that child murders, surely the most extreme form of child abuse, really have fallen from the highs of the 1970s.

## Possible explanations for decline in child homicide

How, then, might we explain the decline in child homicide ? The following section discusses some of the factors which may have influenced or determined these significant changes.

**TABLE 8.3**

**Baby, infant and child (5-14 years) homicide in England and Wales and other industrial countries, 1973-74 to 1991-92**

*(rates per million population)*

| *Years* | *Baby* | *Infant* | *Child* | *Total* |
|---|---|---|---|---|
| 1 | 2 | 3 | 4 | 5 |
| **England and Wales** | | | | |
| 1973/74 | 114 | 25 | 8 | 147 |
| 1991/92 | 34 | 11 | 4 | 49 |
| *Index of change* | *030* | *044* | *050* | *033* |
| **Japan** | | | | |
| 1973/74 | 166 | 50 | 17 | 233 |
| 1991/92 | 72 | 19 | 9 | 100 |
| *Index of change* | *043* | *038* | *053* | *043* |
| **Germany** | | | | |
| 1973-74 | 112 | 18 | 43 | 183 |
| 1990.91 | 68 | 14 | 8 | 90 |
| *Index of change* | *056* | *078* | *019* | *049* |

*(Contd...)*

| 1 | 2 | 3 | 4 | 5 |
|---|---|---|---|---|
| **Australia** | | | | |
| 1973/74 | 50 | 24 | 13 | 87 |
| 1991/92 | 28 | 17 | 8 | 53 |
| *Index of change* | ***056*** | ***071*** | ***062*** | ***061*** |
| **Canada** | | | | |
| 1973/74 | 60 | 29 | 9 | 97 |
| 1990/91 | 46 | 24 | 13 | 83 |
| *Index of change* | ***077*** | ***083*** | ***144*** | ***086*** |
| **Italy** | | | | |
| 1973/74 | 18 | 5 | 5 | 28 |
| 1989/90 | 11 | 6 | 7 | 27 |
| *Index of change* | ***061*** | ***120*** | ***140*** | ***096*** |
| **Netherlands** | | | | |
| 1973/74 | 33 | 4 | 5 | 43 |
| 1990/91 | 25 | 17 | 5 | 47 |
| *Index of change* | ***076*** | ***425*** | ***100*** | ***109*** |
| **France** | | | | |
| 1973/74 | 35 | 11 | 4 | 50 |
| 1990/91 | 40 | 12 | 7 | 59 |
| *Index of change* | ***114*** | ***109*** | ***175*** | ***118*** |
| **USA** | | | | |
| 1973/74 | 104 | 48 | 22 | 174 |
| 1989/90 | 163 | 52 | 30 | 245 |
| *Index of change* | ***157*** | ***108*** | ***136*** | ***141*** |
| **Spain** | | | | |
| 1973/74 | 8 | 2 | 1 | 1 |
| 1989/90 | 18 | 3 | 10 | 31 |
| *Index of change* | ***225*** | ***150*** | ***1000*** | ***282*** |

*Source:* Extrapolated from WHO Annual Statistics (1975/1994).

## Hidden deaths

The idea persists that there has been no real improvement in child death rates, either because child deaths have somehow been more effectively hidden by the perpetrators or because they have been lost in the recording practices of the relevant agencies. However, in England and Wales, over 50 per cent of baby deaths are routinely subjects to an autopsy, a figure which rises to virtually 100 per cent where there is any suspicion or doubt surrounding the death of a child. This is very much the picture in the other Western countries, with autopsies carried out in almost all 'doubtful' cases (WHO, 1975-94). Nevertheless, despite improved forensic techniques, a degree of uncertainty always remains, as it does with any other criminal offence. This supposition that welfare agencies are missing deaths is not credible given the historically unprecedented degree of professional and public attention now being given to child protection. Many measures introduced since 1988, such as 'Working Together', have emphasized the importance of interdisciplinary cooperation and communication, and have thus led to a greater degree of inter professional scrutiny (Buchanan, 1994; Hellett, 1995). Of course, there are still weaknesses in these procedures and variable levels of cooperation between professionals and parents (Thoburn et al., 1995) but, despite the discipline almost making an art of self-denigration, the changes in child protection policy and procedures do appear to have had some positive results. It may be asked, however, why, at a time of the fiercest scrutiny of child deaths, there should be an increase in undetermined deaths in England and Wales. Could it be that UK courts, because of events in Cleveland and Scotland, have become more reluctant to intercede by sanctioning the removal of children from potentially dangerous situations ? We do not know. But, while it is possible that a few child abuse deaths will be successfully hidden by their perpetrators, it has never been more difficult to achieve this and it is surely mistaken to assume that the majority of UDs are homicide.

## Socioeconomic context: The interaction of poverty and mental disorder

One aspect must not be overlooked and that is the cumulative impact of poverty, which from what we know about family breakdown should have led to an increase in child abuse and neglect (Jones et al., 1987; McLloyd, 1990; MacFate et al., 1995). While the vast majority of abuse and neglect cases obviously do not end in death, overall child mortality is, none the less, correlated with poverty, both in the USA (Holinger, 1987) and in England and Wales (Judge and Benzeval, 1993). In their seminal work, Judge and Benzeval examined all types of children's deaths from the ages of 1 to 15 between 1981 and 1985, and their analysis showed, unequivocally, increased deaths amongst children of parents in receipt of benefits. This category of family had three times the child death rate of families from social classes 1 and 2, and were even 44 per cent higher than those in class 5.

Another problem which interacts with poverty is that of mental disorder and its interface with child abuse and neglect. This may be considered controversial but, in Kempe's original work which alerted the Western world to 'baby battering' (Kempe et al., 1962; Kempe and Kempe, 1978), in an effort to emphasize the ubiquitous nature of such abuse, the author played down the psychiatric dimension - although later research shows that a significant number of abusers do have mental health problems (Kaye et al., 1990; Somander and Rammer, 1991; Bourget and Labelle, 1992; Samuels et al. 1992; Wilczynski and Morris, 1993; Meadow, 1994). In a careful review of international research, Stroud (1996) showed that more than 40 per cent of all child killers came from this cohort. While citizens in general are in far greater danger from motorists than they are from people with mental health problems – who are far more at risk from themselves - we should not ignore the fact that, in the presence of a mental disorder, especially a personality and / or a paranoid disorder, the risks to those immediately around the disordered person are raised.

Whilst there is a clear need to improve and better fund community care services for people with a mental disorder (Pritchard, 1992c), there is evidence that the best modern community psychiatry is effective (Butler and Pritchard, 1990; Lester, 1993) - a fact which is implicitly recognized by government in their targets to reduce suicide by substantial margins (Department of Health, 1992). Child protection services usually respond promptly when dealing with the interface of child protection and psychiatric disturbance, and I suspect this is an important feature which is reflected in the overall reduction of child deaths. This fact is partly grasped by some critics: 'whilst intervening we might, incidentally is it were, prevent some deaths' (MacDonald, 1995) - this is exactly what I believe occurs.

## The probable contribution of improved child protection

MacDonald (1995), while accepting that the tend of improvement in the rate of child deaths may be valid, questions whether the evidence supports the assertion that it is child protection services that have contributed to the decline. There is a range of empirical evidence which shows some forms of social work practice to be effective (MacDonald et al., 1992; Sheldon, 1995; Raynor et al., 1995), and particularly in respect of child protection (Burch and Mohr, 1980; Pritchard, 1991; Zimrim, 1984, Gibbons et al., 1995). Despite recent criticisms that the initial contact with the statutory services is almost adversarial and inquisitorial for many families (Thoburn et al., 1995), practice experience suggests that, once child protection services are involved, the situation will either be maintained or improved – children generally are protected from extreme harm. When services pursue the twin aims, embodied in the Children Act 1989, of protection and the prevention of family breakdown, their interventions also contribute to the amelioration of those stresses which at their most extreme lead to severe physical injury and even death. It must be remembered that this evaluation is postulated upon the notion of a continuum of damage, with the accompanying recognition that effective early intervention not only limits some of the least severe consequences, but also ameliorates that worst ones. The Department of Health (1992) have already established the concept of health targets aimed at reducing 'preventable deaths' generally, and have thus made public and political the use of mortality statistics as indicators of success or failure. It may not be long before such targets are established and accepted for child protection services also.

In conclusion, the critics who seck to reject and rebut this approach to the evaluation of child protection policies and services have yet to establish a plausible alternative explanation of why child homicides have fallen in England and Wales. Admittedly the data may be imperfect, the methodology not ideal, and there is urgent need for more practice-related research, but there are grounds for continued optimism that current child protection services have brought about a reduction of child deaths. We should, therefore, give some credit to those front line professionals who, along with their clients, face the risk. Social work has a bad press (Franklin and Parton, 1992), and the discipline is frequently used as a scapegoat for more general social problems. Sometimes we are our own worst enemy: we ignore the growing evidence which can be found in consumer studies, such as those made of probationers (Bailey, 1995; Cox and Pritchard, 1995; Ford et al., 1996), single homeless people (Pritchard and Clooney, 1994) and so on, that clients generally are appreciative of the help they receive from social workers. Hence it is time to give due acknowledgement to the commitment and dedication of a service which seeks to bring about change and improvement in the lives of children and families, which cumulatively has brought improvements and which, at the extreme end of the continuum, saves lives. If these efforts remain unrecognized, we run the risk that our work will become increasingly bureaucratized in ways which will limit and erode our efforts to reach out to vulnerable people, and will thus further undermine our effectiveness.

## A note about methodological issues

There are a number of difficulties surrounding measurements in respect to national and international child death rates. All are essentially related to recording systems and possible changes over time (Gelles and Edfeldt, 1986). The first ever international review of child homicides was criticized in respect to changes in OPCS methods of recording (Creighton, 1993; Lindsey and Trocme, 1994; MacDonald, 1995). These are answered in substantial detail, although readers are encouraged to review such criticisms, as well as the reply (Pritchard, 1996). The following notes briefly outline the main issues, although crucially it should be noted that this chapter has incorporated the earlier criticism, and thus permits a greater degree of confidence in the results.

Actual numbers of child deaths over time are used in the temporal analysis for England and Wales (see Tables 8.1, 8.2), though of course they do not account for the changes brought about by variations in population: hence, as England and Wales are two of the few countries, from the mid-1980s, to have had an increase in births, the raw numbers do not show this modifying factor. Conversely, I have used child death rates per million population from WHO (see Table 8.3) for the international comparisons. These rates are derived for each sex, summed and then divided by two to give the overall rates per million. It should be noted that, in every country reviewed in this sample, baby boys are more often victims than baby girls.

Readers might be surprised to find a variation between OPCS and WHO figures. This is partly due to the fact that 'undetermined' deaths are truly that, and that at any given time a number are 'in process'. Incidentally, neither OPCS nor the Home Office figures match. The key, therefore, is to compare the same data set over time. I choose the 'medical-social'-oriented OPCS because of its closer match to WHO, thus facilitating international comparisons. In respect of the Spanish figures (Table 8.3) mismatch may occur because of the possibility that unfavourable social indices might have been suppressed under the older illiberal regime; we do not know for certain that such was the case, but it is important to recognize this contingency. Similar factors might have operated in respect of both Greece and Portugal.

The most important methodological issue are the changes in OPCS Series DH 2 on Causes of Mortality (OPCS, 1975-94), which removed, from 1986 onwards, those neonatal deaths which occurred in the first 28 days of life. However, in Series DH 6 on Childhood Mortality Causes (OPCS, 1986-94), these neonatal homicides and UDs are given. Tables 8.1 and 8.2 have therefore incorporated the neonate deaths accordingly.

# IX

# A PARENT'S VIEW OF PARTNERSHIP

## Introduction

The late 1980s and early 1990s have been a shift in thinking within child protection practice. After fifteen or more years' emphasis on protecting children *from* their parents, social workers and other professionals are now being required to work together *with* parents to ensure the safety and well-being of their children. 'Participation' has become a key word in child protection work. Involvement of parents at child protection conferences and in the implementation of child protection plans is seen as a prerequisite of effective and ethical practice in this field. The reasons for these developments are complex. The ineffectiveness of measures to protect physically abused and neglected children (Department of Health, 1991a) and public concern about excessive professional intrusiveness in cases of sexual abuse (Cleveland County Council, 1988; Orkney Report, 1992) were important factors in this process. At a broader level, the Conservative Government's emphasis on parental responsibility and choice was influential (Eekelaar, 1991). Such ideas were acceptable to welfare professionals who increasingly valued partnership and empowerment as central elements of practice.

This chapter will examine how, if at all, this shift in thinking has filtered through to practice. Research into these developments is now beginning to emerge. Quantitative data shows that there has been a reduction in the number of care proceedings and in the use of emergency protection orders, which may suggest at shift towards greater use of voluntary agreements between parents and social workers (Department of Health, 1994). A major research study (Thoburn et al., 1995) into the implementation of policies of parental participation at child protection conference has shown such participation as working effectively to lay some foundations for cooperative work with families. Some other studies (Rochdale Area Child Protection Committee, 1993; Corby et al., 1995) are more sceptical, questioning the meaning and impact of policy in this area. Farmer and Owen (1995) have carried out research into child protection practice in the post-conference period. They found that there was persistent disagreement between parents and professionals in 36 out of 44 cases studies, and that many parents and children found the experience of investigation, attendance at conferences, and later intervention to be difficult and conflictual. Nevertheless, the authors see parental participation as one of the key means of improving child protection work.

The study presented here to some degree replicates that of Farmer and Owen in that it focuses on the experiences of a group of parents within the child protection system in a period of up to a year after the initial investigation. It is important to note that the research took place between 1993 and 1994 in an agency that had gone some way further in developing participation procedures than those studied by Thoburn et al. (1995) and Farmer and Owen (1995). On the face of it, therefore, there should have been more scope for effective participatory practice.

## Method

The research data presented here is taken from a larger study of parental participation in child protection work, the initial aim of which was to examine the experiences of parents at child protection conferences. Thirty-five conferences involving 32 families were attended, and 29 of these families (3 refused) were interviewed approximately six weeks later. Twenty-four of these families were interviewed again on average ten months after the conferences. This chapter concentrates on data provided by these 24 families at these two interviews. The focus was on parents/carers' perceptions of being involved in the child protection process. They were asked about their understanding of the purposes of social work intervention, and their feelings about, and their evaluation of, their contacts with social workers and other professionals. The data presented here, therefore, is derived solely from the perspective of the consumer. It is recognized that the consumer perspective provides just one aspect of a multifaceted process, and that service users' views cannot be the sole determinant of policy (Gardner, 1989). However, in an area of activity in which emphasis is being placed on participation and on taking parents' views into account, it seems essential to draw on what parents are saying about their experiences.

In what follows, some general data on the families interviewed is presented, with an account of their experiences in the order of the events as they happened: (i) the initial investigation, (ii) the child protection conference, (iii) the follow-up to the conference and (iv) the situation ten months later. Finally, the implications of these findings for child protection policy and practice are discussed.

**Data on the families**

Sixteen of the 24 families in the study had been involved with social service departments before the investigations which led to the conferences we attended, and 10 had been the subject of previous child protection investigations. The conferences were held because of allegations of physical abuse

(11), sexual abuse (9) and neglect (4). In 20 cases, allegations were based on incidents of abuse that had, in the opinion of the professionals, already taken place. In 4 cases, there were concerns that there was a risk that abuse might occur. Children were registered in 15 of the cases and not registered in 9. The alleged abuser was interviewed in 10 cases. Those interviewed in the remaining cases were largely non-abusing parents (usually mothers) and, in 3 instances, the grandparents who had taken over the care of the allegedly abused child. In 9 of the cases, the alleged abusers (all males) had left home.

## The experience of investigation

Being subject to a child protection investigation is almost certain to be an unpleasant experience for parents, whether they be the alleged abusers or not. It is likely to challenge their ability to fulfil a fundamental social role. There is the threat that children may be removed from their case, and there is the fear of criminal proceedings and public disgrace. Nevertheless, following the experience at Cleveland, there has been a greater emphasis on listening to the wishes and feelings of parents (and children). The focus of current practice is on working to secure the cooperation of parents and to ensure their children's future welfare.

In this study, only one of the people interviewed was regarded as a serious child abuser. Over half of interviewees were non-abusing mothers. Nearly all the parents we spoke to who were alleged to have abused their children were believed to have committed minor acts of violence. Given this, it might have been expected that the wishes and feelings of our respondents would have been genuinely taken into account in accordance with the spirit of the Children Act 1989 and the Cleveland Report. However, if this did happen, it was not reflected in the experience reported by most of the respondents in this study.

Fifteen respondents experienced the child protection investigation negatively, 7 positively and 2 were ambivalent. A variety of reasons were given for the negative responses. In 5 cases, social workers were considered unsupportive: 'I didn't feel like anyone was giving me support.' Five parents/carers felt inadequately informed: 'They blame me, but won't tell me what's wrong with the child.' Three parents/carers felt that social workers were overreacting to events: 'They stirred it up like a hornets' nest' –'It was as though she was deliberately digging, nit-picking about things.' In the remaining 2 cases, the complaints were of a more general nature. Experiences were described as 'frightening' and 'daunting'.

A key factor at this stage was the number of changes that took place in the household: 14 of our 24 respondents reported these. In 9 cases (4 physical abuse, 5 sexual abuse), male adults (all alleged abusers) had moved away from households. In 4 cases, children were placed with grandparents, and in 1, the grandmother moved in with the family.

In half the cases where these changed took place, they were unwelcome to the non-abusing parent. This was particularly so where physical abuse was alleged: in these cases, parents felt aggrieved, but accepted that they could not offer any resistance to the professionals' assessment. In sexual abuse cases, there was more agreement between parents/carers and professionals that exclusion of the alleged abuser was the best course of action. In these circumstances, the non-abusing parent was more rejecting of the alleged abuser.

The general impression gained from most of these parents/ carers was that professionals were not sensitive to their clients' individual needs, being dominated by concern for procedures. Consequently, parents felt that they had little influence on events and that their normal parental control and responsibilities had been abruptly suspended.

Those that experienced the investigation more positively referred to the supportive qualities of social workers, and to the clarity and the patience shown by these workers and other professionals in explaining their involvement: 'I don't know what we would have done without the social worker' - 'I have nothing but praise for them this time.'

Nearly all of these respondents were considered to be non-abusers and their children's names had not been placed on the child protection register.

**The child protection conference**

The 1991 *Working Together* guidelines (Department of Health, 1991b) recommend that parents and children should attend conferences, and stress that their exclusion from such discussions needs to be 'especially justified' (para. 6.15). This thinking is in line with the philosophy of partnership embodied in the Children Act 1989, and some see it as useful in empowering parents and involving them more fully in the child protection process (Family Rights Group/NSPCC, 1992).

In the area studied, all parents/carers and children over 13 years of age attended the whole of child protection conferences. Social workers were required to encourage participation, to explain the way in which conference business was conducted and also to help prepare parents and children as best they could. Immediately before conferences, parents and children met with the conference chairpersons, and further briefing took place.

Parents/carers were asked how adequately they had been prepared for conferences by social workers. Although half felt that social workers worked well to prepare them, it is notable that only 5 of the total sample described their experiences of attendance in positive terms. Some respondents queried whether it was possible to be well prepared for an experience of this sort: 'I don't think that you can be [well prepared]. Nothing against the social worker, but you are so emotional and in a state of shock.'

Nineteen of the 24 respondents considered the conference experience to be threatening or confusing. Nearly half found it worse than they had expected. Many of them found it hard to express themselves in the conference setting, and those who did put forward their views felt that these contributions carried little weight. Several felt that the professionals at the conference had already made up their minds about the outcome. These parents/carers clearly did not feel that they had participated in the sense of being empowered. Significantly, of the 5 who felt positively about their experiences, only I was a suspected abuser.

Notwithstanding these findings, most parents/carers felt glad that they had attended conferences, because they could hear what was being said about them. These views could be used to argue the success of the parental participation policy, but, if so, the standard for participation is being set at a low level, in that it does not require any *active* involvement on the part of parents (see Daines et al., 1990).

These findings do not portray the conference as engaging parents/carers in the child protection process. Indeed, there is some suggestion of an alienating effect, in that parents are confronted with the reality of their lack of power.

### After the conference

The post-conference period provides an opportunity to involve parents/carers more fully in the child protection process, even if the investigation has been a difficult experience for them and the child protection conference too threatening to allow meaningful participation.

Parents/carers were asked in first interviews that had happened in the six-week-period following the child protection conference. The focus was on the extent to which their views and feelings were taken into account and the degree to which they felt in control of events - in short, how far they considered themselves to be working in partnership with professionals.

Immediately after the conference, the social worker was the main point of contact for parents/carers. In addition to social work contact, 2 families were allocated a family aide. Other professionals (particularly health visitors and school teachers) were seen at core group meetings (see below). Five families said that they had received no visits during this period (all registered cases) and 6 that they had received one visit only. Some of these were happy at this limited contact and would have seen professional intervention as interference. Others felt frustrated by the fact that little seemed to be happening. 'The funny thing was that after the conference we never heard a flipping thing.' The remaining 13 families reported between 2 and 6 visits during this six-week-period. Some welcomed this degree of involvement, but a few felt that they were being swamped with visits.

Two key issues emerged from the comments about this stage of the child protection process. First, it was clear that many families were looking for help, and second, that almost all wanted to have more control over events.

With regard to the first issue, 4 families unequivocally reported that their contact with social workers during this period was helpful. The following comments demonstrate the sort of response they valued: 'I could ring her whenever I wanted to - she would visit sometimes to see how I was, which was very nice' 'She was a friend more than a social worker.' Nine families specifically referred to the lack of help they received: 'I did ring her up and ask her to come and she said "No". We want someone to sit down and talk to on our own.'

All these respondents wanted their social worker to give them time and listen to their problems. In many of the remaining cases, it seems that parents/carers had already made a judgement that the social worker was not helpful and so did not consider it appropriate to seek support from that source.

The second main issue relevant to the post-conference period concerned the extent of parental control over events. Many parents/carers felt that they had little such control, and little understanding of what was happening. Five said they were unclear about what social workers were trying to achieve. Eight said that they were unclear about the visiting intentions of the professionals. For those who felt in need of help and support from their social workers, this was particularly frustrating. Many parents had low expectations and accepted what was happening in a fatalistic way, such as this mother who was visited by a family aide twice a week: 'It wasn't forced on me, but I'm not happy about it - no one likes being told how to bring up their own kids, do they ?'

Issues such as these might have been tackled at core group meetings of the kind recommended in the 1988 *Working Together* guidelines (Department of Health and Social Security, 1988). These meetings, convened by key workers (that is, social workers), and attended by other relevant front-line professionals, parents/carers and children (where appropriate), are intended to translate conference recommendations into a practical form in cases where registration of children has taken place. The participation of parents in these meetings is seen as an important means of involving them in any action to be taken. According to the parents/carers in our sample, such meetings were held during the six-week post-conference period in 10 of the 15 cases involving registration. None of the parents who had attended these meetings felt that the meetings had helped to clarify aims.

The overall impression of this stage of intervention from the parents/carers' perspective was one of confusion, uncertainty and lack of control over matters such as agreed goals, expectations and time-limits. In some cases, there was little or no activity after the conference, particularly if children's safety had already been achieved by removing alleged abusers from ongoing contact with them. In other cases, where there were continuing concerns, there was more activity, but the focus was on taking steps to ensure the safety of the child by, for example, provision of family aides, contact with family centres, and monitoring by individual social workers. Most parents felt only marginally involved in the process, and the majority felt that they were not being helped.

**Ten months after the conference**

The pattern set in the early post-conference period generally persisted up to the time of the second interviews. Parents/carers reported either no (or limited) contact (11 cases) or that visiting had been maintained throughout the whole period (12 cases). There was one 'no response'. The key issue seemed to be whether or not the child had remained in the same household as the alleged abuser. Twenty parents/carers felt that the contact they had with professionals was problematical. Most felt that they had little control over events and little understanding of the intentions of the professionals. This was particularly true with regard to the timing and content of visits, which were very much in the hands of the social worker: 'We only see her once in a blue moon when she fancies it' - 'She come [*sic*] in for fifteen minutes, said, "Hello, you're all right", and then left' - 'They said they'd do regular visits - then in May last year they stopped calling.'

Only 8 respondents said that they had some agreement with their social workers about the frequency of visiting. In 13 cases parents/carers felt there were no clear plans, and 15 felt confused about what was expected of them.

Another feature of parents/carers' contact with social workers during this period was that it tended to be crisis-focused. In 11 of the 24 cases, there were further causes for concern, including 2 incidents of abuse. Other concerns included additional children being born; 'potential abusers' moving into households; disputes over contact between parents/carers, and carers' illnesses. Events such as these precipitated visits by workers where previously there was little or no contact.

Throughout this period, 17 of the parents/carers reported feeling blamed and 16 said that they felt judged by the professionals: 'I'm just an item, I'm not really being asked what I want. I don't feel like I'm the girls' mother' - 'They've made me feel inadequate as a parent. I haven't been counselled. I haven't had any help. I've done a good job from my point of view looking after the kids because I've had them all my life. 'This feeling of inadequacy was echoed by many of the parents/cerers, including non-abusers as well as alleged abusers.

In general terms, these parents/carers did not feel involved in the child protection process. Indeed, the opposite was true in most cases. If anything, the picture was bleaker at ten months after the conference than before. Issues of blame and responsibility often remained unresolved. There was still a good deal of bitterness in some cases over the fact that individuals had been forced to leave the family home (very few had returned by the time of the second interview). Few parents expressed the feeling that they had been helped by the protection process, and this was true of several non-abusing parents as well as of those suspected of being abusers. There continued to be a lack of clarity about the purposes of visiting, and little certainty about how long intervention would continue.

## Discussion

For many parents (particularly those who are suspected of abusing their children), the experience of child protection intervention is a negative and problematic one. The overwhelming impression given by parents/carers of their experiences of the child protection system was one of alienation. Two factors seemed to prevail: confusion and disappointment. The confusion resulted from uncertainty about what was required to demonstrate good parenting. The disappointment resulted from a general lack of provision of the help and support that parents had somehow expected to be part of professional intervention.

Given the values underpinning the social work profession, these feelings may be surprising. Why did the social workers in our study seem to fail to engage most of the parents with whom they worked ? It could be that they were particularly incompetent practitioners, lacking the skills needed to work with people in conflictual situations. However, there was no evidence to suggest that this was the case. A more plausible answer is that the tasks of investigation and policing which arr an important part of the child protection role cannot easily be reconciled with the qualities of empathy, sensitivity and support which are normally accepted as part of good social work practice (see Horne, 1990). This is not a new issue for the social work profession and has been the subject of much debate elsewhere (see Davies, 1994). Recently, applying the concepts of participation and partnership with parents (and children) has been put forward as a practical response to managing this 'old conflict'. However, the findings of the study presented in this chapter raise considerable doubts about the effectiveness of such an approach.

While there are more participative structures in the child protection process than before, for example parental (and child) attendance at child protection conferences and at core group meetings (and the local authority in the area under investigation had a thorough approach to the implementation of a participation policy), very few of the parents/carers in this study felt that these mechanisms gave them a genuine sense of working in partnership. Ironically, the main impression gained was of social workers busying themselves to meet the increased bureaucratic demands of participation. For instance, at the investigation stage, many social workers were seen as concentrating on issues as writing reports and briefing parents about conference procedures, but in the process significantly failing to respond to parents' needs for support and understanding in what was often a traumatic experience. At each of the later stages of intervention (conference, the immediate post-conference period and ten months later) parents generally perceived a lack of responsiveness to their particular concerns and needs. It is notable that farmer and Owen's (1995), study had findings that were similary negative in respect of parents' responses to participation. However, they like Thoburn et at. (1995),have faith in the potential benefits of participation, provided it is based upon the efforts of appropriately skilled practitioners and supportive agency policies.

As noted already, our study was conducted in an agency that was more advanced in implementing its participation policy than were those agencies studied by Thuburn et al. and Farmer and Owen, and we have no reason to believe that the professionals involved in the practice we researched were any less committed to participation (or any less skilled at implementing it). This leads us to feel that our findings have particular significance precisely because they are drawn from an analysis of those qualities and procedures which would normally be regarded as good participatory practice. We are, therefore, less optimistic about the benefits of participation under current arrangements and question whether a system developed to protect children from their parents can accommodate participatory/partnership approaches without some substantial retink of the aims and purposes of social work intervention in this field of activity.

At present, the child protection system is tending increasingly to focus on the assessment of risk (Department of Health, 1988), and the main theoretical base for this assessment is one of individual pathology (Corby, 1991). The reason for this emphasis lies in the recent history of child abuse and child protection work which, through public inquiries, has highlighted the dangerousness of parents (Dale et al., 1986). Unfortunately this focus can reinforce professional power and inhibit cooperative work with parents. In these circumstances, it is rare for parents to get clear messages from social workers about the acceptability of their parenting. Restructuring of families can seen a safer option for social workers that working with families as a whole. Parents' needs for help and support can remain unmet, partly because they have low expectations, and partly because the provision of such help becomes a low priority in child protection work. It is very hard to see partnership working effectively under these conditions.

## Conclusion

What are the ways forward ? One suggestion may be that social works need to adopt a more sensitive and responsive approach to the parents/carers they are working with. This might be brought about by training which is focused on the individual skills necessary to achieve this goal. However, while more training in this aspect of practice should not be discouraged, such an addition is unlikely to be sufficient because it does not address the deep sense of uncertainty that is associated with the way in which child protection practice is currently conceptualized and structured. Judging from our study, there is a fundamental lack of clarity about when harm to children should be deemed sufficiently abusive to warrant professional intervention - particularly in cases where neglect and moderate physical injury are concerned. Because of this, there is vagueness about what is required to parents/carers in order for them to demonstrate that they can look after their children safely.

It is essential that professionals operate with definitions of child abuse which can be clearly communicated to parents. Besharov (1981) and Wald (1982) have defended the value of more precise definitions of abuse. This is not easy to achieve (see Giovannoni and Becerra, 1979), but if it is not addressed communication and shared understanding between parents and professionals in child protection work will continue to be deeply problematic. Professionals should be in a position to give parents unambiguous messages about what is expected of them as parents. Protection plans therefore need to be clear, specific, properly shared with parents and, ideally, agreed upon by those parents. Greater clarity in these respects would have benefited many of the parents/carers and children in this study, and it would have given social workers a better basis for intervention.

Although the tensions and dilemmas which are to some degree inherent in child protection practice cannot be entirely eliminated, communication with parents/carers can be enhanced as a result of working to diminish any ambiguity and its associated indecision. If professionals were clearer about what they meant by 'abuse' and the continuing risk of it, the conditions for a limited form of parental participation would be improved. The details of such changes must be the subject of further analysis and debate, but it is important that this is done as speedily as possible. The sense of alienation shown by many of the parents/carers in this study is not conductive to any form of partnership, and the lack of clarity, which is partly responsible for this alienation, does not provide a good basis for effective work with children and families.

# X

# CHILDREN WHO SEXUALLY ABUSE OTHER CHILDREN

## Introduction and background to the research

The Child Sexual Abuse Consultancy in Manchester, England, is managed by NSPCC (National Society for the Prevention of Cruelty to Children) and for eight years has been running a programme of assessment, management and therapy with sexually abused children. In recent years there has been an increase in the number of children between 8 and 12 years of age who were referred because they may have been sexually abusing others. Their histories, and their needs, were so varied that we decided more information was required.

## Studies of children and young people who sexually abuse others

### Definitions of abuse

The National Children's Homes set up a Committee of Enquiry in 1990 to look at the problem of children who sexually abuse other children (National Children's Homes, 1991). They found difficulties with the issue of definition but believed that, if the concepts of true consent, power imbalance and exploitation were explored, then an understanding of what constituted an abusive event would become easier.

One of their first recommendations was that all professionals should take seriously allegations of sexually abusive behaviour by children against other children and proper investigations should be made.

This enquiry was followed by a 'Survey of Treatment Facilities for Young Sexual Abusers' (National Children's Homes, 1992). Again definitions were varied, many facilities using a legal definition which did not then apply to children below the age of criminal responsibility (10 years in England and Wales). This definition colluded with the denial and minimization of abusive behaviour in children under 10 years of age.

We decided that our definition for inclusion of children in the research was that a child should be 12 years or under, and should have acted in a sexually abusive way with another child. We defined 'sexually abusive' as meaning that force or coercion had been used upon another child to ensure participation. We took into consideration the issues of power imbalance, exploitation and true consent.

**Who are the children who abuse ?**

Glasgow et al. (1994) studied children alleged to have sexually abused other children, but found that by far the largest number of children reported for abuse was in the 13 to 17 age band. They found that almost all the reported young people were male. They concluded that 'high risk' children might be identified very early on so that intervention might prevent their sexually abusive behaviour.

Cantwell (1988) found that although it was clear that young children were abusing others, there was a great reluctance to accept the behaviour as potentially serious. Most of her 'perpetrators' were male, but in her 'cycles of abuse' she found some abused girls who, in turn, molested younger children.

Ryan (1989), looking at the effects of childhood sexual abuse, quoted many studies of adult and adolescent abusers which have shown that abusers claimed that they began molesting other children by recreating their own experiences of abuse.

Two studies in Washington State (Kahn and Chambers, 1991; Smith, 1988) each found that a third to half of the abusing children had been sexually abused themselves and half had been physically abused. Both studies found a high proportion of prior aggressive behaviour, although no prior serious criminal behaviours. Again most children were male, the racial composition reflecting the census figures for the state. Smith found that many had witnessed violent or abusive behaviour within the family.

**What intervention is available ?**

Debelle et al. (1993) studied the literature on intervention programmes for juvenile sex offenders (mainly in the USA) and concluded that most therapeutic strategies for these young people had been derived from experience gained with adult sex offenders. The authors suggested that programmes suitable for adults might not be suitable for adolescents.

The NCH Survey of Treatment Facilities (National Children's Homes, 1992) found that treatment in the UK was extremely variable. Staff felt that they were doing worthwhile work because it prevented further abuse, but that much abusive behaviour by young children was going undetected or unrecognized.

Toni Johnson (1988) describes SPARK (Support Programme for Abuse Reactive Kids) at Children's Institute International in Los Angeles. This programme is for children from 4 to 13 who have a pattern of sexually overt behaviour in their histories, and who have used force or coercion to commit sexual offences against other children. Children and parents are assessed, using extensive tests, and mandates are given by the courts to keep families in therapy, much of which is in groups and is largely behaviourally orientated.

The Leaps and Bounds project in Britain provides residential care for some young sexually abusing children, and individual therapy is also provided (Ogden, 1992). The project recruits and prepares adoptive parents and offers post-adoptive support.

In *Sexualized Children* (Gil and Johnson, 1993), the authors agree that people working with this group of children need a firm grounding in both victim and offender dynamics, and they endorse intervention either individually or in groups. They confirm that the therapy must reduce the problematic behaviour of such children and explore the underlying psychological concerns. They stress the involvement of carers and schools in the process.

At NSPCC Child Sexual Abuse Consultancy we assess all children using interviews and creative therapy techniques (Bannister, 1992a; Bannister et al., 1990). We also use these techniques in individual and group therapy and, in addition, we run a confronting behavioural programme for each child alongside this. Carers are involved as much as possible.

## The research focus

Our research focused on:

- children's histories to see if patterns could be detected which might alert us to children who were 'high risk' for future abusive behaviour;
- the offences themselves to see if a behavioural sequence could be identified which might alert carers;
- the therapeutic interventions to see which were deemed helpful or otherwise by children and carers.

We included children of 12 or under who had been referred to NSPCC teams in north-west England for assessment or therapy.

## Method

### Sampling

We included a child in our research only if the child's NSPCC social worker was satisfied that a non-consensual abusive sexual act had taken place between the referred child and another child.

We explained to each NSPCC social worker the concept of the 'unit' which we wished to interview. This consisted of the child, the NSPCC worker and the child's carer. If the child's sexually abusive behaviour had started whilst he or she was with another carer they too were included, where possible.

The NSPCC Regional Database showed a high referral rate of adolescents who had sexually abused others, but a much smaller number of younger children. This reflects other studies, especially Glasgow et al. (1994). We found great resistance from workers and carers when we asked to include cases which had been closed for more than a few weeks. One mother was representative of other parents when she wrote: 'I am grateful for the help, but I think that bringing things up again for C would not help her as she is very concerned about talking to people about what happened.' Eventually six 'units' were included in the research.

### Data collection

Our two interviewers used an interview guideline but encouraged interviewees to give as much information as possible.

Interview I was with the NSPCC social worker to elicit the history and details of the proposed intervention at referral.

Interview 2 was with the carer at the time of the first referral and Interview 3 was with the child. These three interviews were repeated at the end of the treatment. Current carers were interviewed in instances where the carer had changed between referral and the end of treatment.

### Analysis

All the data was fed into a database and analysed according to a systematic framework. Because we carried out this qualitative research using a holistic approach, the text was particularly rich and, where possible, we included direct comments from interviewees. They very small sample size and subjective nature of the analysis must be taken into account when assessing the results.

### Results

#### Age, gender and ethnic group of children

Half of the children in our study were aged 11 and half were aged 12. The fact that this was at the upper limit of our age range did not surprise us, since we found that the greatest resistance of accepting sexually abusive behaviour in children concerned younger children. We should, however, bear in mind Cantwell's point (1988) that early abusive acts which are ignored can mean that many more children are abused.

Five of the children in the study were males and I was female. With our small sample we cannot compare percentages with other much larger studies, but our picture is similar to other studies cited.

We had 1 child who was African Caribbean in our sample; the others were white. This ratio of 1 black child to 5 white children reflects the ratio of black/white children referred to NSPCC Child Protection Teams in north-west England.

One child in the study was in Special Education and 1 other was in a special needs class of a mainstream school.

## The children's histories

Five of the children had reported that they had been sexually abused. In 2 children it seemed likely that this abuse had begun when the child was aged 2 years or less. The duration of abuse ranged between a few weeks and three years. The people who abused the children were close and extended family members, family friends or other carers. All abusers were male. The sexual abuse the children had suffered included violent penetrative acts, mutual masturbation and being shown pornographic material.

Half the children were physically abused, occasionally in bizarre ways. At least 1 child had been seriously neglected. These figures (for sexual and physical abuse) are not dissimilar to figures in studies already quoted, but the figure for sexual abuse is higher because most children are referred to NSPCC teams due to their own abuse, rather than their abuse of others.

All the children had suffered other trauma which they felt was significant. Half had been abandoned by their birth fathers early on in their lives. Two fathers or father figures had abused several children in the family, and this had been witnessed by the subject child. Another child had witnessed his father beating his mother. Two children described poignantly how they had felt emotionally abused by their father or father figure. These events are in addition to the fact that some fathers or father figures had been the instigators of physical or sexual abuse of the subject children.

Although we were not told of any physical or sexual abuse by mothers, 1 mother had contributed to the serious neglect of her child. Only 1 child had disclosed his or her own abuse to the mother, most having disclosed to teachers, NSPCC workers or foster parents. This could indicate poor emotional ties between mother and child. Several children expressed anger at mothers who had not protected them or their siblings.

Two mothers appeared to have an overprotective relationship with the child.

Sibling relationships wee problematic. One subject child had sexually abused a sibling and there was very severe sibling jealousy in 2 other cases. One child had been sexually abused by older siblings. Some children expressed a sense of loss about siblings who had died or whom they had never known or from whom they had been removed. There was little contact with remaining siblings, and only in the case of the child who had been abused by older siblings was it possible to state that siblings were also sexually aggressive.

Many children today live with lone mothers or in reconstructed families (Clarke, 1994). Half of our children were living with both natural parents at the time of the first abusive incident. One was with a lone mother, 1 with a mother and stepfather and 1 with adoptive parents. At the time of our research interviews the situation had changed for 2 children – 1 child had moved from two natural parents to a single foster parent, while the other child had moved from a mother and stepfather to residential care.

All the children had exhibited aggressive, angry behaviour in their past. In 4 cases this was severe (lighting fires, running away, bullying, racially abusive language, sexually abusive language to women). These findings are similar to those of Smith (1988).

Five children were described as bullies of siblings or school friends. One mother said: 'He is very dominating, he is always threatening people... like his dad...'

Four children had threatened teachers and their parents with physical violence. Two of the children had undoubtedly been bullied themselves. One of these had also bullied others. One child said: 'I get called fat and black and the teachers won't do anything... I cry on my own.'

In fact, every child had been involved in bullying either as victim or aggressor or both. However, a recent study (Butler and Williamson, 1995) found that bullying was a common experience for many children, and so it may not be especially significant. The anger or repressed anger that this suggests, however, should not be ignored, since most subject children described feeling particularly angry at the times when they sexually abused other children.

We asked about other sexulized behaviours: 1 child had used sexually abusive language to a female carer, and another had grabbed the breasts of a female carer. Another had suggested and sex to two different professional male carers. These children had also masturbated in public and used sexually aggressive talk to adults and children.

**The abusive incidents**

Four basic behaviours were described, with some additions. Two children had aggressively attempted to overcome another child and to simulate intercourse. Another 2 children had aggressively attempted to fondle another child's genitals; 1 had persuaded another to participate in mutual masturbation. Three children had aggressively attempted to penetrate another.

Some children had perpetrated different sexual behaviours on several occasions. The highest number of recorded incidents for 1 child was 22. Several children had 4 or 5 recorded incidents; 1 child had only 1 recorded incident. The incidents had occurred when the children were between 8 and 11. All incidents had been witnessed by teachers, other children or other adults, except for 1 between siblings. In this case the victim reported it to a social worker and the abusing child admitted it. Victims were siblings, school friends or cousins, although 1 child chose victims from a wider circle of acquaintances.

Most victims were female, although 2 children had each abused children of both sexes. Most incidents were reported immediately. This is, of course, different from abuse perpetrated on children by adults. This is seldom reported immediately and is hardly ever witnessed.

Although there was much variation in the frequency and severity of the incidents, it is clear that all the children had expressed strong angry feelings in other ways, some more violently than others. We have noticed this in our clinical work and it is implied in the SPARK programme (Johnson, 1988). This is expressed well in the Dysfunctional Response Cycle described by Ryan (1989) as a response to being sexually abused.

Ryan describes early life experiences of helplessness, loss and betrayal being re-experienced in current events such as situations of humiliation and powerlessness, which trigger 'bad feelings'. These feelings move on through withdrawal to anger and then to attempts to control or blame others. Plans are then made to express the anger through sexual assault, exploitation (bullying), drug abuse, eating disorders, violence and so on. Ryan quotes Summit's 'accommodation syndrome' (Summit, 1983) to explain how sexual abuse not only involves emotional betrayal and psychological distress but may also melt a vulnerable child's need for attention, thus creating psychological confusion. Female victims often internalize their control-seeking behaviours, whereas male victims externalize them with aggressive behaviours.

Our clinical experience leads us to believe that psychological confusion and feelings of guilt and isolation are present not only in sexual abuse but also in emotional abuse. Emotional abuse is notoriously difficult to define (Bannister, 1992b), but may occur when a carer appears to provide a nurturing, non-abusive environment, but then secretly exploits a child to provide nurture for him or herself.

It may also occur when a carer ignores or diminishes the impact of loss upon a child.

In this study we asked a question of all participants (workers, carers and children) about the events immediately preceding the reported incident of abuse. The answers appear to fit into the Dysfunctional Response Cycle. One child said: 'My mum and dad were having a fight. I was frightened. I went out and saw M (the victim) and took her to the park.' Another said: 'I felt mad and were getting me own back for what happened [to me].'

**The therapy received by the children**

Four children had received some previous intervention, although this had sometimes occurred before their own abusive incidents had taken place. Three had been seen by psychiatrists - mostly for short assessment periods - for behavioural difficulties which sometimes included the sexual aggression. One had been sent by a psychotherapist (in relation to their own victimization) some time before the abusive incident had happened. One child had been seen by an educational psychologist.

Two of the children were seen for short periods of up to three months by NSPCC as part of an assessment carried out for the local authority. They were included because the assessments were seen to have a therapeutic component by workers, carers and children. In each case further intervention had been recommended by NSPCC. The other 4 children had been assessed and were being, or had recently been, helped by NSPCC. The duration of this work was from six weeks (terminated when a child refused to attend further sessions) to eight months. All therapy was individual, but sometimes more than one worker was involved. One child received parallel work on his own victimization and on his victimizing behaviour by two separate therapists. Another had a worker observing the therapy, and another had two workers to offer gender choice to a child.

All work was described as 'creative therapy' or was assessed as this. Drawings, drama, stories and puppets were used. In 4 cases (including one of the short assessment cases) educative or behavioural work had also been included in order to address offending behaviour.

This diversity of therapy is reflected in previous studies (Debelle et al., 1993). Debelle et al. point out that there is little to show that one approach or component or combination is better than another. It would seem that a very flexible approach, individually tailored to each child, has the best chance of success at present. What does seem to be important is the wide knowledge and experience necessary in the workers providing the therapy to enable this to happen?

The most comprehensive treatment programmes do include individual, group and family work. Behavioural and cognitive changes in children must be reinforced by systems changes in families, and the children must have a chance to practice these changes in groups with other children. Most workers with behaviourally disturbed children recognize symptoms such as dissociation and post-traumatic stress disorder, and it is clear that workers must be trained to help children to deal with these. Donovan and Mclntyre (1990) stress that workers must be aware of normative developmental behaviours in children in order to understand what is outside the norm. Gil and Johnson (1993) discuss transferential and counter-transferential issues which have a great bearing on work with abused and abusing children. There is no doubt that workers who do not receive training in all these areas are at a disadvantage.

**Comments on the therapy received**

Five of the children made positive comments about the therapy they had received at the NSPCC's consultancy centre. These ranged from: 'She really listened to me' to: 'When I had problems they were there. They understood what

I said about L who abused me. We made an agreement and I was allowed to say what went into it. We made a folder of all my work and drawings and writing.'

One child said it was hard to talk about some things and that NSPCC had not been able to stop the child's own physical abuse. This same child recognized that more help was needed with 'my problem' but thought the time spent at NSPCC was 'too long'.

Most of the other children felt that the time spent with NSPCC was 'OK' or 'about right'. The 2 children who had only received assessment both recognized that further work was necessary. Some of the carers had a different view of the time spent at NSPCC. Two felt it was too short, although 1 accepted that the work had ended prematurely because the child refused to attend any longer.

Most of the children were happy to describe 'the best bits' of the therapy, such as drawing, acting out stories and using puppets. One said: 'I liked having the sessions videoed so that at the end we could see what I had done and how much better I was...'

The 2 children waiting for longer-term treatment from local authorities were described by their carers as being calmer and less aggressive after their assessments by NSPCC. Similar comments were made by the other 4 carers but 1 stated that, although the initial effect was calming, some of the child's behaviour had now deteriorated. One carer thought the timing of the therapy had been wrong because at the time the child was moving to a new school, which made it less effective. One carer felt that the work was: 'Not deep enough, not pushy enough, they let him decide what he was doing in the sessions, they didn't ask him much about his own abuse.'

Other carers pointed to the value of the support given to

the child, the opportunity to express feelings, and the educative experience. One carer felt the child's behaviour had improved 'drastically' – he was calmer, less giggly and much less aggressive.

All the other sexualized behaviours were presented by the children far less or not at all.

### Recurrence of behaviour after therapy

We did not include a follow-up period in this study. However, half of the interviews took place over a period of up to six months. One child was investigated for further allegations of sexually abusive behaviour during the research period, and was investigated for further allegations of violence after the intervention - and the research - had finished. This child said to our researcher, before the further offences were alleged: 'I think it might happen again.' Another child commented: 'I think I might need more help with this problem.' The latter was a child who had refused to continue therapy and had only had six sessions. Both 'assessment' children and their carers and workers recognized the need for further work.

The 2 remaining children present the most optimistic picture. One had not been reported for further sexually aggressive behaviour in the period of about a year which had elapsed since the end of treatment. The other, whose research interviews had taken place over four months, had no reported reoffences. Since that child's therapy did not start until nearly a year after the last offence, both carer and social worker were optimistic about the future. Both these children expressed positive hopes for the future and one said: 'I don't feel so mixed up now. I've grown up a lot.'

We believe it may be significant that these 2 children are the only ones who were offered, and accepted, a full dual programme lasting several months, where they were treated both behaviourally - for the offences - and empathetically - for their trauma. In addition, the current carers of these 2 children had been fully included in the work and were very supportive.

**Discussion**

We wish to focus on four areas which have raised questions in our minds and which we feel need further work.

1. Our research has confirmed the work of other quoted researchers and has confirmed our clinical experience, which is that children, their carers and childcare professionals are uneasy about taking sexually abusive acts by children against other children seriously. We endorse the comments made by others which state that this is unhelpful to children, and that all known incidents should be investigated within child protection procedures.
2. We found, like other researchers, that the abusing children have varied histories and, as with adult perpetrators, there is no typical profile. However, in common with other studies, we found it is rare for girls to be referred as sexual abusers. We found that children who abuse others are likely to be children who have themselves been abused, and the 'abuse cycle' should not be ignored. Children who witnessed abusive behaviour in families and children involved in bullying figure largely in our sample, and also children who have especially difficult or non-existing relationships with their fathers. More research in these areas might be fruitful.
3. Children who are very angry, and have no acceptable way of expressing this, seem more at risk of expressing the anger in sexually abusive ways. This high level of anger seems to be closely connected with frustration

and powerlessness. Children who are expressing anger in physically abusive ways may be in danger of committing sexually aggressive acts also.

4. As therapists, we endorse the work of most treatment programmes, which include cognitive behavioural work on the abusive behaviour in addition to more creative, psychotherapeutic work on the child's own traumatic life experience. We accept that this must go alongside supportive, educative work with carers and families. We believe it is most important for young children, whose own traumatic experiences are very recent, to be offered empathetic exploration of their concerns, in addition to the behavioural work which adolescent and adult programmes use to address offending behaviour. These younger children need to have an opportunity to express their angry feelings, in an acceptable way, in order for this to be witnessed, and then these feelings need to be processed. This is probably a better way of building rapport with a child who cannot have a full understanding of the consequences of sexually abusive behaviour. There is no doubt, however, that a programme of intervention is incomplete without a component which focuses on the abusive behaviour and provides alternative coping mechanisms.

# XII

# TERROR AND THE STOCKHOLM SYNDROME: THE RELEVANCE FOR ABUSED CHILDREN

## Introduction

'I'll make you suffer just like I suffered': this is the constant message of a mother to her 4-year-old son (Doyle, 1995a). The mother herself had suffered physical and emotional abuse when she was young. Now she rains down verbal invective and denigration on her own child, blaming him for all her problems. It is difficult for many people to comprehend how parents, when they themselves known what it is like to be abused, go on to mistreat their own children. The majority of adult survivors of child abuse want their own and other people's children to have a better start to life than they experienced. Nevertheless, there are a number of such adults who, having been mistreated as children, then become abusers themselves. In a study of 110 emotionally abusing families, 73 per cent were found to have had at least one parent who had suffered substantial childhood abuse (Doyle, 1995b).

In order to understand how some former victims become abusers themselves it is helpful to understand the psychological process to which people can be subjected when they believe themselves to be trapped in a situation of terror and physical and/or mental pain. The phrase 'Stockholm syndrome' has been used to describe the way in which individuals can form an attachment to their persecutor. The victims endeavour to protect their abuser. They show gratitude and loyalty towards them, turning hostility away from their oppressor and onto potential rescuers. Some eventually adopt the abuser's values and beliefs and emulate their abusive behaviour.

The same process can be seen in children who are abused. In most cases, children are so powerless in Western society (Pilcher, 1995) that, potentially, they can be readily trapped in an abusive situation. This may be in the home - where to tell outsiders would be to betray the family - or in an institution - where children may believe that no one else will care for them if they complain. Alternatively, they may be trapped by people outside their home who make them swear secrecy and render them too fearful or indebted to tell. This chapter examines this process of emotional entrapment, termed the Stockholm syndrome, and its possible effects on abused children.

## The Stockholm syndrome

The term 'Stockholm syndrome' derives from events during and after a bank robbery in the Swedish capital in 1973, when bank employees held hostage showed loyalty and affection to the robbers and used their own bodies to protect them from police fire when the robbers surrendered. In a similar manner, some long-standing concentration camp prisoners admired the Nazis, found justifications for their policies and tried to emulate the SS guards by copying their uniform and treating weaker or newer inmates oppressively (Ochberg, 1978; Bettleheim, 1979). This ability of abused people to form an attachment to their abusers is now so well recognized that negotiators in hostage situations will not rely on the hostages to assist in freeing themselves. 'Police negotiators cannot confide in the hostages if an assault is planned' (Ochberg, 1978)

The syndrome can be observed in people from a wide spectrum of cultures and classes, equally in men and women, young or old. The Stockholm syndrome can similarly be seen in abused children whatever their colour, creed, class, disabilities or abilities.

There are certain circumstances when people perceive a danger and can see on immediate means of escape or source of help. In such cases - faced with a terrorist touting a machine gun and hand grenade, the perimeter fence of a concentration camp or, for a child, a powerful, skilfully manipulative adult - the only response may be to freeze.

The inability to escape can be real or perceived. Faced with a robber waving a gun, bank customers are likely to respond with frozen fright if they believe the gun is loaded. In reality, it may be unloaded or an imitation, but it is the customers' belief which is important. Similarly, adults may see that children have an easy escape route from an abuser - 'Why didn't the just tell his mother ?' - but, from the child's perspective, there may have been no obvious deliverance. The child believes he is trapped and in the abuser's power.

In relation to anti-discriminatory practice, the pressures on black and ethnic minority group children have to be recognized. The position is perhaps summed up by Charmaine, whose parents originated from the Caribbean. 'I couldn't tell about my dad because I loved him and I didn't want him to get into trouble and I thought white people would make racist comments' (Rouf, 1991). She recognized the racism inherent in a predominantly white society, and this increased her sense of entrapment.

Some children with disabilities may also additional factors which can contribute to their sense of entrapment. Often there are practical problems about escaping, as one survivor explained: 'Because of my physical disability I can't get off my back without help, so all he had to do was force me to the ground and I was fair game for him and his friends' (Corcoran, 1987). At other times, the messages given by society to children with disabilities serve to entrap them. Margaret Kennedy (1989), for example, explains how the effects of deafness can make some children feel isolated and rejected, leading to withdrawal and a loss of self-esteem and confidence. Being abused can lead to the same feelings and perceptions and thus the child is doubly oppressed, and even less able to seek help.

**Compliance and denial**

The inability to escape leads to frozen fright, which is not just a suspension of emotional response and activity. Rather, all the person's energy and attention are focused on the source of threat. In that state, the victim will become quiet and compliant. Frozen fright and obedience make sense because energy, which could be used later if flight or fight become possible, is conserved. Moreover, it is probably much safer than trying to resist when the odds are overwhelming and the abuser is determined to exert power. This is illustrated by an extract of conversation between a researcher and a hostage taker:

> R [*Researcher*] 'But what you are saying, it seems to me, is the same thing, that what's important is that people obey you'.
> H-T [*Hostage-Taker*] 'Absolutely. You - you have to have control. If I've got six hostages and one of 'em is causing dissension in the group, to sacrifice that one draws the others into line'. (Knutson, 1980)

Compliance is also reinforced by a process called 'psychological contrast'. Solzhenitsyn illustrates this process when describing the torture of prisoners in the Gulag Archipelago:

> The interrogator would be extremely friendly...suddenly he would brandish a paperweight and shout 'You rat ! I'll put nine grams of lead in your skull!' Or as a variation on this two interrogators would take turns. One would shout and bully, the other would be friendly, almost gentle. Each time the accused entered the office he would tremble - which would it be? (1974, p. 448).

Similarly a hostage-taker explained how he ensured compliance on the part of his hostages: 'We played the game just like the police do... whoever was like guarding the hostages, one would be like the bad guy and the other one would be the soft-spoken good guy' (Knutson, 1980).

Psychological contrast or the tactic of 'good guy/bad guy' has long been recognized as a method of obtaining a victim's submission. It occurs in many situations of child abuse. In some instances, the abuser, often a parent, is kind and caring, then suddenly threatening and exploiting. In other situations, the abuser is allied to another person who is affectionate and gentle. This is particularly in evidence where there are two parents. The non-abusing parent, feeling unable to seek outside help, does his or her best to alleviate the situation and comfort the child. It can also be identified in institutions where two members of staff are jointly involved in the abuse. Finkelhor et al. (1988) describe how the head of a nursery sexually abused the children in an overtly cruel fashion, while her assistant also sexually exploited the children but in a gentle, nurturing manner. However manifested, psychological contrast further ensures the obedience of the victims.

In this state of compliance, victims may be forced by the captors to violate or assault others. Children may be ordered to abuse other children. This occurs most commonly in large or extended families, institutions and in organized abuse. The victims are likely to have very little option but to comply. However, this entraps them further because now they are accomplices. The abuser's guilt is their guilt; the abuser's abhorrent behaviour is their abhorrent behaviour. In order to tolerate their own behaviour, the victims must minimize the seriousness of the abuse. They can only accept themselves if they believe that, in some senses, the abuse was justified. In British public and some state schools, the flogging of pupils was perpetuated for generations by making the older boys flog younger ones. As Robert Dougall wrote:

> This was the first of several canings but the worst were always from the Prefects....Once I cut a rugger practice and the Captain of the 1st XV, who was an enormous boy of about nineteen, damn nearly cut me in half. I was black and blue for weeks. (1975)

For anyone, child or adult, to cause extensive injuries and severe pain to a child for a minor peccadillo is clearly abusive and yet, as Dougall added: 'It never occurred to any of us to bear a grievance. It was just the accepted thing'.

Another early response to any horror or threat is denial. The frozen fright gives way to a sense of unreality and numbness which results in a denial of the reality or the severity of the situation. As one hijack victim recalls:

> They shouted at us that the plane was hijacked... they told us to lock our hands above our heads. We sat like that for hours. Funnily enough nobody seemed afraid. Perhaps everybody felt as I did that it was too much like a gangster movie to be taken seriously. (Dobson and Payne, 1977)

This is a useful temporary state which helps people from being overwhelmed by the terror of the situation.

Denial can, however, become less than helpful if it becomes an entrenched state. For some, like Sylvia Fraser (1989), the victim of sexual abuse by her father and a lodger, the denial is so complete that they develop two or more personalities in order to cope. Sylvia had one identity - a perfectly happy girl who had no memory of abuse - and a second one representing her father's lover. Other victims who have an awareness and a memory of their maltreatment may deny that what they experienced was abuse - as the extract from Robert Dougall's autobiography illustrates. They may deny the severity and pain of what happened to them. In addition, they may dismiss the serious effects of the abuse. Simon, a 74-year-old paedophile, despite several convictions including a term in prison for sexual offences against boys, felt his sexual love for boys had developed fully through habitual childhood sexual activities with other boys in a boys' boarding school. He felt it was 'normal' and in no way damaging (li et al., 1990).

If abused children remain in a state of denial for any length of time they may dismiss the severity, pain and distress of their abuse and, like Simon, may see no harm in other children being treated in the same way. They can therefore become abusers themselves, without any recognition of the damaging nature - both to themselves and to their victims - of their behaviour.

**Coping with fear and anger**

Frozen fright, shock, numbness and denial are all passive emotions. This state of passivity does not always continue. These responses can be replaced by more active, and possibly more painful, emotions, notably fear and anger.

The uncomfortable feeling of powerlessness is all the greater if the victim fears the abuser. In order for the level of fear to be tolerated, it is usually repressed. In hostage situations 'Frequently these feelings of fear are transferred from fear of the hostage taker to fear of the police' (Strentz, 1980). And, as Symonds comments:

> Hostages in their psychologically traumatised state never view negotiations for their release as benevolent. The victim would immediately give all for his release

> but he interprets and experiences any negotiations as endangering him...nonloving and threatening behaviour by the very people who are negotiating for his release. (1980)

There is a similar transfer of anger. Gerard Vanders was a hostage whose life had been threatened during the siege of a train by Moluccan terrorists. He commented: 'There was a growing sense that the authorities were mishandling the situation. They sent us food, but no utensils' (Ochberg, 1978). It was only some considerable time after his rescue that 'his negative feelings about the way the government handled the case have abated'.

In the case of abused children, this process can lead to an anger against 'society' or the helping professions, rather than the person who abused them. It can lead to a rejection of all adults and authority figures. For children with disabilities, it may be an anger and distrust of all people who do not share their disability. One sex abuser, Nick, had had an abusive childhood and acknowledged his 'earlier hate for the adult person, just sheer hate . . . I like kids because, I didn't have any other, real great experiences with adults when I was a kid' (Li et al., 1990).

But, conversely, anger can also be projected against other vulnerable people, especially other children, who remind survivors of abuse of their own frailty and powerlessness. This again can lead to a belief that 'weak' people deserve to be mistreated and exploited.

## Hope and gratitude

Elizabeth Kubler-Ross (1970), working with terminally ill patients, noted that those faced with imminent death maintained hope. The same is true of hostages and many abused children. In order to preserve hope, those who are held captive and mistreated have to convince themselves that the person in whose power they are is basically good, and ultimately concerned about their welfare.

This means that hostages and abused people will look for evidence of goodness and suppress any reminder of their captors' malevolence. Sheikh Yamani, along with other OPEC ministers, was taken hostage in 1975 by the terrorist Carlos the Jackal. He recalled:

> I scrutinised his [Carlos'] face. I found that the expression was full of mockery and sarcasm. But then I tried to convince myself that he really was being honest in his words and that because of my own fears I was reading fanciful interpretations into what I read upon his face. (Dobson and Payne, 1977).

Similarly, from the other side of the Arab-Israeli divide, Sarah Davidson, a Jew who was a passenger on the hijacked Air France Flight 139, noted her reactions to the terrorist leader, Bose:

> [He] adopted a pleasant manner. He was a concealed enemy, pretending, tempting his victims to believe in his good intentions... [He was] so affable that after my conversation with him, I found myself accuring myself. (Dobson and Payne, 1977)

There is also a sense of gratitude for 'small mercies'. Of Stalinist concentration camp prisoners, Solzhenitsyn wrote:

> In the morning the jailer came in [with a pail of gruel]... and greeted them quite humanely - no it was even more precious than that 'Good morning !'... grateful for the warmth of that voice and the warmth of that dishwater, they drifted off to sleep until noon. (1974).

In some cases, abusers threaten the victims' lives. Maya Angelou (1984) recalls how, when she was only 8 years old, her mother's boyfriend raped her, then threatened to kill her and her brother if she told anyone. In hostage situations, there is 'a highly credible threat to life... from the moment that it's not carried out, we have the beginning of the gratitude that builds up on the return of one's life from the individual who made a credible threat and nevertheless is not acting upon it' (Bahn). For abused children, the threat may not be directly to their life but to other things that the child holds dear. And each time the threat is not carried out, the child feels gratitude.

The victim has by now learned to view the abuser as good, well-intentioned and worthy of gratitude. This can lead to the victim believing that not only is the abuser good but their behaviour and beliefs are equally good. As noted, this process is so powerful that even some concentration camp prisoners believed that the SS guards' Nazi policy was correct and began to identify with and adopt the Nazi viewpoint. It is perhaps less than surprising that some maltreated children adopt the values of their abusers and start to abuse other children.

**Deserving, deprecation and depression**

The statements by Sheikh Yamani and Sarah Davidson also demonstrate another feature of the Stockholm syndrome. In both cases the speakers felt a degree of self-contempt. Many victims come to a logical conclusion that, if their tormentor is good and yet they are suffering, it must be because they are bad or have in some way deserved the ill-treatment. In the context of child abuse, this can lead children to mistreat their peers. They may believe that all children deserve to be treated badly and excuse their bullying behaviour on these grounds. Or, if victims see a child behaving as they have done, they may consider it right to punish or exploit him or her. The behaviour of the perfects of Dougall's (1975) example illustrates these points.

Victims of abuse often become depressed as they turn their anger and self-deprecation inwards. This too has its dangers. Sexual activity and some physical activities are very pleasurable, or participating in them can cause a surge of adrenalin. Several paedophiles record that they have sex with children to alleviate emotional pain and loneliness: 'I think God's given - let me do this thing [sex with children] . . . to satisfy me, to not let me suffer too much' (Li et al., 1990). Another paedophile explained: 'I was feeling emotionally insecure, I was feeling emotionally starved really... and perhaps this pushed me to break the barriers of the conventions' (Li et al., 1990). For a child who feels depression and self-deprecation, sexual activities or physical and emotional bullying of another child can provide a sense of power, of control and of satisfaction. This, however, may be a vicious circle (Doyle, 1994), because guilt about their activities can lead to further self-deprecation and internalized anger, which in turn can lead to a greater need to regain a feeling of strength, power and control, and hence to repeated abuse of other children.

### Accepting and adapting

The final stage for many people trapped in a frightening situation can be one of acceptance. This was identified by Kubler-Ross (1970). She found terminally ill patients often reached the point where, although they were not happy about their situation, they nevertheless experienced a calm acceptance of it. They were no longer angry and afraid, nor particularly depressed. They did not blame themselves, nor other people.

Acceptance is a helpful adjustment for terminally ill patients. For people in concentration camps, there is value in the ability to live from day to day without wasting precious energy on anger, fear or self-deprecation, and without railing at the injustice and degradation of their situation.

However, there are dangers for abused children who reach this stage. They are less likely to complain about their treatment and are less motivated to seek to escape from their situation. They are also much less likely to be recognized by adults as having difficulties. A child exploding with anger, one who is constantly fearful and flinching away from adults, or one who is patently withdrawn and depressed will usually be noticed by adults. But a child a state of acceptance will often seem to be functioning well, and will not attract attention.

Even if their mistreatment is discovered, they may not be offered effective help and protection. The Children Act 1989 requires a case to be made that the child is suffering, or is likely to be suffering, significant harm. Harm is usually measured by the child's responses. If a young person seems to be coping well, appears emotionally calm, makes no complaint about his or her treatment and has made developmental progress within a broad 'norm', then experts will pronounce that there is no evidence that the child is suffering, or will suffer, emotional harm. The fact that the child has been so severely or chronically abused that he or she has reached the final stage of adjustment escapes the notice of the protective agencies.

There is a final hazard for children who reach this stage. They have an unquestioning acceptance not only of their treatment but also of the values, justification and behaviour of their abusers. This means that they are less likely to view the abuse of other children as wrong. They may indeed believe that it is right and so may consider it their duty to engage in sexual activities with other children themselves, or, like the prefects described by Dougall (1975), believe it right to hurt and humiliate other young people.

Additionally, they no longer feel that they are in control of their own behaviour or destiny. They have reached a state of extreme powerlessness. For some, they are then able to justify their own loss of control and abuse of others on the basis of their helplessness as a victim. Ryan (1989) recognized this in relation to young people who sexually abuse other children, but it is also in evidence in other forms of abuse, including physical and emotional bullying (Doyle, 1995a).

## Individual variations in victims' experience of the Stockholm syndrome

In studies of hostages and captives, the Stockholm syndrome is present in differing degrees and manifestations in different individuals, while some appear to be free of any sign of the syndrome. Researchers have yet to explain these differences. The length of time spent in a situation of entrapment appears not to have great significance. In a study of the victims of the hijack of TWA flight 355, the passengers development of attachment to the hijackers was not dependent on whether the passengers had been freed after three hours or held for the full 25 hours, only being released after the hijackers surrendered (Strentz, 1980).

The depth of the sense of entrapment does not seem to be a major determining factor. This means that children from minority ethnic groups, or those whose disabilities cause them to feel a greater sense of entrapment, are not more disposed to develop aspects of the syndrome, and there is no evidence that they are more likely to abuse other children.

One important factor appears to be the nature of the relationship with the abuser. Hostages and captives who 'had negative contacts with the subjects did not evidence concern for them, regardless of time of release' (Strentz, 1980). It appears that, where there are no positive aspects to the relationship, the syndrome will not develop. This may explain why children are often able to protest about mistreatment by a newly arrived abusive step-parent, a rejecting parent who only has a harsh disciplinary role or a casual ^cquaintance who mistreats them from the outset, and from whom they have received no affection or care.

Some hostages who have not developed the syndrome have had a very strong sense of identity and have created their own world, insulating themselves against the negative pressures. One survivor, a British Ambassador, absorbed himself in the role of the Queen's representative. Children who are able to escape into their own fantasy world or carve out a positive role or hold on to a positive identity may be less vulnerable. But 'as yet there is no identified personality type more inclined to the Stockholm syndrome' (Strenz, 1980).

Children will therefore vary substantially in whether or not they will develop the syndrome. Those who do will also move through the different stages at different times and at an individual pace. Some may remain stuck in a state of permanent denial that they have suffered mistreatment, or one of perpetual anger. Others will range freely backwards and forwards between the various stages, for example at one moment showing depression, at another anger, all overlaid perhaps with a degree of denial. This variation depends on a complex interplay of circumstances: behaviour of the abuser, the victim's relationship with the abuser and, to a lesser degree, the victim's individual temperament, life experiences and inclinations. A similar multifarious set of factors is needed to explain why one child develops the Stockholm syndrome to the extent that he or she becomes an abuser, and why another child is very similar circumstances does not.

## Conclusion

Many abused children perceive themselves to be trapped by a person more powerful than themselves in a situation of fear often amounting to terror. In these situations they are likely to experience a psychological process that many threatened and entrapped people experience. This process has been termed the Stockholm syndrome. It is apparent where the victims show an affection and protectiveness towards their abusers.

Sometimes the process leads to the victims identifying with the oppressors, adopting their values and emulating their behaviour. For abused children, it can mean that some mistreat other children when ordered to, in a state of compliance. It can also mean that they deny the ill effects of the abuse on themselves and other children. They view the perpetrator as behaving with justification and can come to believe that children should be treated in an oppressive manner. They can also end up accepting totally the rightness of the perpetrator's behaviour, and justify their own mistreatment of other children by citing their abuser's values and opinions, while excusing their own loss of control on the basis of their helplessness as a victim.

We should remember, though, that not all young people, even those who can be seen to develop the Stockholm syndrome, will abuse other children – just as the majority of concentration camp survivors did not identify the SS, nor do the majority of hostages threaten fellow hostages. It is only the minority who espouse the cause of their oppressors and, in turn, become oppressors themselves.

# XII

## RESPONDING TO LOSS

Child abuse is a complex, multifaceted phenomenon. However, one dimension of the subject that has received little or no attention is the status of the experience of abuse as a form of loss. This can be seen to incorporate a variety of losses, not least that of trust. This chapter examines the significance of abuse as an experience of crisis and loss, and considers a number of questions that arise from this analysis:

- To what extent can behaviours and emotional responses associated with abuse be linked to responses to loss ?
- If children are not helped to grieve their losses effectively, can this result in destructive behaviours (perhaps including the abuse of other children) ?
- What does the literature on loss tell us that could be usefully adapted to working with abused children?
- What are the implications of this analysis for child protection practice?

I shall explore a number of key issues in relation to the experience of loss as they apply to abusive situations. From this we can begin to develop a better understanding of the significance of loss as a factor in developing high-quality standards of practice in child protection.

Loss is, of course, closely associated with death, and much

of the literature on loss relates specifically to death. Walter discusses the view that death can be seen as a form of social threat, an undermining of what we take for granted:

> Arise, like Gorer, argues that death is inevitably problematic; along with sex, it is one of the major ways in which 'nature' threatens 'culture'. Death must therefore be 'tamed', which societies traditionally do through religion and through ritual. But over the past few centuries, individualism, romanticism and secularism have undermined the rituals, and the modern individual is left naked before death's obscenity. (1993)

Death represents one of the ways in which nature impinges on society, one of the ways in which human endeavour and values can be undermined by what is, in so many other ways, a positive and beneficent force.

There is a direct parallel that can be drawn between this image and the experience of abuse at the hands of someone who is otherwise loving and caring - a parent, for example. A child, who sees the parent as a source of love, security and esteem, can, at the onset of abuse, be threatened by what appears in other respects to be a positive aspect of his or her life-world. It is not surprising, then, that such experiences should so often be characterized by confusion, insecurity and diminished self-esteem. As Corby comments:

> Clinical accounts suggest that the more closely related the abused child is to the abuser the greater is the degree of harm likely to result. Thus, intra-familial abuse is likely to have a more harmful effect than extra-familial abuse, and abuse perpetrated by a natural father more than that perpetrated by an uncle. (1993)

There is, however, a more general parallel between the notion of death as a threat to society and culture and child abuse as a threat to social mores. In a society where children are valued, rhetorically at least, the widespread abuse of children can be seen as a destabilizing social force. The 'discovery' of child abuse in the 1960s, and of sexual abuse in the 1980s, can be seen to present, therefore, not only a threat to the children concerned, but also, at an ideological level, to the basic fabric of society (Parton, 1985).

Child abuse can be seen as a phenomenon that is closely related to loss in a number of ways and at a number of levels. For example, Stewart (1994) draws links between loss and the experience of abuse in adults. Such losses associated with abuse are many and various. They include:

- boundaries;
- trust;
- hope;
- feelings and what they mean;
- intimacy;
- childhood;
- spontaneity;
- privacy;
- self-respect;
- confidence and serenity;
- family;
- happiness;
- identity.

Although Stewart's ideas relate to his work with adults who wee previously subjected to abuse, the same argument can be seen to apply to children who have experienced abuse. That is, the linkages between abuse and loss need to be understood in terms of the immediate effects of trauma as well as their long-term implications in adulthood.

The following passage from Rouf vividly captures the intense sense of loss that child abuse can instil:

I am no longer I.
If I look depressed he will hit me.

He will slap my face like he did this morning.
Doesn't he know why I'm depressed?
He wants me to be his puppet. I am his clown.
I am not allowed to have any emotion. (1990)

The association between the experience of abuse and that of loss is therefore a very strong one, and yet one that has received little or no attention in the literature to date. This raises a number of issues that are very significant for child protection workers, issues that are worthy of much closer attention.

The work of Parkes (1986, 1988) presents loss as a psychosocial transition that can have the effect of shaking the entire world-view of the person experiencing the bereavement. For children, this can be seen to be particularly significant insofar as their world-view is still in the process of construction, and is therefore more vulnerable to the ravages that a significant loss can bring. We should therefore be ready to accept that a loss for a child may have profound consequences. Consequently, we should be wary of simplistic aphorisms along the lines of 'Children are resilient' or 'Children don't suffer in the same way as adults.' As Eth comments:

> Society generally views childhood as a naturally happy time, free of responsibilities and worries. But the implication that children are somehow protected from the emotional effects of traumatic events is tragically false.... Children are, in fact, as susceptible to trauma as adults, even though their suffering is commonly overlooked. (1989, p. xi)

The tendency to underplay the significance of loss and grief in children (Thompson, 1995) can add to the pressures abused children experience, by devaluing or 'disenfranchising' their grief (Doka, 1985).

This can be better understood by reference to Prior's

concept of the social distribution of sentiments. Prior (1993) argues that the experience of grief is not simply an individualized psychological process - it also needs to be understood in terms of social factors. Different societies permit or encourage different responses to grief. But what does this mean for children who have experienced loss as a result of abuse ? What socially approved avenues are available for the expression of grief ? Clearly, this is a difficult area to address in view of the issues of confidentiality surrounding child abuse and child protection. This is a point to which I shall return below.

A similar set of issues arises in relation to Marris's argument that the severity of grief depends, to a large extent, on the degree of social disruption caused by the loss. Marris (1986) draws links between the experience of loss at an individual level and at a community level (through public disasters, for example). He argues that a common theme is the loss of meaning that a bereaved person experiences. Meaning derives, to a certain extent at least, from our social networks. When these networks are also disrupted by the loss, then the loss of meaning can be intensified. In a child abuse situation, the response to the abuse by officialdom can be extremely disruptive of the child's social circumstances, particularly where the child is removed from home or where the perpetrator is a family member and he or she moves from the family home as a result of the abuse coming to light. Ironically, then, attempts to protect the child from abuse may well heighten the experience of loss brought about by the exposure to an abusive situation.

Having considered a number of issues that link loss with child abuse, we can now move on to explore some of the responses to loss that can also be seen to apply in many child protection situations. Responses to loss include:

- anger and aggression;

- guilt;
- depression;
- idealization;
- sleep disturbances;
- appetite disturbances;
- absent-mindedness;
- social withdrawal;
- restless overactivity.

Experienced childcare workers should have little difficulty in recognizing in this list a number of responses not only to loss, but also to abuse, thereby underlining the significance of the relationship between loss and abuse.

The overall list presents a range of important questions to be addressed in working through loss issues with abused children. However, for present purposes, I shall limit myself to considering three: guilt, depression and idealization.

Guilt can be seen as an internalization of aggressive feelings, anger turned inwards upon the self. A common response to abuse situations is for the victim to experience a sense of guilt, to wrestle with feelings that they somehow invited or effected the abuse. This is particularly significant, I would argue, in relation to sexual abuse situations. This is because the dominant patriarchal ideology incorporates and perpetuates such myths as 'she was asking for it' or 'she led him on'.

Guilt is a non-pathological response to a loss situation. As Littlewood comments:

> Guilt, over acts or omissions, is another experience which often follows the death of a loved person. Guilt in connection with not being kind enough to the dying person or not being present at the death are particularly common. (1992)

Guilt can be seen as a means of handling a flood of intense feelings, an attempted solution rather than necessarily a problem, in the sense that it can, in the short term, play a constructive part in coming to terms with the loss. However, if it persists over a period of time, its presence may indicate complications in the grieving process.

The fact that, in child protection work, we also encounter a great deal of guilt in children who have been abused reinforces the central tenet underpinning this chapter - the importance of recognizing the experience of abuse as a form of loss.

Depression is a further basic element in grief responses which also arises quite frequently in the aftermath of abuse. Depression can be seen as a psychological response to loss. It is defined by Thomas and Picrson as 'feelings of hopelessness, sadness, tearfulness and intense anxiety' (1995). They go on to comment that:

> Depression affects people in different ways. A person suffering from depression can feel sadness, how self-esteem, hopelessness or something more extreme, such as feelings of total despair, complete worthlessness, intense guilt and constant irritability. Tasks require extra effort; thinking becomes more difficult; and thoughts can centre on SUICIDE or be preoccupied with fears of serious illness. Speech and physical movements can be slowed drastically, while at the same time the sufferer is tense and restless, with pronounced interruption to sleep patterns. (1995)

Children who have been abused may at times manifest some degree of depression through their actions and emotional responses. Again, this can be seen as part of the process of adjusting to an experience of loss. However, there is one significant difference. In mourning the loss of a loved one, the bereaved person can understand why he or she is depressed - the feelings, although profoundly negative, none the less make sense to the person concerned. In abuse situations, however, where the losses experienced are less explicitly acknowledged, any feelings of depression may be experienced as more threatening or destabilizing because the reason for such feelings is less clearly understood (by the person concerned and others involved in his or her care).

Idealization is a process that sometimes occurs when the loss of a loved one is experienced. This involves a bias towards remembering only the positives about a person's character and our relationship with him or her, while shutting out any possible negative thoughts or memories of the person who has died. A certain element of idealization is not uncommon in grief responses generally, but can, in some cases, be taken to extremes - it can become a dominant feature of the grieving process.

Once again, there is a clear and strong parallel with child abuse. For example, a child who has been abused by his or her father may see the father in an unreasonably positive light. He becomes idealized, as the traumatic feelings associated with the abuse are 'compartmentalized', set to one side because they are too painful to deal with. In this respect, idealization can be seen as a form of denial.

Extreme examples of the idealization of the perpetrator can create barriers for the child protection professional in trying to make progress in working with the child. However, even where the idealization is less extreme, there are dangers that the worker must become sensitive to. For example, it can be very problematic and destructive if the worker refers to the perpetrator in negative or derogatory terms. Despite what the perpetrator has done to the victim, the child may none the less have a very deep love, or at least strong attachment, for that person. The dilemma that the child experiences - trying to reconcile feelings of love with the experience of abuse - is a very difficult one, and an insensitive negativity towards the perpetrator may lead to a response of idealization. Such matters therefore have to be dealt with very carefully and sensitively.

The recognition of abuse as a matter of loss and grief represents an additional element of theory that pressurized child protection workers need to address in their practice. However, this recognition also gives us access to an existing body of knowledge and practice experience that can be amended and adapted to inform child protection work. I shall use the model of Worden (1991) as a worked example to illustrate the understanding that can be gained by drawing on theories of loss.

Worden's approach is based on the notion of 'tasks' that need to be achieved in order to move through the grieving process. There are four such tasks: accepting the reality of the loss; working through to the pain of grief; adjusting to an environment in which the deceased is missing, and emotionally relocating the deceased and moving on with life I shall address each of these in turn.

*Accepting the reality of the loss* This refers to the need to work through and beyond the first stage of the crisis, the 'impact' stage which is characterized by a sense of disbelief:

> This initial stage is characterised by stress and confusion and a sense of disbelief. The situation seems unreal. Comments such as 'I can't believe it's happened' or 'It hasn't sunk in yet' are not uncommon. Profound feelings of emptiness, loss and disorientation are experienced. (Thompson, 1991)

One problem that can occur here is the use of denial to avoid accepting the harsh reality of the abuse. In younger children, in particular, this may manifest itself in the use of fantasy as a means of mediating or counterbalancing reality. Alternatively, it may be the *meaning* of the loss that is denied:

> In this way the loss can be seen as less significant than it actually is. It is common to hear statements like, 'He wasn't a good father,' 'We weren't close,' on 'I don't miss him. 'Some people jettison clothes and other personal items that remind them of the deceased.

> Removing all reminders of the deceased... minimizes the loss. It is as though the survivors protect themselves through the absence of any artifacts that would bring them face to face with the reality of the loss. (Worden, 1991)

Worden's comments here relate to the loss, through death, of a person. However, the same comments can be seen to apply to situations that involve the loss of a person through other means (imprisonment, for example) or to other forms of loss associated with abuse.

A first step towards integrating the experience of abuse can be seen as an acceptance of the reality of what has happened. This may be problematic for some children who have yet to reach a cognitive level at which they can comprehend an abusive situation. Ironically, in some abusive situations – those that come to the attention of the child protection services – the official response to the abuse may be even more confusing and difficult to understand than the actual abuse (Thompson, 1992).

*Working through to the pain of grief* Loss is characterized by intense emotional pain, and it is a well-established principle of bereavement counselling that it is necessary to work through this pain in order to begin to come to terms with the loss. That is, if the pain is suppressed or avoided in some way, the necessary 'grief work' will be held back.

Depression can be seen as one way of avoiding the pain by numbing all emotional responses, leaving the person in a psychological state that resists all forms of emotional stimulation. The depression often associated with abuse can be seen to play a very similar role.

The skill of the worker can be a very significant factor in helping children to deal with painful feelings and avoid the need to repress them. A basic part of this skills base is the worker's ability to listen. This may sound relatively simple, but in dealing with a person who is grieving, there is a strong temptation to focus on *doing*, rather than listening. Active listening is more important than activity for its own sake:

> When humans are faced with a crisis, the urge-to-do can tempt us into rushing to 'make it better' with a platitude or other unhelpful response. But it is, of course, not action but reception which comforts. It is a counsellor's task to help a client give words to his sorrow.
>
> It is not easy to find the words to express grief and the listener can easily react to her own anxiety, letting it get in the way and thus prevent the words being found. There is a special quality of reflective silence within a relationship, however, which can enable the griever to find his [or her] own words. (Lendrum and Syme, 1992)

*Adjusting to an environment in which the deceased is missing* Loss brings about not only emotional changes, but also significant changes in the 'environment' or life circumstances of the person concerned. This means that an abused child has to come to terms with the changes brought about first of all by the abuse itself and subsequently, as noted above, by the abuse coming to light and being dealt with through official procedures.

Although there is no actual 'deceased' person, the adjustments to the loss can be equally demanding for the child to make, particularly as loss through abuse can lead to very significant, sometimes dramatic, changes - police involvement, for example. In addition, although an actual death has not occurred, a key figure in the child's life may have left, particularly where the abuser is a member of the family. Adjusting to that person's absence can be a major task in its own right. Where the person's absence produces a confused set of feelings (relief mixed with regret, for example), the complexities of adjustment can be extreme.

An important problem that needs to be prevented where possible is the tendency for the person experiencing the loss to avoid making the adjustment to their changed environment. This can occur, for example, where, instead of adapting to new circumstances, the individual resigns him- or herself to a narrower, more constricted set of circumstances. That is, they make little or no attempt to adjust to certain absences - preferring, instead, to exclude those aspects of their life from their new environment. They create, physically and/or emotionally, no-go areas.

*Emotionally relocating the deceased and moving on with life* It is understandable that we should hold on to memories of a person close to us who has died. However, these feelings may need to be set in a new context, to allow us to move on with our lives. As Worden comments:

> The counselor's task, then, becomes not to help the bereaved give up their relationship with the deceased, but to help them find and appropriate place for the dead in their emotional lives - a place that will allow them to go on living effectively in the world. (1991)

In situations of abuse, there can also be this task of 'emotional relocation', and may require skilled help to achieve. Johnson (1989) argues that this process of 'resorting' can be particularly significant for adolescents. The process involves reconstructing the present on the basis of changed perceptions of the past, and this is specially relevant for adolescents who are in the process of leaving childhood behind and engaging with adult responsibilities and expectations.

These, then, are the four 'tasks' of grieving, as set out by Worden (1991). Once again, we can see that are clearly discernible parallels between loss as a result of death and the losses brought about by child abuse. This is not to say that the two sets of experiences are identical, but there are sufficient similarities for us to take seriously the lessons that can be learned from identifying abuse as a form and source of loss.

There are a wide range of implications that can be drawn from the recognition of this parallel. The most fundamental is the need for child protection workers to be sensitive to children's experiences of loss, to become attuned to the possibility or likelihood that the abused child they are working with is also a grieving child. The literature on loss and loss counselling can then be brought to bear to help increase our understanding and skills in this aspect of practice.

Another important implication is the need to recognize that such grief, where it does occur, is *disenfranchised* grief (Doka, 1985). That is, it is a form a grief that is not socially recognized or culturally codified, and therefore presents greater difficulties in finding expression. In particular, the confidentiality surrounding child abuse situations may erect substantial barriers to effective grieving, by narrowing down the range of people who can share the grief.

The experience of bereavement is often cushioned to a certain extent by the existence of culturally-specific rituals. These have the effect of helping to affirm that, although one member of the culture has been lost, the sharing implicit in the very notion of culture can be part of the process of beginning to come to terms with the loss. The absence of constructive, supportive to come to terms with the loss. The absence of constructive, supportive rituals for responding to the grief associated with abuse can have the effect of further reinforcing its status as a form of disenfranchised grief.

In addition, the child is unlikely to be the only person experiencing loss and grief. My focus in this chapter has been on the abused child, but an argument could be made that everyone involved experiences, potentially at least, some degree of loss. This would include family members, other relatives and friends and, of course, staff involved in the child protection system. As Morrison (1990) has very ably demonstrated, child protection is an emotionally highly charged type of work. A profound sense of grief can at times be one of the emotions experienced - a fact that raises important questions in terms of supervision and staff care.

Perhaps one of the most fundamental aspects of the linkage between abuse and loss, and one that perhaps forces all practitioners to reconsider their approach to practice, is the notion of a quest for meaning. At times of loss, our sense of meaning, purpose and direction can be profoundly shaken, leaving us feeling insecure and vulnerable (Morgan, 1993). This, too, can be the reality of abuse - with many unanswered questions, little sense of meaning or purpose. Abuse can leave a child wondering 'Why ? Why has this happened to me?', with child protection workers also at times overawed by the sense of tragedy, meaninglessness and loss that child abuse can so powerfully create within us.

# XIII

# EFFECTS OF TRAUMA ON CHILDREN

## Normal child development

Trauma is an inevitable experience throughout our lives but there are many things that may determine how well or how ill we survive it. For children, the cost of survival may be very high indeed. They may have to distort their developing self so severely that they are unable to gain maturity and make a successful transition to adulthood. Often the result of their trauma is never properly detected by those who care for them (Terr, 1990). This chapter will outline what happens to a traumatized child and how it is that the trauma 'doesn't show' very easily.

A child is not born with a ready-developed sense of self. This has to be acquired through experience. Just as cognitive and physical development is required before a child can move from gross jerky motor movements to finely tuned and skilled ones, so there is the necessity for cognitive structures to develop in order for the child to acquire a sense of self, to build expectations of the world, and to form patterns of action and interaction that rely on establishing a memory system. The building blocks for this sense of self and mental development, including memory, are the interactions a developing infant has with him - or herself and other objects in the environment, especially transitional objects (Winnicott, 1960) and significant human and animal objects. A child learns about turn-taking, the basis for interaction with others, through peekaboo games. A small child uses mirrors to learn about self but also to learn how to distinguish between self and other. This is achieved adequately between 10 and 24 months of age if development is not interfered with, prevented or skewed.

In the early development stages, an infant's experience is stochastic - that is, disjointed, like the frames of an old movie. Infants have to learn to build patterns and sometimes even the illusion of continuity that is necessary for their sense of well-being. Until they do this, they inhabit a world of part objects, dissociated islands of experience and extremes of emotion: things are either wonderful or terrible (Kohut, 1984; Stern, 1985, 1990; Winnicott, 1960). A great deal of development of memory and other mental processes is required to integrate the extremes of good and bad and establish gradations of perception and experience, especially in one person and especially in the self. Object Relations theorists describe how, in the early stages of development, an infant is only able to hold one extreme at once, and during the stage of attempted integration will use 'projection' (projecting feelings and attributes but onto others) and 'introjection' (bringing feelings and attributes into the self) repeatedly in attempts to accommodate an integrated mixture of both into the self. It is like the development of any skill - learning to drive, for example. At first one can only cope with one thing at a time - the clutch, the accelerator, the steering - since integrating and coordinating them takes time. Even with the steering, one either goes too far to the right or too far to the left; achieving the integration and control to move smoothly throughout the range of steering possibilities, while managing to stay mainly in the middle of the range, takes development (McIntee, 1992).

Psychological research now demonstrates that a baby is learning about some aspects of its environment even before birth, but following the birth there is a much greater opportunity for the child to utilize an increased range of experiences in its development. Stern (1985) has shown that even very new infants are beginning to make distinctions and build up a world-view that moves from gross to finer distinctions and patterns. The developing child is beginning to differentiate between self and other from around 10 months of age, but the self does not become consolidated until around 2 years of age (Mahler et al., 1975). Complete establishment of self and independent functioning may be a lifelong task, and for many it may never be accomplished

Adolescence is a period in which the early development of self is revisited and reworked at a very fundamental level in preparation for separate living. There is a return to a dichotomous (all-or-nothing) world-view that is similar to that held in infancy. Things are perceived as extreme: pop bands may be seen as the best one week and the worst soon afterwards. There is a reworking towards integration, usually after separation as an individual at some greater level has already been achieved.

## Traumatic effects

Mclntee's trauma model (Mclntee, 1992), schematized in Figure 13.1, is set in the context of trauma being an inevitable part of human experience, beginning with the natural trauma of birth. It is also assumed that the possibility of unwanted trauma may even occur in the pre-birth period.

This model is also based on a developmental perspective that assumes that 'narcissistic injuries' (Kohut, 1984) - what we may think of as disappointments and let-downs (normal trauma) - are a necessary part of the separation process and are in fact one of the mechanisms by which individuation is achieved. Mclntee (1992) describes successful accommodation of the effects of, and recovery from, trauma as the outcome of a ratio between the quality and quantity of trauma and the sum total of internal and external resources available to process it.

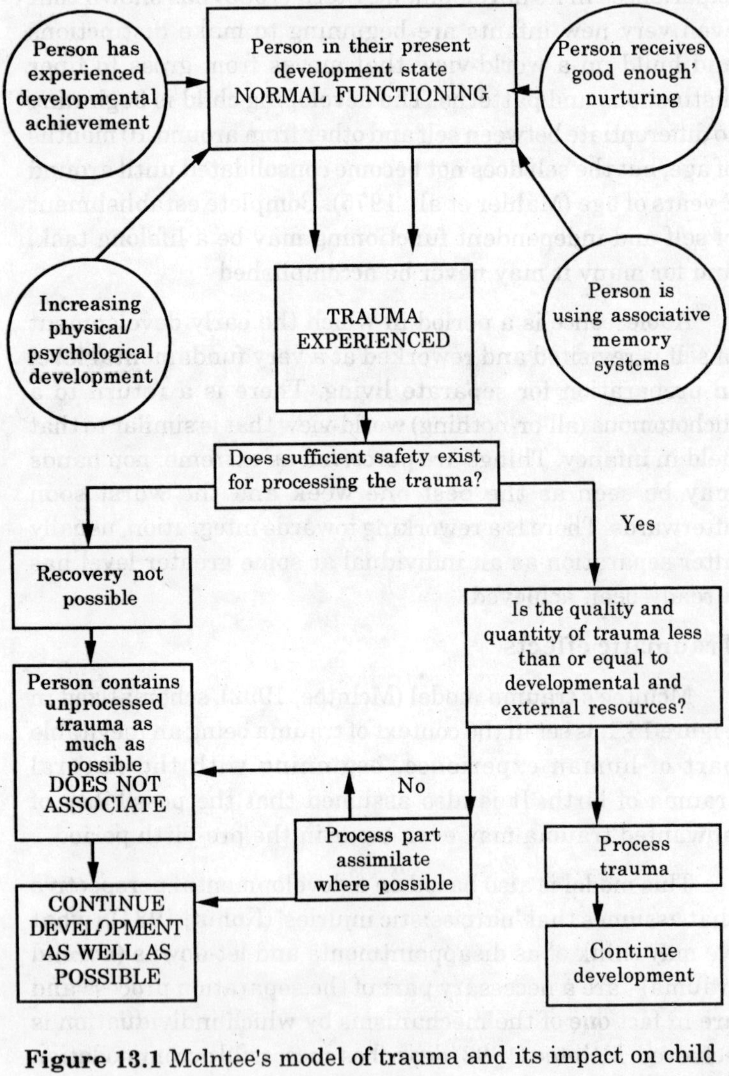


**Figure 13.1** McIntee's model of trauma and its impact on child development

A positive outcome occurs when the total effect of the quality and quantity of the trauma is less than or equal to the internal and external resources of the individual who is traumatized. Where trauma overloads the capacity of the individual in his or her environmental support system, development is distorted. It is not difficult to see how many small traumata or a single large trauma may easily outweigh the capacity of a small child.

## A 'good enough' environment

Child development is seen as a process by which the child intuitively takes the necessary steps for growth, if the immediately nurturing persons and environment can provide a 'good enough' (Winnicott, 1960) psychological and physical holding. Research has shown that primate infants require the warmth of touch, cuddling and physical holding in order to thrive and reproduce successfully (Harlow and Suomi, 1970). Winnicott (1960) has shown that a similar need exists on the psychological level. While a child requires positive interaction with a carer, the carer does not have to be perfect. However, they do need to have provided 'good enough' positive input for the child. If this is the case, the child will have been able to internalize the 'good' sufficiently well to advance to the transitional stage, where the source of the 'good' may be psychologically transferred from the original provider onto an object (dummy, blanket) or onto an action (behavioural routine). Either of these transfers will remind the child of the continued existence of the 'good' and help to sustain the comfort and security derived from it, until it can be fully internalized. The authors' clinical experience of treating trauma victims suggests that the birth mother appears to hold a special significance in this holding, presumably because some form of pre-birth bonding takes place, even where this is not further developed after the birth.

### Psychological holding

'Psychological holding' means providing a psychological space or relationship for the developing child. Good psychological holding should be a safe space and relationship in which the child can find nurturing and can grow. Poor psychological holding will still provide a space or relationship but instead of it being safe, it may have many inconstancies and dangers. Instead of it meeting the needs of the child, it may serve the interests of the adult.

Ideally the 'holding' should be adequately supporting but not confining. It should be like psychological scaffolding - removed unobtrusively only when it is no longer required due to the developmental achievements of the child having made it redundant. Underprotecting - taking the scaffolding away too soon - will cause the child to be low in confidence and self-achievement. Such a child will develop a false and extreme pseudo-independence or an anxiously insecure overde-pendence on the carer or, as an adult, on partners. When the scaffolding is held in place too long, it becomes confining, causing the child to feel suffocated and squashed. This impedes psychological development and individuation.

### Adolescent separation

Pubertal development sees a reworking of the adolescent's earlier individuation with greater depth and achievement, the aim being a balanced, stable sense of self that is essential to permit intimacy and fully independent functioning suitable for rearing the next generation. Distortions at the pubertal and emerging parental stage of life will result in patterns of dysfunction that may be unrecognized by the self. Where they are recognized, they may result in under - or overcorrection. This is one of the vehicles by which dysfunction is transmitted to the next generation. An example of this is found with Annie who had suffered very badly at the hands of her physically abusive father. She recognized the problem, was determined not to repeat that pattern and very carefully chose her partner to be devoid of any of the same tendencies. The problem was that she overcorrected in her choice of partner and, although things were fine until the children came along, she then found he was leaving all of the boundary-setting to her. The failure of this to become a shared responsibility caused an imbalance in their relationship, similar to that which had existed with her parents, but with the male dominance being substituted by female dominance. The result was that Annie felt overloaded with disciplining the children and she became more and more stressed. Upon reaching the extent of her capacity to cope, she became violent towards her children in an escalating manner. Annie became very distressed because she began to realize that, in avoiding the choice of an abusing husband, she had inadvertently performed the abusive role herself, having failed to resolve the abuse dynamic.

**Memory**

The developmental model of memory that underpins McIntee's theory of trauma (see Figure 13.1) is associative. This means that the human brain will store experiences in some form, build them up into patterns of repeatedly similar experiences and adapt behaviourally according to these predictable patterns. For example, if you become accustomed to regular meal times, your body becomes hungry according to the pattern you have learned. Patterns have to be developed and refined through repeated experiences, where parameters and common denominators are worked out. For example, if you have been driving the same car for ten years and you change to a new one, you will quickly recognize the common items: steering wheel, accelerator, clutch, brake, gear lever. Things may differ by a small amount or by a large amount – for example, a steering wheel-based gear lever versus a floor-based lever, or manual transmission versus automatic. Knowledge of these items relies on their shape, size, colour, function and position in space in relation to each other: for example, how often do you drive a left-hand-drive car instead of a right-hand-drive–or vice versa - and go to reach for the controls in the wrong place, thus demonstrating your learned patterns of behaviour that have become automatic?

**Mental map of the world**

Psychological research suggests that experiential patterns are reflected by the development of internal mental constructs, an internal map or mirror to the world. An example of this would be the way a small child will build up a pattern in their brain that translates into 'biscuits are kept in the blue tin'. These internal constructs reflect the external object relationships (for example, mummy has dark hair and wears glasses) and are mediated through the subjective lens of experience of the particular infant: for example, the picture one child may draw of 'mummy' may be quite different from that drawn by another child when drawing the same person. Obviously some of the difference is accounted for by differences in the respective infants' ability to draw, but much more is likely to be a reflection of the subjective perspective of the child. Similarly, different witnesses of a road traffic accident would give differing accounts.

Mclntee's model assumes that cognitive development will be needed to permit a gradual formation of these internal object relations from the gross to the refined and that two-way interactive distortions may occur. The child may bring their own experiential perspective to bear, causing distortion, or distortion could be brought about by external means. An example of a subjective distortion is the way in which children misuse language in their effects to communicate. A friend's little girl, whilst in a cafe, said to her mother: 'I can't eat any more, I'm fed up.' It took a little while for her mother to realize she meant that she was 'full up'. An example of distortion created from outside is a client in his mid-twenties who, when first seen, had no ability to detect or label some of his bodily sensations and most of his emotions. He did not know when he was hungry or tired, and he did not know what it was like to experience happiness or sadness. He had apparently tuned out these sensations at a very early age to avoid pain. It is not uncommon to hear a child say 'I'm hungry' and to hear an adult reply 'No you're not, don't be silly!'

We are often unaware of how our perceptions and learning of patterns have occurred, and sometimes these are very difficult to change. All those who have had difficulty with changing eating or smoking patterns will understand this very well. Patterns are built up according to the subjective experience of the child within their home context. There is an interesting story about the idiosyncrasy of family patterns that became loyally repeated and became automatic, even when the need for this had ceased to exist.

A man asked his wife why she always cut the end piece off the roast joint and threw it in the bin before serving dinner. She replied that she did not know but her mother had always done it that way. The husband went to his mother-in-law and asked her why this practice was adopted and she gave him he same reply: 'Because my mother did it that way.' He then went to the grandmother and discovered that she did it because her oven overheated on one side and always burnt the joint on one side, and so the end piece on that side had to be discarded. The next two generations were loyally repeating patterns adopted without question or rationale.

## Trauma and the physical and psychological processes

Trauma causes higher animals, including human beings, to produce a fight or flight response to moderate threat (see Figure 13.2). This response includes adrenalin flooding the body in order to increase the blood supply and enhance physical performance. Where the threat is even greater, this response reaches overload and a shutting down or freezing response is produced instead. This includes a decrease in the blood supply and an almost total reduction in organic functioning. This prevents memory and other cognitive processing from operating. It is hypothesized that the neocortex functioning is reduced to a minimum and the organism relies on more primitive, instinctive responses that are located deeper in the brain. The hypothalamus – situated at the base of the brain – is a very complex structure, responsible for the control of the autonomic nervous system, reflex integration and organization of behaviour related to survival (Carlson, 1994).

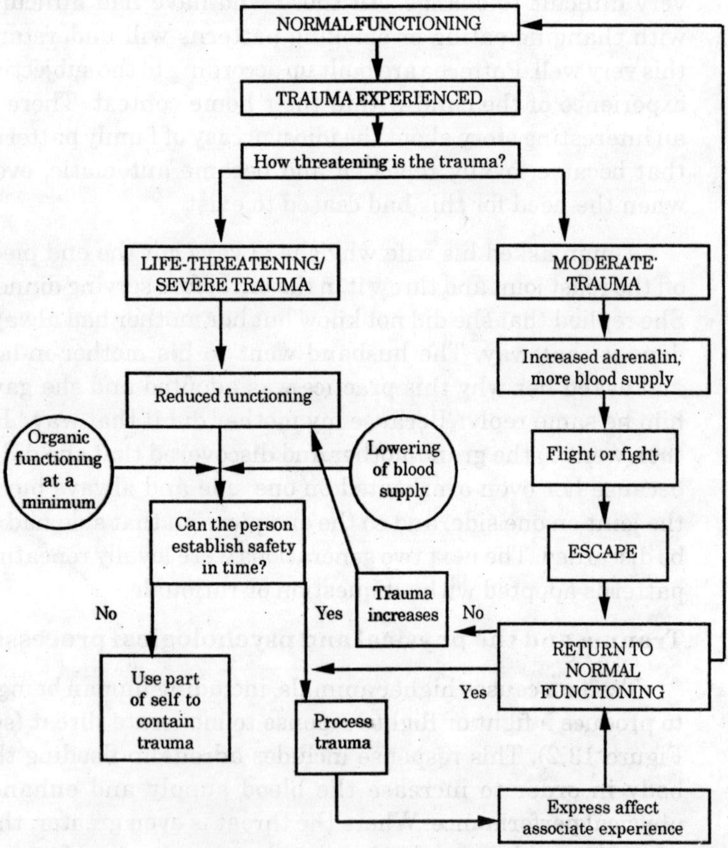


**Figure 13.2: The trauma process**

McIntee (1992) proposes that a reduction of functioning and the existence of a 'red alert', survival mode of functioning means that events re not being fully experienced and processed by the brain. The brain normally requires 20 per cent of the heart's blood supply so that, under these 'frozen' conditions, with blood supply on minimal functioning, processing cannot be performed until the danger is past and the psychophysiological canditons have returned to a more normal state.

Recovery will automatically begin once safety is re-established and the psychophysiological homeostasis has been achieved. Recovery is seen as requiring assimilation and accommodation of the events, the expression of the associated affect (emotion) and the reworking of damaged cognitive and behavioural development that may have suffered regression.

Recovery can only take place if the 'red alert' situation can be changed to one of relaxing safety, and then only if the combination of internal and environmental resources is sufficient to deal with the quality and quantity of trauma that has been experienced. If the person undergoing trauma does not possess sufficient such resources, processing will be partial or minimal.

It is proposed that loss of memory, of any degree, of traumatic events may occur for a number of reasons:

1 Processing may have been only partial and chunks of experience may not have been 'experienced' by the brain's integration-processing mechanisms. This may account for recovered memories or experiences being manifested years later in therapy or elsewhere as 'happening right now.

2 The emotion caused by the processing may be intolerable. Denial processes, such as disbelief, may be invoked to assist with accommodation or to delay

further processing. Repeated cognitive reworking and minimizing may also help in accommodating events. Recovery of these events has for the person concerned the quality of 'having always known about it but having failed to realize its significance'.

3 Processing may have occurred but in an incomplete way so that, when the emotional experience is too damaging, a repression mechanism is invoked to create either a partial or substantial amnesiac effect. Repression may overlap with the partial processing described in (1) above. It is as yet unclear if these are separate psychological mechanisms.

### Dysfunctional families

An abusing family eclipses the development of the child's body or mind by requiring the child to serve the needs of the adult. This results in a loss of the appropriate boundaries, where the child's body or mind becomes used by someone else in the service of that person's own needs. This can range in severity from a parent or carer who, when a child says 'I'm hungry' or 'I hurt', denies the validity of their sensory processes, through to severe emotional, physical and sexual abuse. The loss of appropriate boundaries prevents the development of individuality and maintains the child in a somewhat undefined state, always close to 'red alert' in order to adapt to external demands.

Where the usual separation process or split into 'self and other' (usually achieved within the first two years of life) has been prevented, it may occur internally instead. This results in the most severe form of Dissociative Disorder, Dissociative Identity Disorder (DID) (formerly known as Multiple Personality Disorder). Clinical experiences of clients with Dissociative Identity Disorder show internal self structures that contain self and other development but seem to lack that individuation in the clients' external relationships. As abused child may develop a self part to whom the abuse has happened and who is experienced as 'not me'. This is either to create distance from the associated affect or because there has been a failure to process this and integrate the experience into the 'true' self. Winnicott (1960) suggests that this gives rise to manifestations of 'false self'. At the same time, there is often found to be a lack of self/other differentiation externally. Such clients are often unable to tell whether anger or other emotions are their own or belonging to someone else. In relationships they lose all sense of themselves and are subsumed by the other person, experiencing abject loss of self and existence if the relationship is not present. In cases of DID, such splits or self parts often seek expression and may take on identities and needs, therefore competing for control of the body and mind. The extent of their development appears to relate to how much they have been developed and reinforced through use. For example, if a child is repeatedly raped and has developed strong dissociation for the part of the child's self that experiences the rape, yet that part is required repeatedly to cope with these incidents, the part is likely to become experienced as a personality entity in its own right. Because of the dissociation, however, this part is unable to integrate into any more developed personality structures without therapeutic succession.

Clinical experience and self-report from DID clients (McIntee, 1994) suggest that the separating on the inside is accompanied by the building of internal object relations to reflect the external people/objects and their abusive and conflictual behaviours. The internal objects or 'parts of the self' behave conflictually towards each other. This process prevents associative and integrative functioning developing. These isolated internal objects or self parts remain isolated from each other, and their behaviour and world-view become idiosyncratic and extreme. The possibility of developing a shared reality is low and, in some cases, non-existent. The

Structured Clinical Interview for DSM-IV Dissociative Disorders (Steinberg, 1994a) assesses five main aspects of experience resulting from the use of dissociation as a survival response to trauma:

1 **Amnesia** A specific and significant block of time that has passed but that cannot be accounted for by memory.

2 **Depersonalization** Detachment from one's self, for example a sense of looking at one's self as if one is an outsider.

3 **Derealization** A feeling that one's surroundings are strange or unreal. Often involves previously familiar people.

4 **Identity Confusion** Subjective feelings of uncertainty, puzzlement or conflict about one's identity.

5 **Identity Alteration** Objective behaviour indicating the assumption of different identities or ego states, much more distinct than different roles.

For discussion of the subjective experience of this see Mclntee (1994).

Attempts to solve internal conflicts may occur externally via repeated, compulsive behaviours or internally by way of arguing voices or acts of self-harm. Research suggests (Kluft, 1985; Ross, 1989) that abuse would need to be early and repeated for this to occur to such an extent. Mclntee defines abuse as the withholding of care, belittling and the existence of inappropriate boundaries, emotional, physical or sexual. Severe abuse can create an apparent lack of differentiation between people, place and time to the extent that past, present and future become completely malleable. This may lead to the initiation of self-abuse on the victim's part in order to give an impression of control and time process. However, this attempt at control is dysfunctional and so it fails to break the abusive cycle; instead, it merely perpetuates it, providing temporary rather than permanent relief.

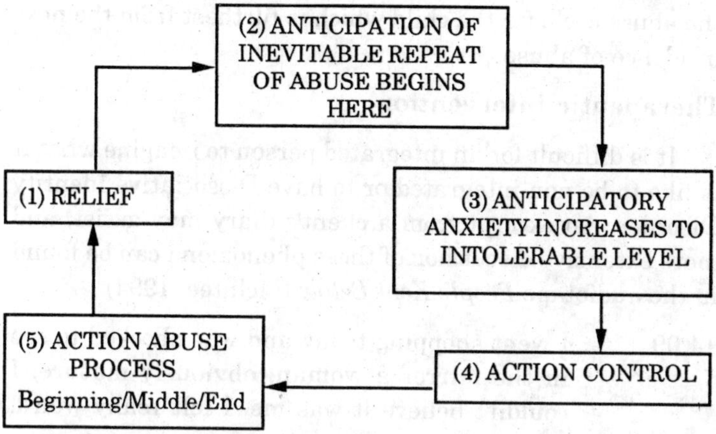


**Figure 10.3**: The self-abuse cycle

The most difficult phase in the abuse cycle (see Figure 13.3) is not the abuse itself but the anticipation of it. The stress caused by not knowing what is going to happen, by whom, and when, provides a human being with an intolerable level and build-up of anticipatory anxiety (3). An ordinary example is the anxiety after a first date, waiting to see if a call will follow. A job interview or application may have the same effect. Often people go into 'premature closure', convincing themselves of the worst in order to avoid the need to tolerate the uncertainty, and waiting for what they feel will be a disappointing or intolerable outcome (2). For an abuse victim, it gives a sense of control to behave proactively within the abuse cycle (4). A child may deliberately 'provoke' his or her carer to the point of physical abuse since, once the abuse process has begun, the child knows he or she is nearer to the point in time at which the abuse will end. By acting in this way, the child forces the abuse cycle forward from the 'worst place' (5), which is the abuse itself, to the 'best place' (1), where the 'best place' immediately follows the abuse process. This point is so called because it marks the stage in the abuse cycle for the child which is furthest from the next incidence of abuse.

**Therapeutic intervention**

It is difficult for an integrated person to imagine what it is like to be non-integrated or to have Dissociative Identity Disorder. An excerpt from a client's diary may assist, and more extensive discussion of these phenomena can be found in the audiotape *People Kept Below* (McIntee, 1994):

14.09 I went shopping today and was shocked to see in the mirror a woman, obviously mature. I couldn't believe it was me. I felt really weird. Who is this mature woman ?

20.09 I have just found Serenity.
She is so beautiful.
She can get us all together, if only we would give her a chance.
It is her love that has kept us alive.
She is the one I saw in the mirror in the shop.
Serenity is chairman of the board.
I think, constantly, she is there behind the scenes while the others are behaving and reacting.
I fear they will try to keep her out.

Another person with Dissociative Identity Disorder, now well on her way in her recovery process, wrote the following poem as part of her therapeutic creative writing. She is describing her selves, and speaking to all of those with whom she had contact: parents, foster carers, social workers and so on. Unfortunately, because she was also abused many times after being 'taken into care', there is a double significance for her:

**A Plea from the children within**

We tell you no stories, we tell you no lies, we tell you only what we see through our eyes or hear through our ears.

We are the innocent children you sent away. You are the grown-ups who chose not to listen.

We were not born with knowledge or thoughts we brought to you. We knew nothing of men's or women's private parts, of the nasty things they do.

We told you only what we had seen or been taught. We were not born so distressed or distraught with our lives in a mess.

We are human beings just like you with true feelings and thoughts. We are after all small versions of you who needed to be cared for and protected from all the evil people who did us so much wrong, not turned away or ignored just because we were small.

We are the children who never grew up because we were left with so much pain, fear and sorrow. You were the grown-ups who left us holding all the guilt and shame because you turned us away and did not listen when we came to you, leaving us believing we were all to blame. You are the grown-ups who were supposed to be our guardians of love, care and protection instead of turning us away, calling us liars and story tellers with huge imaginations.

We are the children who ended up feeling crazy or insane, keeping secrets because we dared not tell you as you chose not to listen when we tried so hard to tell you about our journeys through hell, causing us to become so split up and divided inside, it's a miracle we ever survived.

Because severe Dissociation has resulted from very early and severe trauma, it has interfered with, and distorted, the normal psychological developmental process. Therefore, therapy for Dissociative Identity Disorder needs to be psychodynamic in its basis but eclectic in the management of thoughts, feelings and behaviours that are dysfunctional. It should also be in the interests of maximizing integrative development. The client with DID has so much development to achieve and so much traumatic material to process that a very comprehensive package of therapy is essential. Although there are differing opinions about how long therapy will take and whether integration of subjectively separate self-parts is the desired goal, the International Society for the Study of Dissociation (1994) suggest that therapy will typically be in the region of five to ten years. Our clinical experience concurs with this view and suggests that therapy can be very demanding of both client and therapist.

There are many general principles of therapy generated by this theoretical model. The task is so comprehensive that it draws on many other theories and established techniques, bringing them together in a paradigm that informs the therapy for Dissociation, and which allows for the existence of prodigious individual differences. The less experienced and confident psychotherapist finds it hard to accommodate this level of complexity and seeks to simplify the task by concentrating on generalities that inform practice and create the illusion of security and recipes for intervention. This is profoundly limiting for the therapist, and especially for the client, who will still not experience unrestricted growth even though their therapist recognizes and knows 'what to do' with DID?

Successful work with Dissociation requires a highly skilled psychotherapist with the confidence to know that he or she does not need to know everything and that the 'doing' belongs with the client and not the psychotherapist, even when the client is suffering from such a profoundly disabling and developmentally delayed condition. Like all nurturing, it is the quality and capacity of the psychological holding of the client and the tolerance of uncertainty that permits growth in both the client and the psychotherapist. This also means that sufficiently nurturing holding is required for the psychotherapists themselves. It is necessary for every psychotherapist treating Dissociative Identity Disorder to have a supervisor with extensive experience in this clinical field. The severity of the trauma and the complexity of the therapeutic task mean that the transference and counter-transference have a quality that is often too extreme for the therapist to hold alone without distortions affecting their capacity as a therapist. It is of great benefit to have not only an experienced supervisor but also the guidance of a supervisor who does not have direct contact with the client. As expert help is not yet very widely available in the UK, this may mean resorting to the use of supervision by telephone if no source of expertise is locally available. A good theoretical framework does help client, psychotherapist and supervisor hold on to such complex and sometimes bizarre information as is generated in Dissociation cases, and to provide guidelines as to the course of therapy and its pitfalls. That a professional can develop the awareness to identify Dissociation is in itself a great help to the client and permits the professional to assist the client in locating a suitable therapist. A common mistake, once one's awareness is raised, is to experience a very strong need to rescue, or make up for, the client's past professional or service losses. This may result in beginning therapy by default, with no certainty of continuance or competence, and may do more harm than good.

For the potential therapist, new to this clinical field, there is a great advantage in demonstrating to the client that no matter how urgent for terrible the content of the client's distress, it can be held and tolerated whilst appropriate boundaries and other therapeutic considerations, like supervision, are secured.

# XIV

# LISTENING TO CHILDREN: APPRECIATING THE ABUSED CHILD'S REALITY

## Introduction

Buscaglia's words alert us to the powerlessness of childhood, to the total dependency of infancy and to the effects with may persist into adulthood. To begin to work effectively with abused children we must hear the child's voice and listen to it. We have to begin to appreciate how the world looks from a child's perspective. If we fail to take this step into the world of children, then we do violence to their experience by superimposing our own meanings and intentions without any consideration of their understandings of what has happened, or is happening, to them. That child protection is a contentious field is without doubt but, in all of the debates and arguments, we should be careful to hear what children themselves have to tell us. Otherwise, the consequence, as Boyle has noted, is that amidst 'the clamour of professionals crossing swords, it is hardly surprising that the voice and the experience of the abused child is the most silenced voice of all' (1991). This chapter therefore considers some of the barriers to effective communication. Its core theme is that, without an appreciation of the reality of the children with whom we work, we will adopt approaches and procedures which will be insensitive, ineffective and even counterproductive. In short, we will fail children.

**Being prepared**

Preparing oneself to work with abused children is not an easy task. There is no easily learned process for the task is never completed - it requires a continual willingness to be open to change and to appreciate the reality of another person's experience. It must be recognized that this type of work cannot be sustained successfully without organizational commitment and support. The emotionally charged content of child protection and therapy goes to the very heart of the worker's sense of self. Without adequate support and opportunity for reflection it can prove overwhelming. Nevertheless, we can identify some of the significant issues and indicate their likely consequences.

**Barriers to communication**

We focus here upon some of the most common barriers to communication with children who have been abused. Probably the biggest barrier arises from the reluctance of adults to acknowledge the relative powerlessness of children. In daily life children cannot fail to be aware of this imbalance but, because of their particular experiences, abused children may be extremely sensitive to this. They may have learned to watch adults very carefully indeed for the slightest signs of disapproval, aggression or threat. In its most extreme from this can be seen in the ultra-quiet and conformist behaviour described as 'frozen watchfulness'. In contrast, the insecurity of other children may lead them to adopt behaviour which tests the adults' reactions. Thus a child who has been sexually abused by several adults may greet a new person by overtly sexualized behaviour, such as tongue kissing, and sexual rubbing of themselves or the adult. In doing so, they may be repeating previously learned patterns of behaviour which they believe are either normal or necessary in such situations, or alternatively, are checking out the adult as a potential threat. Such behaviours are often misinterpreted by workers. In our experience they are as much about the exploration of power, and attempts to make sense of the child's inner confusion, as they are about sexuality.

While workers can never entirely abolish the power difference between themselves and the clients, they can minimize it to some degree (Pugh, 1996) and, most importantly, can communicate to the child their willingness to proceed on the child's terms. Workers should be sensitive to:

- how they physically position themselves in relation to children;
- their language and the words they use;
- their tone of voice;
- their appearance;
- their gender;
- how they introduce and present themselves.

It is crucial to allow children the space and the time to develop conversations as they wish. This, of course, is where the use of toys and other forms of play create opportunities for workers to be with children and engage with them in relatively non-threatening ways. This is not play therapy as such, but is better described as play-related communication (Wilson et al., 1992).

Avoiding direct questions and intrusive eye contact, together with responses which echo the child's statements, usually help children to feel more at ease and less threatened. When the primary aim is communication it is important to understand that, when such communication begins, it is a process rather than an event. When approached with sensitivity and care it can represent the first part of a therapeutic process which begins with an opening out and sharing - a willingness on the part of the child to contact distressing and confusing experiences within themselves and share them with the listener. This process, encompassing the sharing of painful material, is often a necessary first step towards subsequent protection of the child. It can represent a first stage too, towards helping the child to enter into a therapeutic relationship with the listener, where that is appropriate, or with some other person who can go on to help the child make sense of these experiences. The primary aim of therapy may be described as one where: 'The emphasis is thus on enabling the individual to move from a sense of being at the mercy of hidden feelings to gaining some mastery [*sic*] over them' (Wilson et al., 1992).

Although the promise of therapeutic help for such children may not fall within the scope of the adult listener - who may, for example, have a limited investigative role – it is nevertheless vital to acknowledge that such processes may already have begun. It is therefore crucial to ensure that roles are clear and that further opportunities are afforded for the child to continue the process within safe boundaries.

Our capacity to hear what children are saying, especially for inexperienced workers, can be limited by our sense of revulsion and distaste at the things we encounter when children reveal their abuse to us. The ubiquity of abuse as well as its nature are shocking to all of us who were fortunate to have had safe childhoods. Such events may fundamentally challenge our perceptions of society and parenting, particularly when we realize that the abusers rarely conform to the stereotype of the stranger with monstrous appetites, but are the apparently ordinary mothers and fathers who might pass by unnoticed and unremarked in any street or supermarket. Furthermore, we need to recognize that, while many children who have been involved in exploitative sexual experience are aware of some sexual taboos and consequently may be unhappy about what has happened to them, they are often confused about sexual behaviour and the context in which it has occurred.

So, while the horrors of their abuse remain overarching and oppressive in the experiences of some children, for others it is confused by the fact that it may have taken place within a relationship which also contained some emotional comfort and warmth. The experience of abuse, for this latter group, confined as they are by their own limited experience of the world, may be that it is relatively 'normal'. After all, their parents/carers are the only ones most of them have ever had, and whatever else happens, they represent 'normality' and home. Consequently, abused children may develop confused and ambivalent feelings about their own sexuality and its implications for other people. In some instances, adult carers may find that gentle boundary-setting linked to sex education is the most effective response, whereas, in others, where children perceive themselves and their bodies as dirty or worthless, there may be a more fundamental task of re-establishing some basis for the child to begin to value him - or herself. Whatever the most appropriate response, in all cases the crucial first step is to seek to establish communication with the child on his or her terms, not ours. If not, a child's perception that he or she is somehow responsible for what has happened, coupled with an awareness of social taboo, can - when combined with a more or less explicit injunction against disclosure from a powerful adult - create a powerful barrier to disclosure and is often a major hurdle to be overcome in therapy.

Perhaps the most pervasive barrier to communication arises from the different social realities which adults and children inhabit. The tendency to interpret the behaviour and language of other people solely in our own terms frequently obscures the meaning it has for them, or debases the messages they are conveying, as in the case of Zoe, aged 5, who spoke of her fears:

> Well, this is getting more seriouser everyday. More seriouser. You've got to help the little girl. She has the spider disease. And there are poisonous spiders in her tummy. And it's full of, full of, poisonous spiders and soon her tummy's going to burst open and the poisonous spiders will fly out everywhere and poison every human in the land. (Bray, 1991)

It would be easy for an adult listener to ignore the child's reality or immediately attempt to construe it in adult terms – and thus shape the dialogue in these terms - by asking the child to explain what the 'spiders' were. However, by accepting the child's subjective perception of events and attempting to explore it, in this case by asking how the spiders get into the girl's tummy, the worker elicits the following response: 'They came in a hole in her mouth and in her tummy and the naughty man put them in there with the white stuff.' It later became apparent that Zoe had been sexually abused by her father, and her ideas about what had happened to her were further confused by her lack of knowledge about human reproduction. This does not mean that, in coming to our considered view of what such narratives represent, we uncritically accept them, nor should we simply assume that such stories are necessarily metaphors for sexual abuse, but simply that, when children say things like 'a worm came into my bedroom last night', or speak of 'poisonous spiders', we should not automatically deny or attempt to 'correct' their accounts. Instead we should listen carefully to what they have to say and attempt to construe what meaning it might have for them.

## Sexuality and listening to the narrative

It is well recognized that attitudes to sexually are often conflicting, sometimes ambiguous and frequently uncertain. It is unsurprising, therefore, that in our dealings with children we communicate such varied and sometimes confusing messages. There are two central issues in respect of practice with abused children. The first is to acknowledge that we need to be aware of our own personal feelings and ideas about sexuality and thus do not allow these to obstruct our work with children. Being prepared therefore involves the development of an open and pragmatic acknowledgement of sexual language, taboo and behaviour. Workers should be prepared to use whatever language children feel happiest with and should learn to recognize how difficult it may be for children to speak out about their experiences. One training exercise which one of the authors of this chapter has used is to ask workers, in pairs, to discuss a recent sexual experience. Few find it easy. How might children feel, therefore, when we ask them to recount their own experiences ? How can we listen to an abused child's account, if our own discomfort and inhibitions obstruct our 'hearing'? The following extract shows just how shocking some children's experiences may be, even to experienced workers, but also demonstrates how important it is to listen openly without attempting to deny or suppress the narrative:

> 'It were them little ones that hurted, weren't it, Jess?' James ventured matter-of-factly. 'You know, the ones you cut your nails with, with the pointy ends, weren't it, Jess?' He pressed his older sister for confirmation. 'The other ones what you sew with, the big ones with the jaggy bits. . you know . . . round the sides, well they never really cut as much, did they, Jess? Cos there was no points on the end probably,' he added wisely. Jessica sat, detached, twisting a blade of grass around her finger.... The scene was the foster carer's garden. I was collecting information for a court report. James, aged six, was explaining... the relative merits of pinking shears over nail scissors as instruments of anal penetration. It was becoming clear that the children's father hat not limited himself to penile or digital penetration in this sexual assaults upon them .... Such events, it seemed, had been a matter of routine in James' life. I struggled to regain composure. In the meantime James' mind had moved on to another subject. 'Have you seen my hamster?' (Bray, 1991)

The second issue central to practice with abused children is to acknowledge that such children may themselves have sexual feelings. However, recognition of this possibility is potentially fraught with danger because it can be misused by abusers themselves. Consequently, we should not allow exploitative adults to expropriate this possibility and use it to legitimize their perception of children as sexual beings for their own purposes. Nevertheless, we need to acknowledge that not only has the behaviour of some children been sexualized by their abuse by adults or other children, but also that some victims of child abuse may have learned to take pleasure from sexual activity, and/or the intimacy which may have accompanied it.

This socially premature consciousness by some children of their own sexuality is not universal amongst abused children, nor, obviously, is the experience of abuse always pleasurable for them. In fact, the damaging and harmful consequences are usually all too clear. But we have to accept the reality that not only will some children repeat and rehearse the sexually inappropriate behaviour which they have learned, but also that some are potentially capable of taking pleasure from these activities. This realization is frequently a disturbing one for carers and workers to confront, for it erodes their idealistic notions of childhood innocence. After all, the most common construction of childhood is one which perceives children's bodies, minds and emotions as immature, and thus tends to preclude the possibility of sexuality, or, alternatively, views it as evidence of some deeper disturbance (de Mause, 1991).

While the difficult questions about whether we describe such sexualized behaviour as 'dysfunctional', 'precocious' or 'premature', and about how we should understand and theorize such behaviour, are beyond the scope of this chapter - especially since it requires some knowledge of what is perceived as 'normal' (Lindblad et al., 1995) - we cannot ignore its existence. A reluctance to recognize the fact that George, a 7-year-old, gets pleasure when he 'rubs his willy like Sam done' (Bray, 1991) and is quite prepared to act sexually with other children, leaves us badly placed to discuss and respond to the problems this may cause - complaints from other parents, exclusion from school and rejection by ill-prepared, poorly informed and overwhelmed foster carers are unfortunately all too common in such cases. Apart from the obvious risk that such behaviour may pose to other children, it remains risky for the child who exhibits it, since its continuance unchecked and unaddressed almost invariably results in social condemnation and isolation.

Preparedness therefore requires that workers develop a professional persona which is authentic - in that it is genuinely based upon their own personality and character - but one that remains unshockable and allows them to hear the child's narrative with relative equanimity. There is, however, a danger that, in developing this aspect of professional persona, workers may become desensitized to the pain that children suffer. The implications for staff care are clear: it is vital that professionals are provided with opportunities for support and reflection upon the impact of their work upon their own lives. If children perceive that workers are shocked by or displaying revulsion at what they are hearing, or suspect that there is, however unwitting, any form of negative response, including insensitivity, then it is likely that their narrative will be inhibited (Glaser and Frosh, 1988).

Of course, there may be a clear need on the part of the worker to show the child that they disapprove of the actions of the abuser(s), but workers should be wary of unwittingly displaying judgemental attitudes and of rushing to offer judgement. This may be particularly dangerous in cases where a courtroom appearance may be in prospect, and where such responses may be open to scrutiny and challenge. It may have the effect of undermining the credibility of the worker's evidence because of the apparent prejudging of the issue. In this latter respect, as with all communication with children, one should attempt to move at their pace and take one's cues from them.

Based upon her own practice, Bray presents a model of disclosure which describes a typical process through which many children pass. This is by no means an inevitable sequence, nor even a necessary one, but it is common:

> At the beginning, blocking behaviour such as foot-tapping, hysterical giggling or averted eyes - the child would keep its dilemmas very close to its chest and would resist any adult attempts to make contact.... Gradually, then we would move on until the child began to test the ground tentatively and trust began to develop, then would come the sharing part when we began to face the problem head on and share it, and I would learn for the first time precisely what it was and gain a measure of what the impact had been upon the child's life. Soon we would experience discharge when an outpouring would occur, often in the form of a torrent of words, anger and actions which led to confrontation.... The end of the process saw a plateau, a calm resolution, a putting down of the baggage and moving on. Time and time again, we would move backwards and forwards across this continuum as the child's own inner healing strength offered its own answers and dilemma after dilemma sought resolution. (Bray, 1991)

The crucial point is that, while workers may have sound ideas about the likely processes of disclosure and therapy, the cues for the content invariably come from the child themself. For example, one child, Tracey, who was being shown around a police station because she was worried about the consequences of revealing what had happened to her and - as became apparent later - wanted to know what would happen to her abuser, asked to be locked in a cell alone for a few moments. The adults present were understandably somewhat surprised by this request but acceded to it: 'After a little while she banged on the door. "Let me out now." We opened the door. She stood, a tiny form in the doorway. "He can't get out," she said triumphantly' (Bray, 1991). Thus, it is only from a close hearing and sensitive understanding of children's narratives that we can guess what their confusions and problems are. They worker, therefore, is not the possessor of the answers, but is a catalyst for change. As Bray later comments in regard to successful outcomes: 'The child did all the doing - I just made a place where it could happen, and let it be' (1991). Given that the extended extract above describes a set of processes which children commonly undergo when a constantly listening adult affords them the opportunity to share in this way, it is perhaps salutary to note how difficult it can be for this to occur within existing 'unfriendly' adult-constructed frameworks of investigation and evidence-gathering.

## The contradiction between professional procedures and the child's needs

The practice guidelines provided in the *Memorandum of Good Practice* (Department of Health and Home Office, 1992) ascribe a dual role to child protection agencies in respect of children at risk, one of 'protecting their interests and dealing effectively with those who would harm them'. However, there are two questionable assumptions which underpin the guidance protocol:

- Children like James and Jess will be able to talk about their abuse, accurately, at a time that is administratively convenient, and in a form that adults can use to protect the children's interests and deal effectively with those who cause them harm.
- This process of disclosure can be successfully achieved under artificial conditions, in front of a camera, in a short period of time, lasting little over an hour, since workers

who wish to continue with disclosure will need to be in a position to justify further interviews from material obtained in the first session.

It is our contention that the protocols and the formal processes of gaining evidence ignore the reality of how children actually respond to formal intervention by child protection agencies. Put simply, such procedures ignore the reality of how children think, speak and act. Furthermore, the statutory emphasis - enshrined in the Children Act 1989 - upon participation and cooperation with parents, whose interests must be seen to be afforded demonstrable consideration and respect, introduces another complicating factor to this aspect of investigation in cases where it is the parent(s) who are under suspicion. James and Jess, for example, live their lives in a distorted world. Their abusive experiences may be so much a feature of their everyday normal life that it literally may become 'unremarkable' to them. Even when such children are aware of the distortions which beset them, they may develop coping strategies which deny or downplay the significance of what has happened, or is happening, to them. They may cope psychologically with the uncertainty, or the possibility, of overwhelming distress by, for example, distancing, denial or blocking: that is, by having it 'not happen to me'. Helping children such as this to express their pain, and thus providing us with the evidence and means to protect them, is often a lengthy and immensely delicate process.

The case of Michael, a small, undernourished 3-year-old boy whose eating patterns were unusual - sometimes biting but not swallowing food, and sometimes vomiting it up again and playing with his vomit as if he were trying to examine it - shows how ham-fisted existing procedural guidelines often are. Concern about Michael arose from circumstantial evidence that he would not let anyone take him to the toilet, nor take off his clothes to allow doctors to examine him, and appeared to be frightened and wary of men. Michael's mother, Annette, had reported that her partner, Stephen, was violent towards her and intimated that he also treated Michael harshly in comparison with his own children. There had also been earlier suspicion of possible sexual abuse of Michael's sister, Kerry Ann, but no conclusive evidence. Annette, though frightened of her partner, gave her consent for Michael to be interviewed without Stephen's knowledge. A specialist child abuse consultant was called in to conduct the interview with the aim of establishing whether there had been any abuse and, if so, to gain evidence which would justify statutory intervention. During the informal interview held at the day nursery Michael attended, he quickly became absorbed in playing with a number of different toys available in the consultant's specialist toy-box. Unprompted, Michael enacted a scene of considerable domestic violence. Amongst the ordinary toys were several anatomically complete dolls of which he was initially unaware, but which became the focus of his attention when he discovered them later in the session. Again unprompted, Michael began to play with the adult male doll:

> Totally involved. He pulled the penis hard and twisted, jamming the now naked doll in between the radiator and the wall. He ran forward, picked up the yellow plastic sword and thrust it deep into the man's groin. He cut and twisted and pummelled at the genital area, twisting the penis round and round with furious grunting noises. The doll fell to the ground. I knelt down beside him. Silently he paused for breath, starting at the devastated spectacle on the floor. He looked at me. Glassily. Eyes empty. Mind eleswhere....For some time Michael considered my face. From the frenzied odyssey a victor was emerging....He stood across from me, still measuring my face. He reached out towards me and, still whispering (to himself), placed a small grubby finger on my lips....Michael had not yet spoken a word (to me). In his world, speech has superfluous.

> His language was the language of play. Michael was introducing me to his explosive and precarious world....He pulled my arm and, male doll in hand, beckoned towards the window....'You open', he said....'Michael, if we open the window I shall have to hold on to you. We're too high up and I can't let you fall.' He nodded...I opened the window and held on to him tightly, my hands around his tiny waist...he raised his arms. The cloth doll balanced momentarily above his head and then fell, hurled downwards towards the ground far below. 'Man dead', he said...'Man dead. Naughty man dead', he repeated. 'Michael, has the naughty man got a name?' No reply ... I tried again. 'Michael, can you tell me, where does this man live?' Michael shook his head. I could feel him withdrawing from me. Things were becoming unsafe. We both knew it. Now he would retreat to safety within himself, and close the door. Much against my better judgement, I persisted. 'Michael, does somebody hurt the little boy?' Panic flooded his face. He stood before me, eyes moving everywhere. His hands reached automatically to cover his penis. (Bray, 1991)

As feared, after the end of this session, whicn was suggestive of abuse but did not in itself provide unequivocal evidence of it, Annette appeared to respond to threats from Stephen and forbade any further contact with the worker. While 'common sense' might persuade us otherwise, we must not rule out the possibility that Michael was receiving adequate care and protection in his own family – no one working in childcare can be unaware of the dangers of jumping to unpalatable conclusions, but the critical point is that further exploration of the possibility of Michael having suffered abuse was obstructed in this case, as the local authority's judgement was that an approach to the court was unlikely to be successful. Although Michael was a very young child, he was able to give us a glimpse of his fragmented world. Given further time, trust and confidence, he may have provided information about who did what to whom within this disrupted world he inhabited. With continued access to him, the provision of such information remained a possibility, but it could not, and would not, have happened in a single hour within a video suite.

Among the views expressed in the study of the implementation of the memorandum of good practice on video interviewing of child witnesses (Department of Health, 1994) one respondent stated that 'There is a lot of commitment, but also a lot of anxiety about the lack of results' and concluded that 'children don't tell stories the way the Memorandum suggests. They often tell some of it before and then repeat and expand on video. However, that is not technically how it is meant to happen.' Indeed, practitioners might wonder whether, in the current climate, exploratory play sessions should even take place at all. If Michael's case were being investigated today, he might well be considered too young to represent a view via an interview conducted in accordance with the memorandum guidelines, and the case might not proceed beyond this initial decision.

## Conclusion

The Bridge Consultancy's report into Gloucestershire Social Services' handling of the children cared for by Frederick and Rosemary West (who were arrested to several charges of murder) once again emphatically reminds us to the crucial importance of listening to what children are saying. It concluded that this aspect of practice was: 'probably the single most important matter in this report' (1995). The report stated that:

> The social work staff, lawyers and police who listened to the West children, evaluated their comments and acted, should be commnded for their ability to respond objectively and for their willingness to risk their professional reputations on the basis of what they were being told. It would have been so easy to do nothing rather than take the risk because the comments of the children appeared bizarre. (1995)

While the West case is admittedly extreme, even by the horrific standards of so much 'ordinary' child abuse, it is galling to realize that even the most recent review of the research into child abuse and protection (Department of Health, 1995), with one notable exception, makes little reference to the voices of children. This exception acknowledges children's disappointment at the lack of effective response in some cases. It notes their sense of powerlessness, and recognizes that they often blame themselves for what has happened to their families after social services and the police became involved. But in the practical exercises suggested at the end of this review, while there is one of communicating with parents and carers, there is no mention of actually communicating with the children themselves.

Current practice, both at the personal level of practitioner preparedness and in terms of the procedural guidelines for establishing and gathering sustainable evidence, may be incompatible with the practical reality of how children actually communicate difficult information. Unless we recognize and address this disparity by better preparing novice practitioners for their work, by lobbying for more child-friendly statutes, and by developing reality-based procedures which allow the child's voice to be heard properly, we should face the uncomfortable reality and acknowledge that current practice continues to leave some children in dangerous situations without adequate protection.

We acknowledge that 'the interplay between fulfilling the requirements of a legal or a therapeutic system presents a constant dilemma for those involved in sexual abuse assessment work' (Keary and Fitzpatrick, 1994). However, we are firmly of the view that the current guidelines are unrealistic when working with young children because, in the most fundamental manner, they fail to observe one of the most basic tenets of sound practice - which is to start from an appreciation of where the client is, that is, the client's own psychological and emotional position in relation to the experiences they have undergone. Nevertheless, our view derives more from direct case experience, and we recognize that it is not unequivocally supported by research (although there are a number of studies which point up the importance of interviewing styles: Dent and Stephenson, 1989; Jones and McQuiston, 1988; Keary and Fitzpatrick, 1994: Quinn et al., 1989). In our view, the question of the 'balance of rights' in terms of what constitutes acceptable grounds for statutory intervention remains central. Contemporary practice does not best serve children's interests since the main arena for deciding such matters - the court system in England and Wales - is premised upon an adversarial contest instead of an inquisitorial search for 'truth'. This system is often destructive of children's testimony, because it sets out, not with the primary aim of establishing the veracity of such testimony through inquiry, but with the presupposition that this can only be tested by a process of challenge.

Finally, while professional practice in case of child abuse is most obviously conceptualized in terms of adult notions of protection, safety, respite and prevention, we should also consider the child's position and perception of events. In many interventions their position of powerlessness is continually confirmed by the processes which swamp them - their voices remain unheard. We know that some children are wary of disclosing what has happened to them for fear of the consequences for, and from, their families, and that others having disclosed abuse are sometimes unhappy about the ways in which allegations are investigated. For example, a small study of older children who had reported abuse while they were in public care, which uniquely asked them to talk about what they thought of the investigation, revealed that the children felt considerable dissatisfaction with what happened of them (NSPCC, 1996).

It is our contention that listening to children and

appreciating what they are saying is not simply a matter of getting better evidence, but is a small step towards empowering relatively powerless people. Since most abuse, whether of children or adults, is readily understood in terms of the abuse of power, we should always consider this dimension in our work with children. Simply listening carefully demonstrates our appreciation of their position. Hearing their narrative in the way in which they wish to tell it signals respect. This alone can begin to help some children regain a sense of personal worth because, apart from the cathartic effects of ventilation and disclosure, they have some element of control in their interactions with us. Let us not forget that it is we adults who, by dint of our age and understanding, mandate politicians and public servants to establish the statutes, structures and processes which purport to respond effectively to the pain of some of our most vulnerable children.

**Footnote**

While reference to anatomically complete dolls is made in the description of the case of Michael, we knowledge that, since that time, there have been considerable misgivings and a vigorous debate about whether, or when, such dolls should be used. Nevertheless, it is our view that they remain a valuable aid to communication in some circumstances, but that workers should not use them as if they were a diagnostic test of abuse, especially because of the dangers of adult imposition of meaning which might be mistaken and unjustified. For a fuller account of the issues we recommend Everson and Boat (1994). None the less, it is worth nothing what a curious and fascinating phenomenon it is, that 'ordinary' dolls routinely do not represent the reality of the human body. This 'bowdlerization' of the human form for the most part passes unremarked. What does the desexualization of the doll signify - an adult perception of idealized childhood, or a manifestation of adult fears and sexual taboo?

# XV

# SHORT-TERM FOCUSED GROUPWORK FOR YOUNG MALE ABUSERS

## Introduction

Many intervention programmes with adolescent males who sexually abuse have been carried out in group format. Programmes used in the USA by Ross (1987), O'Brein (1992) and others have a large component of groupwork in their make-up. Many programmes in this country have used groupwork as well, sometimes for assessment as well as intervention.

The advantages of groupwork have often been listed. Ryan and Lane (1991) suggest that many of the common characteristics exhibited by young offenders are effectively addressed in a group. These include: denial and minimization, isolation, poor social skills, inaccurate sexual education, distorted beliefs and victim stance. Ryan and Lane feel that connecting with other group members and using confrontation and challenge, together with role play, support and education, can help deal with many of these issues. They are particularly keen on the 'combination of confrontation and support' as it 'originates in the peer group [as] adolescents are less resistant when challenged by their peers than in similar interactions with adults' (1991). While groups are often used to work with adolescents who abuse, there is very little in the way of evaluative work to suggest how effective they are compared, for example, to individual interventions.

For the confrontational aspects of a group to be effective, they need to be genuinely created by the group members themselves and not simply put to the group by the facilitators. Groups of adult sexual offenders involved in long-term intervention - and probably under a legal mandate to attend– often can provide such challenges, especially when some members of the group have been involved in the intervention programme longer than others. Adult groups, such as those run in the past by the Gracewell Institute on a residential basis, and by various probation services throughout the country, can provide not only such challenging but also a level of support (Beckett et al., 1944). One of the major concerns in looking at groupwork with adolescents was the possibility that such groups would be less likely to create appropriate challenges and could even become counterproductive.

There are a number of reasons for this. The first of these relates to the power imbalance in the adolescent group situation. Such a group is always facilitated by adults who have a level of power and control over the young people involved. However it is presented, the adults are in charge of the group. While this may be acceptable to adults who have been convicted of abuse, adolescents may be more likely to respond to their own peer group pressure and attempt to challenge the adult facilitators or take over control of the group. Given that adolescents do respond readily to such pressures, and given that many of them do not have the impulse control to avoid or recognize the negative nature of such a response, it is possible that working with a group of adolescents who had abused could become a very difficult and unhelpful experience.

The second difficulty, in our specific setting, arose because many of the adolescents were not, in fact, on criminal orders. Some were in care, but most were cautioned for their sexual abuse, and any intervention carried out was done solely on the sanction of the case conference and with the agreement of the young person and their carers. This means that there was little compulsion for them to attend the groups. While some workers who run groups may feel this to be a disincentive, it can be seen in a positive way: if the young people involved in groups have a personal commitment to attending, then the work they do is likely to be much more effective. However, this means a good deal of hard work in making the groups very positive without losing the challenging nature of the work and, certainly, without colluding in any way with the offending. It also suggests the need to keep the groups relatively short. An adolescent's attention span is limited in any case, and a long-term group would seem destined to fail unless there was a compulsion to attend. On the other hand, a long-term group whose members *were* compelled to attend would seem likely to be much less effective as the young people would either seek to take over the group and disrupt it (subtly or directly) or simply 'opt out' and take little part in, or pay little attention to, what was going-on?

Previously, one of us had acted as a consultant for a longer-term group which had tried to cover issues relating to offending pattern, sexual education, relapse prevention and victim empathy work. In the dozen or so sessions, it was very clear that these issues could not be covered appropriately and that some of the young people simply 'opted out' and avoided certain areas altogether. Because the schedule was so full, many issues were not covered. In discussing the difficulties raised by this group, it was obvious that a longer period of time was needed to deal with each issue, but that this would then make the entire group unacceptably long in its duration.

The answer, then, appeared simple. Shorter groups, dealing with specific parts of the abusing behaviour, would enable us to provide a concentrated input, allowing group members opportunities for both challenge and support but avoiding any bid to disrupt the group due to the novelty or initial motivation wearing off. A shorter period would commit the young people to a definite number of sessions with a clear end in view and this, if presented in the right way, should enable workers to hold their interest right to the end.

It was also clear that there were some parts of the work which should not be undertaken in groups. Fantasy work is a good example - there were fears that young people would share fantasies or become aroused by each other's descriptions of the abuse. There seems to be little or no direct research evidence on this point, but it is easy to imagine adolescents trying to outdo each other in their descriptions of abusive fantasy just as they do in reality in boasting about their sexual exploits. It would be likely that there would be some offences - such as rape of a girl of nearly the same age as the offender - where such boasting (once the offence had been discovered) would enable the young person to minimize the abuse and place the blame on the victim. Although most sexual offending against children is secretive and not usually shared with peers, there is a significant risk that simply using groupwork to address such offending could 'normalize' it to an extent and, ultimately, be counterproductive. It is important that individual work gives a young person the chance to examine their own motives and recognize their own patterns without distractions from others.

## Setting up the groups

In setting up the short-term groups we were clear that individual work with a young person should continue alongside any groupwork. We were also clear that, for each group, there would be specific requirements and that a young person would have to have achieved specific goals before attending a group.

We decided that there were four areas in which groupwork could enhance the individual work we were already undertaking with young people: Sex Education, Planning the Offences, Victim Empathy and Relapse Prevention. These four areas would provide four short-term, focused pieces of groupwork. Young people could progress through each group, if that was felt to be appropriate, but it seemed more important to be able to feed them into groups at a time that fitted with their own needs. While the group was operating, individual work would continue, and feedback to the individual worker would be given from the facilitators. We were able to set out quite clearly the requirements for, and the aims of, each group, and both local authorities involved put forward the names of young people to be considered for each group.

The requirements and aims were as follows:

*Overall aims*

1 To add a further dimension to individual work with young people who abuse by enabling:

- support from peers and peer group challenge to take place, as appropriate;
- young people to make quicker progress, thus supporting individual work with them;
- intervention methods to be used which can enhance individual work with young people who abuse.

2 To assist in training workers by:

- increasing skill and confidence in groupwork situations;
- providing appropriate support and supervision for designated workers.

3 To provide a new and cost-effective resource for each participating area which it would be unlikely to provide on its own, in line with 'Working Together' and the provisions of the Children Act 1989 to cater for 'Children in Need'.

*Objectives for groups*

Objectives for each group focus on specific issues, but overall objectives include:

1 Assisting group members to change their behaviour in the context of taking responsibility for their actions.
2 Improving self-esteem and social skills for group members.
3 Enabling group members to challenge each other appropriately about their excuses and rationalizations for offending.
4 Enhancing and emphasizing the individual work being carried out by local authority workers.

*Objectives for workers*

1 To utilize the four suggested group modules in intervention with those young people who abuse who, it is felt, will benefit from groupwork.
2 The evaluate each module both through the self-report and questionnaire responses of the young person and through the worker's own evaluation.
3 To feed back information to individual workers to enhance and focus their interventions with young people.

*Aims of groups*

1 Sex Education group, At the conclusion of this group, a young person should be able to:

- demonstrate that they understand the following terms: abuse, mutuality, cooperation, compliance, consent, relationship, rape, sexual assault;

- distinguish between sexually appropriate and sexually inappropriate behaviour and explain the reasons;
- demonstrate an understanding of the way attitudes towards men and women, boys and girls affect behaviour;
- question some of their own attitudes about sex, sexuality and gender;
- understand the legal situation with regard to sexual offences and abusive behaviours;
- demonstrate an appropriate understanding of contraception and sexually transmitted diseases;
- discuss, with tolerance and understanding, issues around developing sexuality and sexual orientation.

2 Planning the Offences group At the conclusion of this group, a young person should be able to:

- describe in full their offending pattern and the ways in which they were able to set up and carry out their offence(s);
- describe and challenge their original excuses, rationalizations, justifications and minimizations;
- identify other areas where they may be reluctant to take full responsibility of their actions and the consequence of these actions.

3 Victim Empathy group At the end of this group, a young person should be able to:

- demonstrate a real and genuine understanding of the thoughts and feelings of their victims(s);
- write an appropriate letter to their victim which does not use blame, excuses or justifications;

- demonstrate an understanding of the short-and long-term effects of sexual abuse for victims;
- identify the questions and concerns which victims will have about their abuser;
- incorporate an appropriate concerns for past and potential victims into their strategies for avoiding reoffending.

4 Relapse Prevention group At the end of this group, a young person should be able to:

- clearly state alternatives to offending;
- identify various practical ways out of their offending cycle;
- demonstrate the existence of external supports in preventing reoffending;
- have an appropriate and rational view of their potential for reoffending;
- state and understand the consequences of further offending for victims, family, self and society;
- have a positive view of themselves in a future without abusing.

*Initial requirements for short-term focused groups*

1 Initial requirements for Sex Education group:

- assessment has suggested that relationship and attitude education work is needed.
- young person has skills in reading/writing and understanding to cope with several written questionnaires;
- young person is willing to participate in a group;
- young person is able to make a brief statement to the

group (can be worked out with individual worker) about their reason for being there.

2 Initial requirements for Planning the Offences group - the young person:

- has completed Sex Education group and achieved its aims *or* has achieved similar aims through individual work;
- is able to draw out their cycle of offending and to include some (i) grooming/targeting behaviours (ii) excuses and rationalizations;
- has acknowledged the importance of fantasy and masturbation in setting up their cycle.

3 Initial requirements for Victim Empathy group - the young person:

- has completed Planning the Offences group and achieved the aims of that group *or* has achieved the aims required of that group through individual work;
- is *not* a bullying or sadistic offender - workers need to be clear that the young person does *not* gain pleasure directly from hurting or overpowering others;
- is prepared to acknowledge responsibility for offending directly to the group.

4 Initial requirements for Relapse Prevention group - the young person:

- has completed Victim Empathy group and achieved its aims *or* has achieved the aims required to that group through individual work;
- has recognized and acknowledged to the group that there is a real chance they could reoffend;
- has at least started individual work on fantasy modification if appropriate.

From the management side, it was important to have an agreement that allowed this 'cross-boundary' model to succeed. Given the current financial position, the only type of agreement which was possible was a no-cost agreement. Each local authority agreed to release two workers to be involved with the groups. The time required included meetings to plan the groups, the group sessions themselves and additional time after each session for debriefing and final evaluation meetings. In addition, while one local authority provided the premises for the group (a room with video recording facilities and an observation room), the other undertook to transport its young people. This was always done separately from the workers – it is not feasible to run the group and debrief afterwards if young people have to be transported home as well. From both workers' and managers's viewpoints, the other benefit of this groupwork system was in training workers. We used four workers for each group. Workers with little experience or workers who had groupwork experience but had not worked with young people who abuse were able to become involved in observing, facilitating and planning alongside others who had had significant experience in both areas. This was a very real 'plus' for workers and for managers, who thereby created inexpensive training for their own workers.

In each session, therefore, we had two facilitators and two observers - the observers being, for the most part, in the observation room and not present in the group. However, because we alternated facilitators, all the young people knew all the workers, and we met together at the start, at the end and during the break in the middle of the session. From the feedback after each of the groups this approach was seen as positive by all the young people.

**Gender balance of workers**

After much discussion, we decided that the only group

where it was important to have both a male and female co-facilitator was the Sex Education group. It seemed essential that this group, designed to examine attitudes to men and women, should provide an appropriate role model. In subsequent groups, this model was not pursued as we felt that there the gender balance was much less important and preferred to mix up the workers according to their own interests and skills.

**Running the groups**

One of the difficulties often faced by workers in creating groups is that there are not enough young people available at any given time to form a group. This means that young people can wait around for a group when all the evidence suggests that, to avoid build-up of denial, avoidance, minimization and justifications, work needs to be started quickly, and the impetus of the initial assessment should not be lost. By combining two local authority areas, this becomes much less of a problem. We felt that a group should be composed of between three and eight young people - certainly no larger.

The basic session plan for the groups was devised to allow for the short-term concentration of the young people and to make each session as interesting as possible. We therefore included a number of different activities. The group started by talking briefly about the positive or negative experiences they had had during the week. This was followed by a group game, not necessarily a serious one, and then the first part of the working session. A short break - for drinks and crisps, at which all observers and facilitators were present - was followed by the second working part of the session. A final game, either to calm the group or to get them moving about, followed by feedback from the observers and (usually) five minutes' relaxation, brought the group to a close. The techniques used in the working sessions included discussion, video, drawing and drama.

## The Sex Education group

The main aim of the Sex Education group was to begin to challenge attitudes to males and females, but it was also designed to provide updated sexual knowledge. We evaluated this group by means of a simple questionnaire about sexual knowledge - in fact, most of the group had the basic knowledge before the group began and there were no major improvements on what were reasonable scores initially. We used video clips, discussion and games to disseminate information and worked in a 'sound bite' way which seemed to hold the attention of the young people involved. Two of the group were dyslexic, so we built into our group model ways of working which did not pick out or disadvantage those two young people. This involved, for instance, always reading out any written information and sometimes utilizing all four workers to ensure that everyone understood their tasks.

## The Planning the Offences group

This was probably the most demanding group - the 'cycle' group. In it, we aimed to work through a typical offender's cycle, with each young person identifying the parts which related to their own offending pattern. This involved some careful work around the 'fantasy' part of the cycle to ensure that young people did not share their own fantasies, and it also involved some specific role-play work around parts of their offending. This was very draining, both for the young people and for the workers, but it enabled some young people to add a good deal to the cycle that they had already recognized in their individual sessions.

The challenging that we got was not extensive but the group did seem fairly supportive of each other (although not collusive). We created an 'excuses board' which the group challenged during the last session, but direct challenge during the group itself was rare. It was our conclusion that many of the young people involved in this sort of group would not directly have the courage to challenge their peers.

**The Victim Empathy group**

This group relied almost entirely on role-play work and, as such, appeared very successful. Some of the comments from the young people afterwards were: 'You get to see what it's like from the other person's point of view'; 'It makes you feel better in the group - working it out. The hardest part was at the start... introducing yourself and all that'; 'The worst bit was being the abuser in the role play.'

We asked them what they thought they would remember in ten years' time: 'Role plays'; 'About victims'; 'The other group members'; 'The way you've been working with other people.'

We had decided that it would not be appropriate for the young people to role-play their own offences. Partly this was to avoid recreating fantasy and memories of the experience, and because we felt that it could put too much pressure on each young person. In any case, with five young people in the group we would not have time in six sessions to role-play each individual offence effectively. We therefore created two composite offences, incorporating elements of each person's offending, and spent parts of two sessions on each 'offence', casting, discussing, playing and videoing each one. We were careful in the selection of roles and ensured that each young person had an experience of playing a victim. When a young person played an abuser, we ensured that they were not playing a role which was similar to their own abusing behaviour. This group was set up with the same basic session plan as the other groups.

One of us had also worked extensively with groups for young women who were victims of abuse. She was interested in the comparisons between the two types of groups, not having worked before with a group of young abusers. In the use of role-play, for instance, it was clear that the young abusers' group took readily to the idea and were keen to participate. Using the 'freeze frame' technique to elicit thoughts and feelings at different points enabled the young people to go beyond the here and now in their thinking and to consider gender, societal and cognitive influences on victim responses to abuse. All of the young people felt that it was uncomfortable playing the victim but they also said that they very much disliked playing the abuser. In retrospect, this is exactly the result we would have wished to achieve.

Our facilitator who had worked with the young women's groups observed that, in such groups, while role-play was a very useful tool to developed freedom of expression and disclosure of 'real' feelings, the participants were generally difficult to engage in this activity. It appears that victims have difficulty in taking on a 'tough' role and do not easily adjust to assertive, dominant character parts. However, the women's groups did use peer support to challenge oppression and gained strength from helping each other.

Relaxation and games were used by both groups, with the young male abusers engaging readily in both activities with little apparent embarrassment. The young women, on the other hand, appeared to feel much less safe and found it hard to relax and let go. Avoidance tactics were applied to this part of the schedule, and the group as a whole viewed this as an unhelpful activity.

Attendance at the abusers' group was 100 per cent, without any mandate. This was surprising because it indicated a real level of commitment to the group which might not have been expected. There was real sadness when the group ended. For the young women, it seems that many of them attended because of pressure from their non-abusing parent or from their social worker. Very few believed that attendance was for the benefit of themselves or that it would be helpful. Numbers fell within the first month and 30 per cent, on average, of the membership were lost.

A concern that is often expressed about working with young abusers in groups is that they could create a 'hierarchy of offending'. In the case of this specific group, there was some discussion of each person's offences but there never appeared to be a problem in relation to a hierarchy or a comparison of offending behaviour. We felt that this would only become a possibility if the group had gone on for much longer and that using a six-week group session was one way of avoiding difficulties in this area. The group for victims of abuse was, of course, longer and, in the early stages, it seemed that a 'tariff' of experience evolved, leading to one or two members questioning their group membership. This led to two possible responses by the young women: putting extra effort into group members felt to be more 'hurt' than themselves, or minimizing and dismissing their own need for help and support. The young women needed reminding that the degree of abuse was not the issue and that their feelings were the common denominators, whatever the individual experience.

**The Relapse Prevention group**

As far as the local authority programme was concerned, this was to be the fourth group but, at the time of writing, it has not been operated. Several workers moved on and the impetus was lost. Relapse prevention runs through all the intervention programmes in any case, but this group was designed to reinforce the positive, offence-free lifestyle and to enable young people to role-play difficult situations and avoidance techniques. Plans for the group were made and included a number of visual ways of looking at how to avoid reoffending. A 'relapse prevention' game was created, and it is envisaged that such a group would include role-play work to reinforce coping strategies devised and developed by the young people and their individual workers.

## Conclusion

The three groups seemed to run successfully. With one exception (due to circumstances not within our control as the young man was from third local authority) we had 100 per cent attendance. Only one young person was under any compulsion to attend. He was on a deferred sentence for the Planning the Offences group, but he also attended the Victim Empathy group after he had been conditionally discharged. One young man attended all three groups, another two attended two, but the others came in for groups as indicated by their progress on their individual programmes.

We did feel at times that the groups were not long enough, even though they dealt with one specific aspect of the abusing. On reflection, however, these short-term groups seem to hold the attention of the young people, quite effectively enabling them to concentrate on a particular issue. In addition, the programme provided positive and invaluable 'hands-on' training experiences for workers. The young people's feedback indicated a level of enjoyment which seems more likely to ensure that they relate to and remember the issues discussed. The young people also indicated that the most difficult part of the programme was having to talk about their abusing behaviour by being open and accepting responsibility for their actions.

From our own point of view, the experience of planning and running such groups has been very challenging, but the cooperation and links with other workers who are doing the same has been very positive indeed. The element of training during the time the groups were operating was also important and enjoyable.

From our observations of abuser and victim groups we would suggest that adolescents who abuse are as much in need of a safe, supportive environment as are victims of abuse. Their cognitions, attitudes, values and fantasies need challenging and checking out, but there remain the issues of isolation, rejection, disgust, self-devaluation, guilt, blame and family breakdown which are also experienced by the victims of abuse. This observation does not minimize their behaviour but reinforces the idea that, in order to avoid their reoffending, a whole series of other issues need to be tackled along with the confrontation and change of the behaviour itself. In the victim empathy work, in particular, it was clear that the group helped the young people to rethink their perspective and to create some empathy and understanding, and that this was by far the best way to enable them to make long-term, positive behaviour change.

Immediate feedback on the groups suggested that the young men involved felt that the experience of attending had been an important one for them. Measuring long-term behaviour change is clearly difficult and, in any case, the groups were always intended to run alongside a full programme of individual intervention. None the less, the short-term groups focused the young people on specific issues and enabled them to examine their cognitions and feelings along with others who had also abused, but without the dangers of creating in 'abuse subculture'. Such groups enhance the individual work but are not a substitute for it. Group participants need to be selected carefully and, just as with individual work, workers need to remain fully in control of the content and direction of the sessions. With these provisos, however, short-term focused groupwork with young sexual abusers appears to avoid the pitfalls of other types of intervention programmes involving adolescent groups, and provides a positive experience which can only aid young people in making confident choices not to abuse in future.

# XVI

# THE GROUPWORK SUPPORT OF SEXUALLY ABUSED BOYS

## Introduction

This chapter discusses issues relating to a groupwork project which was set up to support a group of boys who were victims of organized sexual abuse. The boys had to wait for almost two years following their disclosure before giving their evidence in court.

The first part of the chapter relates to factors around male child sexual abuse and initially considers problems relating to its under-reporting. Subsequently the problem of *some* male victims of sexual abuse sexually victimizing other children is explored. It is strongly emphasized that there is a substantial majority of sexually abused male children who *do not* sexually abuse others, and that this issue requires sensitive consideration when working with sexually abused male children. Finally, the influence of structural pressures and societal definitions of masculinity in exacerbating the problems experienced by sexually abused boys is debated.

The second part of the chapter considers the incompatibility between the evidence demands of the legal process and the therapeutic needs of sexually abused children. The *Memorandum of Good Practice* (Department of Health, 1992) has tried to address this issue with the introduction of guidelines for the production of videotaped evidence. However, because this is based only on partial implementation of the Pigot Committee's proposals, children are still required to attend court for cross-examination.

Finally, I offer an example from practice which tries to show that in spite of problems in the judicial system which can hinder supportive, child-centred practice, it is possible to identify and execute certain areas of positive intervention before a trial, without interfering with the reliability of evidence.

## Factors relating to the sexual abuse of boys

From the review of research by Watkins and Bentovim (1992) and others, it would appear that there is a considerable under-reporting of the incidence of sexual abuse of boys (Peake, 1990; Mendel, 1995). The reasons identified include: the victim's fears of homosexuality; a response to the stress caused by abuse through externalized behaviour; the culture of masculine self-reliance, and ideas about youthful male sexuality. There are also arguments that there may be an inadequate response to allegations because of a tendency to blame the boy or even because of a denial of abuse by professionals. In addition, the influence and possible power of the paedophile lobby has to be acknowledged. Other factors which may be involved include loyalty to the offender and pleasure in aspects of the abuse.

The fact that, within a homophobic society, homosexuality engenders widespread fears, confusion and taboos about sexual identity may also discourage openness about the subject. It is important that these and other possible factors in under-reporting should be considered when designing programmes of intervention.

Watkins and Bentovim (1992), in their review of research relating to the sexual abuse of male children and adolescents, quote research (Rogers and Terry, 1984) which describes three behavioural responses which were seen as more or less unique to male victims:

1 Confusion or anxiety relating to sexual identity.

2 Inappropriate attempts to reassert masculinity (compensatory aggression).

3 Recapitulation of the victimizing experience.

Confusion or anxiety relating to sexual identity is described as involving homophobic concerns. Attention is drawn to the importance of distinguishing between fear of homosexuality and the development of homosexual preference. The former is a contributory factor to non-disclosure, possibly enhanced by societal factors and compounded by confusion relating to arousal during abuse. In many cases, sexual abuse is experienced prior to a full understanding or development of sexual identity, which may create the myth that the experience dictates the identity.

Compensatory aggression is described as the most common behavioural reaction. Such behaviours would include fighting, destructiveness, disobedience and hostility. Alongside the research by Rogers and Terry (1984), additional research by Summit (1983) supports this finding. The majority of the research evidence discussed by Watkins and Bentovim (1992) supports the view that sexually victimized males are more likely to show externalized responses than females.

Recapitulating the victimizing experience is described as identifying with the aggressor in preference to adopting a victim identity. That most perpetrators are male enables boys to become more likely to develop such identities.

Watkins and Bentovim (1992) quote conflicting research on the extent to which victims go on to sexually victimize others. One study by Conte and Schuerman (1988) quotes a rate of 2 per cent, although the study is not gender-specific. Other studies, relating to boys alone, ranged from a rate of victimization of others of 13 per cent (Friederich et al., 1988) to a rate of 50 per cent (Sansonnett-Hayden et al., 1987). The pooled prevalence of these studies was 22 per cent.

Statistics quoted in the media and in other arenas sometimes relate to the proportion of adult sex offenders who were themselves victims of abuse. Often these statistics are quite high and can instil considerable anxiety into the male child victim, who may not have sufficient understanding of statistics to realize that the particular example quoted does not accurately relate to the proportion of victimized boys who go on to abuse?

Furniss (1990) refers to sexually victimized males having fears of themselves becoming abusers. The path of victim to victimizer is described as a circular and self-reinforcing process in which fears relating to the abuse prevent the development of normal adolescent relationships. Ryan (1989) refers to victims of sexual abuse experiencing many dysfunctional outcomes: emotional; development; behavioural; an inability to communicate; feelings of helplessness; depression, and somatic complaints. She refers to learned behaviour where victims recreate their own experience of abuse. Such 'traumatic sexualization' is referred to as developmentally inappropriate sexual behaviour (Finkelhor and Brown, 1986). Long-term victims of sexual abuse may have been exposed to the distorted rationale of the perpetrator. This can lead to ritualistic patterns of sexual behaviour that become more rigid and more secretive over time, nurtured by an emotional climate of fear and anxiety. The child's anxiety and confusion lead to an incorporation of the offender's rationalizations and distortions:

'The conflicting physical and emotional sensations, psychological confusion, and feelings of intrusion may

> create a sense of powerlessness and lack of control that reinforce the helplessness inherent in any exploitative experience' (Hiroto 1974). The lack of control may lead to control-seeking behaviours (e.g. eating disorders, self-destruction, or exploitation of others). (Ryan, 1989)

Secrecy and isolation prohibit the child from validating feelings or correcting distorted assumptions (Finkelhor et al., 1986). This is supported by Furniss' (1991) reference to entrance and exit rituals which deny the reality of the abuse taking place in terms of being validated by events outside the abuse itself. This may lead a child into irrational thinking, a declining self-esteem, guilt, confusion, powerlessness and anger. Ryan (1989) refers to such developing fantasies as retaliation in order to regain control. This, in turn, leads to planning negative behaviour such as offending. The identity of an aggressor becomes more comfortable than the pain and anxiety of a victim. Aggression becomes the means of dominating helplessness.

For such a child, the triggers for negative behaviour or sexual offending may be those situations where the child feels out of control of experiences situations which resonate with the abuse. The cycle towards a sexual assault may take the form of a pattern of negative feelings and cognitive distortions coupled with a need to take control. These children may often feel persecuted not only by their own experience of victimization but by other factors such as social isolation, poor peer group relationships or family disruption. According to Furniss (1991), the physiological reward of sexual offending constitutes its addictiveness. The pairing of sexuality with fear, anxiety, helplessness and aggression may lead to future experiences of those feelings becoming the trigger for a cycle that leads to sexual arousal. This reinforces the pairing and can lead to the sexualization of non-sexual problems. For some children, remembering experiences of abuse may entail high levels of arousal. Over a period of time, sexually aggressive fantasies followed by sexually aggressive behaviours become the means to regain control, albeit temporarily, until the initial feelings which triggered the cycle recur and move the child towards repeated sexual offending. For the victim, this loss of control and subsequent emotional turmoil is the *outcome* of being abused. For the offender it becomes the *trigger* for future offending.

Minimizing one's own abuse, denying the abuse, retracting disclosures, accepting the pleasure of the abuse without question, and repressing any subsequent trauma arising from the abuse all serve to create the deception that sexual abuse is not harmful and can be enjoyed by its victims. They are dysfunctional, irrational defences and serve to move a victim along the path to victimization.

Therapeutic intervention must work towards accountability for both the victim and the offender. Any intervention with victims of sexual abuse must focus on placing blame with the offender and must emphasize empathy with the victim. The victim is helpless and needs to be helped to regain control. Ryan (1989) argues strongly that victim empowerment must be based on cognition rather than on feelings. The victimization of another can create a feeling of power but it is difficult for such an act to create an open, rational cognition of power. Ryan is cautious about some of the traditional therapeutic methods of helping a victim. Encouraging a child physically to act out anger may reinforce aggression and support retaliatory behaviours. Victims need to be helped to rethink situations in order to cause a reduction in negative feelings, as scenarios of anger and retaliation can become role plays for future aggression and victimization. Ryan uses the term 'legitimate privacy' to replace the dangerous secrecy of the facts of a child's abuse. It is emphasized that the victim must be helped to identify his own pain and that victim empathy is a key element in therapy: 'The child's power is in self-discovery, strength discovery, and the ability to identify and rely on supportive, protective adults' (Ryan, 1989).

When dealing with child sexual abuse, children and adults may be presenting themselves in states of trauma and distress which require an immediate response in terms of individual support. However, it is important in terms of being able to apply the most appropriate and effective intervention to keep structural factors in mind. For example, feminist perspectives see child sexual abuse in the light of power and gender - an unequal distribution between men and women in a patriarchal society. Child sexual abuse, then, is seen as an abuse of male power and trust. This perspective relates male sexuality to power, control and dominance. Scration (1990) refers to Connell's concept of 'subordinated masculinity' by citing examples of younger men subordinated to their seniors and the subordination of homosexuality to explicitly heterosexual, hegemonic masculinity. Hegemonic masculinity is central to cultural beliefs and orientates policy and formal politics:

> Further, they become the basic currency of entry into the world of work, leisure and social commentary, deeply ingrained in the initiation of induction procedures of political and economic institutions, social clubs and gatherings, and forming the basis of laws, conventions and practices. (Scraton, 1990)

Helping an abused boy contextualize abuse may prevent him from developing some of the compensatory aggressive behaviours mentioned above. The secrecy and shame of sexual abuse may serve to 'subordinate' a survivor's masculinity to the 'hegemonic masculinity' of wider Western culture. Treatment should consider forms of 'alternative masculinity' which help young people become aware of these cultural forces and develop a sense of choice which does not by necessity conform or subordinate itself to enforced stereotypes. Gender, of course, is only one aspect of discrimination which forms the context for abuse. Other aspects of structural disadvantage should also be borne in mind, such as age, race, class and disability.

Sexual abuse is a multifactorial problem implying multifactorial solutions which take account of the interaction of individuals within a cultural framework. It is also necessary to be aware of matters which relate specifically to the male experience of sexual abuse. As with all situations of intervention relating to sexual abuse, it is important to take account of the gender of workers and of the need to avoid creating therapeutic scenarios which resonate the experience of abuse.

For children and young people who have sexually abused other children, their offending behaviour needs to be addressed as a primary focus. When helping boys address their own experience of being sexually victimized, the therapeutic task is to identify and name the experience of sexual abuse as a harmful and painful one whose recipient requires support, understanding and healing. The victim becomes not a victimizer but a survivor. Dangerous secrecy becomes legitimate privacy through a process in which the individual regains rational control.

## Children, evidence and therapeutic intervention

The incompatibility between the evidence demands of the legal system and the needs of children in child abuse cases has been well documented in the literature (Spencer and Flin, 1990; Davies, 1992; Aldridge and Freshwater, 1993). It is generally agreed that children's attendance at such trials is at least stressful, if not traumatic. In cases of sexual abuse, where a child may be in need of therapy, the experience may be particularly traumatic. In such cases, any pre-trial discussion of matters relating directly to the evidence of the alleged abuse is likely to prove difficult if the reliability and spontaneity of the evidence is to be preserved. The child is required not to discuss the evidence but to keep it freshly in mind for repetition at the trial and wait until after the trial before being able to talk through the abuse and receive help.

This problem has not been resolved by the introduction of the *Memorandum of Good Practice* (Department of Health, 1992) following the Pigot Committee, as it is still necessary for a child to appear live in court the cross-examination after admitting evidence in the form of a video-recording. This has been only a partial implementation of Pigot's proposal. He had suggested a second vide-recording of the child's cross-examination in chambers soon after the first video interview. This would have solved the problem of therapeutic work being delayed by slow-moving legal processes.

The current system has the therapeutic needs of abused children and the evidence requirements for a successful prosecution locked in opposition to each other. The task is to maintain a balance throughout a very difficult waiting period. If the decision has been made for a child to go to court, then the balance is already moving towards evidence. The task then becomes a damage-limitation exercise as, inevitably, the child will suffer stress as a result of such a decision.

**A practice example**

The boys served by this project had attended computer clubs set up locally by a man named Harry, who was a computer studies lecturer, and another man named Gordon, who was a legal clerk. These men were known to each other. Harry's club was for boys aged under 11 whilst Gordon's was for 11 and over. Some of the boys had attended both clubs, as moving from one club to next was an established process. The club evenings involved computer activities, games and trips out. Occasionally there were residential trips during school holidays and at weekends.

After concerns had been raised relating to the continued presence of boys at Gordon's house and the behaviour of the of the boys, a joint social services and police investigation was set up - over thirty boys were interviewed. There were clear statements from 11 of the boys relating to acts of sexual abuse which had been committed against them by either Harry, Gordon or both over a period ranging from two months to, in some cases, four years. Most of the boys were loyal to Harry and Gordon, some out of fear, particularly in relation to Harry, while some of the loyalty was a genuine friendship, particularly in relation to the boys who attended Gordon's club. This made the investigation both confusing and difficult.

Because of the legal system, the complexities of the case and possibly the professional status, knowledge and skill of the offenders, the process of prosecution lasted for almost two years. During this period there were several 'warnings' for court appearances, some of which involved the boys attending court sessions which resulted in adjournments. These repeated delays caused the boys a great deal of anxiety and stress. Both men were eventually convicted on a number of counts of sexual abuse and given short prison sentences.

When the Crown Prosecution Service (CPS) had decided to proceed with a trial, a multi-agency meeting was set up. At this meeting the setting up of a support group was proposed by myself and social services colleagues. Following this, it was necessary to negotiate with the CPS about how it would be possible to run a support group without influencing or causing problems with evidence. It was also necessary to advise them that this practice would be in accordance with the child welfare recommendations of *Working Together* (Department of Health, 1991). A close liaison with the CPS was established and maintained throughout the pre-trial phase. The defence lawyers were made aware of the group and were given a basic outline of the programme. There were no specific challenges about the support groups in court, although the accusation of collaboration was an aspect of the defence case.

It was recognized that there needed to be a speedy acknowledgement of the difficulties the boys had experienced so far, and their need for a support system for the future which would reduce their anxieties and break down and isolation. There was also an emphasis on giving the boys a choice about appearing in court.

I was introduced to each family by a member of the initial investigation team. After I had given each boy an initial support interview which gave him and his parents an opportunity to raise questions, further interviews were arranged, at their request, in groups of two or three. This was necessary in order to break down further any fears and anxieties the boys and their parents might have before entering into a full group. The boys chose particular friends from the proposed group with whom they felt they would like to discuss the idea of a support group. This suited the pace of events, as the social services department were still in the process of identifying co-workers for the groups. Two support groups were set up - one for six boys aged 14 and the second for five boys aged 10 to 13. The members of Group One were an established peer group, all members living on the same estate. Group Two members were only acquainted through occasional computer club sessions and some residential trips. I led the group with two female co-workers, one for each group, in order to provide a mixed gender leadership.

The boys welcomed the prospect of attending a support group, especially in view of their not attending any group activity since the closure of the computer clubs. The boys also welcomed the proposal that attendance at a support group was a decision independent of attending court, and that the decision on attending court could be made during the life of the group. This was particularly important for some of the boys who were struggling with their loyalty to Gordon. In some cases, this situation was causing family conflict. Most of the families expressed concern about the boys. Some boys were suffering from disturbed sleeping patterns, were often moody and appeared unsettled. As soon as the boys began to feel that they were being involved in a process of exercising choices and were not being seen simply as court witnesses, their commitment to the process developed and their anxieties began to reduce.

The pre-court stage of the groupwork programme was as follows:

1 *Identifying support and building self-esteem*

This involved the presentation of the group programme with discussion around issues to do with choice. Activity-based sessions were designed to enhance self-esteem and to develop a group identity. These sessions generally alternated with the work-based sessions to offer support through a difficult and distressing programme.

2 *Going to court*

Sessions included the giving out of basic information about the court and the nature of the adversarial process. Also included were visits to local courts, role-plays, identifying personal strengths and discussions emphasizing the importance of telling the truth. Also included were stress-reducing techniques.

3 *Sexuality and sex education*

We embarked on a basic sex education programme using the 'Man's World' board game to facilitate discussions about sexuality, sexual orientation, gender roles, sexism and so on. It addition, these sessions attempted to identify the pre - and post-court areas to be worked on, including the difficulty of not discussing the abuse before the trial. The boys were asked to approach me in the event of any distress which they felt could not be addressed within the group sessions.

4 *Protection issues*

This part of the process focused on discussions about knowledge of good touching and bad touching and the importance of being able to say 'No' to inappropriate contact. In addition, activities were used to help the boys learn to identify safe adults to tell. This whole area attempted to ensure a continuation of understanding and support from families.

This pre-court phase of the programme was characterized by the need to balance evidence requirements and welfare/ protection issues. The boys were asked not to discuss aspects of the abuse with each other. The pre-court phase addressed issues relating of the context in which the abuse had occurred. Most notably, issues were discussed relating to developing masculinity in a society which emphasizes dominance and self-reliance as expressions of masculinity, and which generally supports the expression of homophobia. Such issues have the potential to exacerbate and deepen the anxiety of an abused male. We took pains to talk about such issues supportively but without any direct reference to sexual abuse, with the knowledge that it was likely to be the case that privately held anxieties were being addressed. When, during the post-court phase, these issues were fully addressed in the context of the actual sexual abuse, it was clear from some of the comments and reactions of the boys that they had listened carefully to, and benefited from, the earlier discussions. They demonstrated understanding and made reference to the earlier sessions, and were able to enter into the discussions with some degree of ease.

A group leader attended each trial and supported the boys throughout. Prior negotiations had already been made with the court for the provision of suitable waiting facilities.

The post-court programme was as follows:

1 *Discussing the court experience*

This session involved discussing and explaining the outcome of the trial and acknowledging everybody's contribution as well as sharing feelings.

2 *Secrecy*

Here we looked at the role of secrecy in sexual abuse as a means of maintaining silence, and explored together the advantages of breaking down such secrecy. Again, feelings, anxieties and events were shared.

3 *Abusers*

The characteristics of abusers and their behaviour were explored by the group, focusing on how an abuser can present different faces to different people. Discussions centred on abusive processes, targeting, grooming, and the maintaining of silence. The session also talked about how the abusers set up sexually-oriented games and asked about the boys' feelings towards the abusers now. The session ended with a discussion of how one might identify abusers in the future.

4 *The abuse*

There was an open discussion by each young person of the abuse they suffered. This allowed group members to compare and corroborate their experiences as well as challenge denial within the group. There followed a discussion of feelings about the abuse and a sharing of difficulties as a result of the abuse. We also highlighted the importance of the safety of the group and the advantage of talking.

5 *Further issues of sexuality and sex education*

This part of the programme looked at the nature of sexual assaults on children and compared them to the group members' own experiences. To help in ensuring protection in the future, we identified and addressed sexualized behaviour and sexual messages. Discussions covered a variety of issues, including masturbation, sexual fantasies and memories of the abuse, along with problems of tension-relief and the possible sexualization of non-sexual problems. The session concluded with talks about relationship attitudes, sexism, gender roles and stereotypes.

6 *Fears arising from the abuse*

We explored at some length the fears around enjoying

some aspects of the abuse, and concerns around homosexuality. Issues around loyalty to the abuser and the mixed feelings that were aroused were addressed, as was the fear of becoming an abuser. We emphasized issues of choice and sexuality as a developmental process and the need not to become fixed by one's experiences. The group talked about the importance of talking through difficulties and solving problems, as opposed to hiding them and building up fears. The session also emphasized the harm of sexual abuse and the need for help and guidance in recovery.

7 *Source of future help*

This session acknowledged the importance of family, friends (each other) and the availability of local resources. Members were encouraged to contact group leaders in the future, if necessary, or any other member of the social services department.

8 *Evaluation*

The whole experience was evaluated by the use of questionnaires, discussion and the comparison of earlier group material with more recently completed work. The discussions centred on feelings and the extent of recovery, and the ultimate ability of group members to be able to protect themselves and be protected in the future.

Throughout the unexpectedly long lives of both groups, the group leaders observed increased levels of confidence and self-esteem. This was borne out by comments from the young people to the effect that they felt better and had valued being a number. Topics which had been the subject of personal fears and secret anxieties were finally discussed openly and to the full. Some boys showed a greater level of initiative and independence, becoming more able to take part in discussions and make decisions about group events and topics. There were comments on the evaluation forms about the value of being listened to and having the opportunity to take time to discuss feelings and have questions answered. The attendance rate for both groups was close to one hundred per cent. The artwork towards the end of the group was much more relaxed, relating to hobbies and interests, and no longer showed any sexual comments or sexually explicit drawings of the abuse. Most of the tensions and conflicts between group members had also subsided.

That the boys had to wait for almost two years before giving their evidence meant their having to hold on to deeper anxieties of the abusive experiences for an intolerably long time. This was a clear example of the incompatibility between the demands of the legal system and the therapeutic needs of victims of sexual abuse. Several of the boys openly stated that they felt that their enjoyment of the support groups had to some extent compensated for this. At times, however, their actual experiences and responses spoke against this. Furthermore, these comments were made after the court process had concluded and were a sharp contrast to the anxieties expressed in response to news of further adjournments. The boys had to cope with the knowledge that a stressful event was still to occur at some undefined point in the future, and that this was preventing a full therapeutic discussion of personal experiences and feelings relating to the abuse.

If it had been known at the outset that the delay would be two years, then the process may have been considered to be contrary to the welfare to the boys, and it is likely that the topics of the post-court programme would have been dealt with much sooner. Such a decision, however, would have damaged the prospect of a successful court outcome to the extent that the case may have been dropped. Many sexual abuse investigations fail to reach the court system for reasons relating to the weakness or lack of evidence. This case could have been one such example.

Inevitably, a programme of this length and nature will have an impact on its leaders. This impact will possibly differ between genders. A male worker has to face comparisons with the abuser and needs to identify boundaries and highlight the absence of any personal complicity in sexual abuse. A female worker has to face possible stereotyping and sexist altitudes and can feel isolated in an all-male group. These factors dictate the need for close communication between workers and a well-worked-out and agreed consistent response to situations which may arise. All the workers discussed ways of demonstrating non-oppressive, respectful relationships in their behaviour with each other and with the boys. These factors also highlight the need for the leaders to provide mutual support and to receive joint and individual supervision on a regular basis. Unfortunately, the supervision accrued more on an individual basis than on a joint basis. The mutual support and cooperation between the group workers, to some extent, compensated and replaced this. In view of the unexpected length of the groups, each group worker required and benefited from the sustained support of colleagues from their respective teams.

## Conclusion

The incompatibility between the therapeutic needs of sexually abused children and the demands of the legal system was vividly demonstrated by the experience of the boys in the groups. Throughout the process there were clear expressions of anxiety from all of the boys in relation to the delays in the court process. This highlights the need for social workers involved in this area of work strongly and consistently to advocate and negotiate for priority to be given to the needs of children who are caught up in this manner.

The experience of the boys in this project supports the view expressed in the literature that groupwork is an appropriate and desirable response to male sexual abuse, particularly in relation to organized abuse involving several children. The proposals for such work are likely to require strong negotiation for acceptance by members of the legal system. Detailed plans justifying how the work will give priority to the children without jeopardizing the reliability of evidence are needed.

The project has shown that it is possible to carry out

therapeutic work before a court trial, without interfering with evidence - most notably, areas of work which address issues relating to the context of abuse which have the potential to exacerbate and deepen the child's level of anxiety. The split of a therapeutic programme into pre-court and post-court phases was helpful to all parties but particularly to the boys, who were able to see the difficult areas of work were on the agenda for discussion at a later stage. Such a split is, of course, a compromise and not a solution. The solution requires an adjustment of the legal system to enable a child's role at court to be concluded at a very early stage, to free the child to receive a full therapeutic programme.

The project has demonstrated that many of the problems identified in the literature in relation to male sexual abuse were experienced by the boys in the groups - most notably, the anxieties relating to the legal processes as well, of course, as the personal emotional distress and turmoil already highlighted.

The extension of the group process as a result of the delays had a compensatory spin-off in therapeutic terms, although direct therapeutic work relating to the abuse itself did not take place until after the court appearance. Both groups continued until the full therapeutic programme had been implemented. The workers and boys believed that a degree of therapeutic healing took place through the positive group experiences, in the form of increased self-esteem and, ultimately, empowerment through knowledge and confidence-building. There was visible relief after a positive court outcome when responsibility was finally placed where it belonged.

It is hoped that the boys involved with the project will continue to recover and readjust to a life without court cases, secrets and fears, and will continue to develop along the path of transition from victim to survivor.

# XVII

# EMOTIONALLY COMPETENT CHILD PROTECTION ORGANIZATION

## Introduction

A couple of years ago a middle manager summed up the culture of her social work organizations in terms that have resonated with every audience that I have subsequently shared it with. She described herself as paid for 'doing' - outputs, tasks and so on; as far as 'thinking' was concerned she should do that at home or at the weekend, but as for 'feeling' she should not bother to do that at all. In other words her organization, typical of many social care organizations in the early 1990s, was one in which two-thirds of the domians of human experience - that is, thinking and feeling - were off organizational limits. The consequences for any social are institution are deeply damaging in terms of critical reasoning, planning, working relationships, reflective analysis, staff stress and motivation. The consequences within a risk management environment, such as child protection, are more worrying still: blunted emotional responsiveness, reduced sensitivity, inadequate reflection, and dangerous decision-making.

Emotional competence is therefore not simply a challenge for individual managers or practitioners, it is also a corporate issue for organizations. Indeed, one might ask whether individuals at any level in the organization can remain emotionally responsive and literate in an agency environment that is emotionally illiterate, blunted, or sometimes more deeply disturbed.

The purpose of this chapter is to explore a number of related themes: the philosophical and emotional context in which child protection organizations are currently operating; the impact of anxiety on agencies, practice and practitioners; and the interplay between client-generated stress, practitioner stresses, and agency culture. It concludes with a number of ideas for promoting healthier organizational conditions. It is hoped, therefore, that the material will be of relevance not only to practitioners, but also to those managing these difficult processes, who are only too aware of the increased toll that child protection work is exacting on the workforce.

## The current context of child protection work

It would be hard to overestimate the extent to which the context in which child protection work is operating has changed in the space of only a few years - and certainly since the Cleveland crisis in 1987, and the publication of the subsequent inquiry. There have been fundamental changes both in the philosophy of child welfare and in protection work, as well as in the organizations and structures through which such work is carried out.

As far as child protection is concerned, and sexual abuse more particularly, whilst in the early 1980s the accusation was that intervention was 'too little, too late', post-Cleveland this has given way to a deeper public disquiet that intervention is 'too much, too soon'. Olafson et al. have described such societal responses to sexual abuse in terms of cycles of discovery and suppression in which:

> We behave somewhat like those victims who protect themselves by splitting off and sealing over the memory

> of their childhood traumas . . . despite substantial contemporaneous research on child sexual abuse. (1993)

In other words, there is no consensus from society as to how sexual abuse should be managed.

Events in Cleveland became in turn one of the most potent catalysts to the Children Act 1989, which was designed to redress the balance of power in favour of the preservation and support of the family, and away from paternalistic state intervention. 'Partnership' philosophy was thus seen as the solution to the deficits of the child protection process.

However, the Act also retained much of the previous framework for investigating suspected abuse and intervening to protect children, albeit with more robust safeguards to limit what decisions social services can take without the court's sanction. Fox Handing (1991), in her analysis of the Children Act 1989, describes two contrasting tensions withim the Act: first, increases in the state's right to intervene in family life are juxtaposed with the 'no order' principle of judicial non-intervention. Secondly, the Act's strong emphasis on working with parents, and defence of the natural family, is counterbalanced by the strengthening of children's rights. Thus, three years after the Act's implementation, whilst figures showed a dramatic reduction in the numbers of *emergency* applications for the removal of children from home, the percentage of children on child protection registers who were looked after by social services had dropped by only 3 per cent, from 23 per cent in 1989 before the Act, to 20 per cent in 1993 two years after the new legislation (Department of Health, 1994). Similarly, figures for numbers on child protection registers reveal that despite a substantial 30 per cent decrease between 1991 and 1993 - mainly due to the removal of one general criterion, 'grave concern' - during the same period there had been an underlying increase of 23 per cent in registrations for the other more specific criteria such as physical and sexual abuse and neglect (Department of Health, 1994). In other words, while gatekeeping has generally improved, there remains a fairly consistent cohort of abused children in need of statutory protection, and an increase in some areas of reporting.

Given the philosophical tensions within the Act, and the trends described above, it is perhaps not surprising that it has proved so difficult to find a consistent definition of 'partnership'. In fact, neither the statute nor official guidance defines the term. So why is this apparently 'user-friendly' and straightforward term so problematic to define and express in practice ? The lay person's definition would equate the term with 'joint business' (*Concise Oxford Dictionary, 1976),* sharing, and equality.

However, it is very clear, both in the statue and in the accompanying guidance, that partnership in this context does not mean equality. The state has not abdicated its right to intervene in family life when a child is deemed to be seriously at risk of harm, particularly in cases of sexual abuse, which are seen in the first instance as criminal Acts. The UK has not, for example, adopted the principle of family group conferences as in New Zealand, whose legislation is based on a more radical belief in a non-adversarial response to family difficulties.

Further analysis of the concept of partnership by Howe explores distinctions between notions of participation and empowerment:

> To what extent should helpfulness, empowerment and participation be mentioned in the same breath? Is to speak of one to speak of the others? Although they develop similar characteristics, they ought not to be confused as members of the same species. Their evolutions are quite separate but occupying similar ideological niches they have assumed similar shape and form. Practice is likely to become muddled if workers

> are attracted merely by a concept's looks rather than its intellectual origins. So for example it might be that clients experience participation as fair rather than helpful or that empowerment is a weaselword in child protection if good practice is to be characterised by honest dealings. (1992)

He also contrasts a *therapeutic* definition of partnership based on a psychological contract between the parties for change, and a *social justice* contract based on respect, sharing, openness, clarity of roles, responsibilities, accountabilities and involvement in decision-making. So, whilst there has undoubtedly been a sea change in our approach to child protection, with the shift to a partnership ethos, many unresolved questions remain as to precisely what this means in contested situations.

### Organizational change

Alongside these philosophical shifts there has been a parallel upheaval in the structures and relationships between all the main child protection agencies. Reforming legislation in health, education and social services against a backcloth of harsh fiscal cutbacks has resulted in extensive decentralization, and the creation of internal markets and competition which have fundamentally altered the relationships between those who purchase services and those delivering them. There has been a shift to competitive market solutions based on the primary values of efficiency, effectiveness and value for money, an erosion of state welfare, and a reappraisal of the very nature of professionalism (Yelloly and Henkel, 1995). These forces have in turn placed an almost intolerable strain on interagency work and the ethos of collaboration which has been at the heart of modern child protection work. Given that, even under reasonable conditions, multi-agency work is not easy, current conditions mean that it is facing its sternest test since its importance was first recognized in the early 1970s.

Hallett and Birchall summarize the situation when they describe the:

> atmosphere of chronic overstrain, unrealistic expectations of staff, desperately inadequate resources to cope with rapidly increased reportage of cases and a limited fund of skills and knowledge confronting rising expectations that abuse should always be successfully managed. (1992)

Child protection work is thus being undertaken in an organizational environment which, for many staff, is characterized by rapid and continuous change, occupational insecurity and a preoccupation with survival at both institutional and personal levels. It is the particular impact on practitioners and practice, and the dynamics of managing child protection in an anxious environment, to which we now turn.

### The anxious organization

Anxiety runs like a vein throughout the child protection process. It is present in the anxious or unrewarding attachment that forms the family context in which abuse may occur. It is present in the highly charged atmosphere of the parents' first encounter with professionals concerned about their child. It is present too within the professional system, as child abuse represents a crisis not only for the family, but also for the professional network. But anxiety exists not just at the level of the individual but also, as Menzies (1970) has pointed out, as an *organizational* phenomenon, in the organization's struggle for its own survival.

Menzies' research on 'Social Defence Systems' provides a compelling description of the organizational and human effects of managing in such an environment. She states:

> The success and viability of a social institution are intimately connected with the techniques it uses to contain anxiety. The needs of the members of the

> organisation to use it in their struggle against anxiety leads to the development of socially structured defence mechanisms, which appear as elements in the structure, culture and mode of functioning of the organisation. A social defence system develops over time as a result of collusive interaction and agreement between members of the organisation in order to avoid the experience of anxiety, guilt, doubt and uncertainty which are felt to be too deep and dangerous for confrontation. (1970)

Failures at an organizational level to contain anxiety appropriately can permeate all aspects of the agency's work as well as affecting its relations with the outside world and other agencies. This is demonstrated in the Dysfunctional Learning Cycle described by Vince and Martin (1993).

In this environment, anxiety is seen as unprofessional, a sign of weakness or not coping. As a result, uncertainty is suppressed through fight and flight mechanisms. The absence of forums where feelings and doubts can be safely expressed leads to defensiveness, and a resistance to share and reflect on practice. It also undermines confidence to experiment with new forms of practice. (This may go some way to explain why it has proved so difficult to enable staff to relinquish paternalistic practices in favour of more innovatory and participatory approaches.) Emotional defensiveness then deepens into cognitive distortion whereby the painful reality is warded off via denial of dissonant information and attitudes, offering a temporary but false sense of security. If this process worsens with more wilful and sustained ignorance, it may lead eventually to total disengagement. Such systems have the appearance of being psychologically impregnable. The consequences of prolonged engagement in such a dysfunctional coping cycle are deeply damaging for all involved: families, staff, agencies and, most of all, abused children.

These consequences include:

1 *Depersonalisation* as clients cease to be individuals and become statistics;

2 *Detachment and denial* of feelings as the language of intervention becomes bureaucratised into packages and throughput;

3 *Ritual task performance* concerned only with procedural compliance;

4 *Constant counter-checking* in which cases never get beyond assessment;

5 *Redistributing responsibility* through projection and blaming of individuals or other agencies;

6 *Reframing and minimising* the true nature of concern;

7 *Clinging to the familiar* even when it has ceased to be functional (Menzies, 1970).

As Menzies comments, in an observation that rings very true of the child protection system:

> The difficulty has tended to be handled by increased prescription and rigidity. The greater the anxiety, the greater the need for reassurance in rather compulsive repetition. It is unfortunately true of such defence systems that they prevent true insight into the nature of problems and their real seriousness. Thus too often no action can be taken until a crisis is very near or has actually occurred. (1970)

There is of course a powerful link between organizational and personal anxiety, as external insecurities impact on the internal worlds of individuals, and resonate with their own historical and childhood experiences, fears and fantasies. To quote Menzies again: 'The organisational worlds we inhabit reflect the psychic world, the internal society of images and fantasies, conscious and unconscious' (1989, cited in Yelloly and Henkel, 1995).

For those working directly with abused children and their families, all the above simply compounds an already highly complex and emotionally demanding process. Indeed, it is the contention of this chapter that the processes of transference and counter-transference which occur for practitioners in direct work with abused children are acutely exacerbated by the parallel processes and dynamics which occur in the organizations in which such work is undertaken. As we look now at some of the processes arising from direct work with abused children, we can begin to draw parallels with similar organizational dynamics.

Gil and Cavanagh-Johnson (1993) identify a number of core transference and counter-transference themes in work with abused children. Transference is the process whereby the client transfers or projects feelings, perceptions or behaviours arising from a previous relationship, onto the worker. Parental relationships are a prime source of transference, especially in the client's current relationships with quasi-parental figures such as social workers or other professionals. Counter-transference can be described as the feelings, perceptions of behaviours generated in the worker either in response to the client's transference or the worker's own unresolved issues.

*Transference issues in working with abused children :* Worker seen by child as:

1 *Parent/caretaker:* child tests out, or attempts to provoke abusive responses from, the worker.

2 *Sexual object:* child uses sexual behaviour as strategy with the worker to manipulate meeting of child's needs.

3 *Persecutor:* worker seen or perceived as controlling the child.

4 *Judge:* worker seen or experienced as having range of other powers over child, thus making it harder for the child to invest trust in the worker.

5 *Rescuer:* worker seen as all-powerful, and able to prevent any harm.

6 *Colluder in denial:* especially by abusing children or adolescents.

7 *Focal point for all needs:* thus the child needs to behave compliantly or look after worker to ensure she/he is not rejected or abandoned.

These dynamics, with perhaps the exception of being seen as a sexual object, mirror many of the conscious and unconscious expectations that practitioners may have in relation to their own agency. Few new entrants to social work or healthcare are adequately prepared for the realities of organizational life, and often come with idealized hopes of what working for a 'caring' profession will mean. Sadly, this mismatch between expectation and experience is a major cause of stress at a crucial point in their career, and intensifies the nature of the worker's counter-transference responses to children such as described below.

*Counter-transference responses by the worker.*

1 *Overidentification:* the worker needs to absorb the child's pain, resulting in an absence of psychological boundaries. The child's and the worker's pain are inseparable.

2 *Rescuing:* the worker believes they alone can 'save' child.

3 *Helplessness:* the worker resonates with, and joins, the child's sense of futility and loss of hope.

4 *Anger:* the worker's anger on behalf of the child or him - or herself is, however, suppressed because of lack of permission to express this, and guilt about feeling it in the first place.

5 *Over-controlling behaviour:* This is designed to ward off the worker's anxiety and reflecting of the child's own attempts to control their world.

6 *Victim behaviour:* This is especially likely if the worker

has suffered similar traumas to the child, leading to the worker seeing their own abuser in the child, or feeling actually abused by the child. This may result in feelings of isolation, and fears such as 'Sex offenders are everywhere', 'Something is wrong with my child', or 'Something is wrong with me.'

A poignant example of helplessness was provided in a workshop when participants were asked to draw a road map of their own life history, indicating experiences or themes which may have motivated them to enter social work. One woman, a very experienced childcare worker, soon became distressed, as she realised for the first time why her interaction with children whom she had to take into care was so emotionally cold. She had spent extended periods in hospital as a child and recalled the painful memories of her parents leaving when the visiting period was up. When years later she was required, for the first time, to remove a child from home, she could not stop crying. The transference from the child in terms of abandonment, rejection and loss had provoked an overwhelming counter-transference in terms of helplessness in this worker. The worker resolved never to cry again, as a result of which she had learned to switch off emotionally whenever she was involved in similar tasks, a process which she had long felt guilty about. If a tutor, supervisor or trainer had thought to ask her to reflect on what personal issues childcare work was likely to generate for her, this scenario might well never have occurred.

Many of these dynamics are further mediated by factors of gender, race, disability or sexuality, through which personal and agency responses are differentiated and made more problematic. Thus female staff may well identify strongly with the child's experience of men as violators, whilst male staff may struggle with issues of generalized guilt and shame resulting from the same issue. For both, the experience is one that attacks their sense of confidence, self-trust and safety in doing the work, as well as their ability to work with others.

It is also not hard to see the potential impact on the management of risk. Unattended to, such processes can all too easily result in: distorted perceptions and bias; acting out of unexpressed feelings; impaired communication; blurring of facts, feelings and opinions; ignoring information; inadequate analysis; untested assumptions; action based on personal agendas, and polarization of professional networks. It is a prime source of dangerous practice.

## Professional dangerousness

Reder et al.'s (1993) analysis of child death inquiries has considerably enriched our understanding of the ways in which the dynamics of abusing families interact with professional systems to increase the dangerousness of such situations, resulting in the mismanagement of high-risk families. Two specific characteristics of abusing families, unresolved care and control problems, are discussed. Many parents of seriously abused children have themselves been subject to emotionally depriving care and/or physically abusive punishment, which are subsequently manifested in their own adult and own parenting relationships in the form of unresolved dependency needs, and major conflicts about control. However, Reader et al. suggest that these care/control problems are further played out through the interactions between such families and the child protection network. Four specific processes in family-professional relationships are identified - dependency; closure; flight, and disguised compliance:

1 *Dependency:* Professionals are drawn into meeting more and more demands from parents, thereby obscuring the child's needs and issues of risk. When, for resource or other reasons, such intensive support is withdrawn, this triggers in the parents early feelings of abandonment, anger and withdrawal.

2 *Closure:* Parents who have a precarious feeling of control over their own lives, when forced to engage in mostly involuntary relationships with the child protection system, may respond by distancing, and closing in on themselves, either temporarily or completely, in an attempt to regain control of the outside world by keeping it out.

3 *Flight:* Parents move home, in some cases travelling to another part of the country, in an effort to maintain control over their relationship with child protection agencies by running away from, and thus fragmenting, the professional network.

4 *Disguised compliance:* Parents neutralize professionals' demands by offering an overt verbal compliance whilst maintaining a covert agenda of delinquent and rebellious behaviour towards the child protection agencies. (Reder et al., 1993)

Thus professionals' well-intentioned attempts to provide care and nurturance for deprived parents, and/or to set boundaries to protect children, may, unintentionally, trigger more dangerous responses from the parents as they struggle with the crisis that threatens to overwhelm their fragile defence systems.

There is, however, a parallel narrative to Reder et al.'s story of the way in which professionals can be drawn into dysfunctional family processes. This parallel narrative has its starting point not in the family, but in the dysfunctional organizational processes, described earlier (see Figure 17.1). For, in agencies where anxiety is not attended to, where feeling and thinking are off-limits, and where management processes may be experienced as non-contingent, neglectful or punitive, care and control conflicts can be an endemic feature of agency life. Thus, when such agencies encounter child abuse, their staff's own organizational and personal care and control conflicts may unwittingly be triggered by the very same dynamics in the families whose children they seek to safeguard (Figure 17.2).

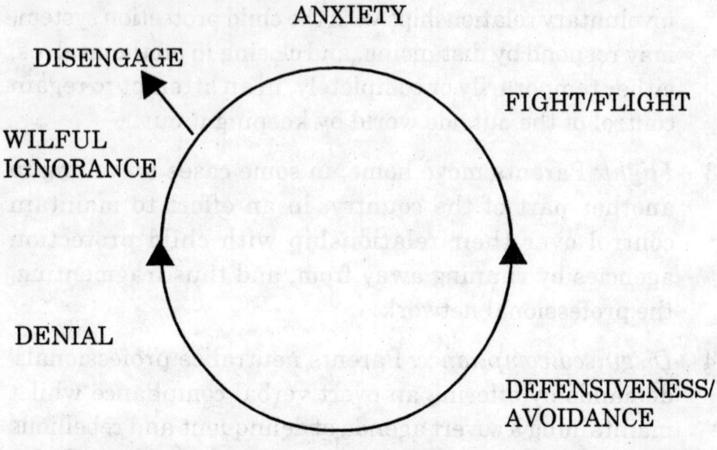


**Figure 17.1**: Dysfunctional Learning Cycle (Vince and Martin, 1993; reproduced with permission of Management Education and Development)

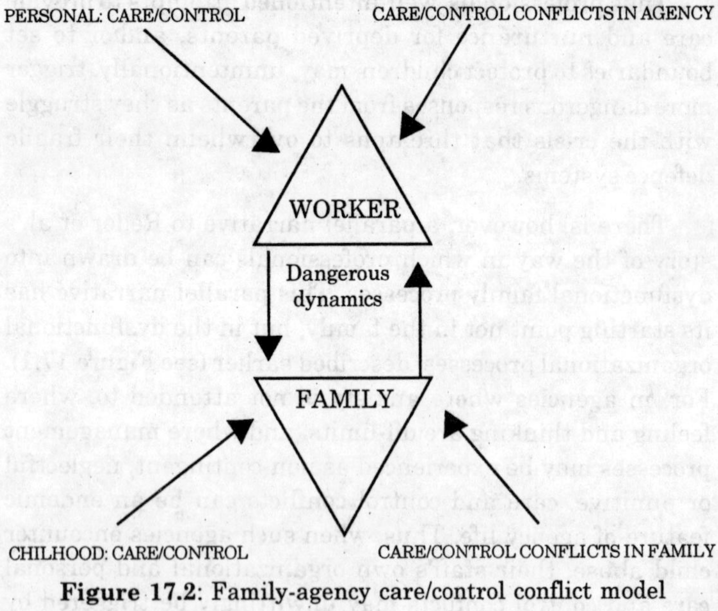


**Figure 17.2**: Family-agency care/control conflict model

In summary, the front line of today's child protection work is potentially a partnership between two parties, families and professionals, neither of whom feels understood, valued, respected, prepared or supported. This has potentially highly damaging, consequences not only for practice, as we have seen, but also for the well-being of staff. To explore this I will to refer to, and elaborate on, an earlier model, the Professional Accommodation Syndrome (Morrison, 1990), to promote an understanding of the interaction between the primary stress of working with abused children, and the secondary stress stemming from the agency's response to these primary stresses.

## Professional Accommodation Syndrome

In 1983 Roland Summit published a seminal paper, 'The Child Sexual Abuse Accommodation Syndrome', which offered a model to explain both why children took so long to disclose sexual abuse, and the reasons for some children subsequently retracting their statement (see Figure 17.3).

Briefly stated, Summit showed how the sexually abused child, living in a family system regulated by the perpetrator's dominance and by secrecy, feeling helpless and entrapped by the abuse, sought to resolve this psychological crisis by shifting responsibility for the abuse from the adult(s) to the child. The function of this accommodation is that by choosing to take responsibility for their own abuse the child can attempt to regain some control over the situation - for example: 'It's too awful to contemplate that my father is abusing me, and that my mother knows about it (even if this is not true), as I am powerless to act. If I assume instead that it is my fault (which is what my father has been saying to me) then, if I am good, and do what my father says - that is, keep the secret - then maybe it will stop.'

The effect of accommodation in this way is, unfortunately, further entrapment in the abusive relationship and ensuring delays in disclosure. Because of this, and the conditions under which a disclosure may emerge (family crisis, running away, psychosomatic complaints), the eventual disclosure may be seen by professionals as unconvincing and thus be disbelieved. Faced with doubting professionals and the mounting family crisis surrounding the disclosure, for which the child is now also made responsible, the solution is for the child to retract. The perpetrator's denial and the rule of secrecy are thus sustained, both of which serve to deepen the child's future vulnerability to abuse. The inadequate response of the professional system acts as a secondary form of victimization, and worsens the damage done by the original primary source of victimization.

(5) RETRACTION

(4) DELAYED OR UNCONVINCING DISCLOSURE

(3) ENTRAPMENT AND ACCOMMODATION

(2) HELPLESSNESS

(1) SECRECY

**Figure 17.3**: Sexual Abuse Accommodation Syndrome (Summit, 1983)

However, Summit's powerful model can be adapted to enable us to understand more general processes of victimization and staff stress, and it is particularly useful for child protection staff because it draws on the dynamics of abuse. It can be applied to managers, teams and organizations, not just in social work agencies but in virtually any care setting. Thus, in its reworked version, the Professional Accommodation Model works as follows, based on the same five stages:

1 *Secrecy:* Many staff hesitate to speak about the impact of the work on them because they feel or know that the agency or colleagues covertly or overtly deny them permission to do so.

2 *Helplessness:* Staff who feel helpless in relation to their work, or in the face of stress arising from it, feel a sense of shame. They experience the agency's rejection and dislike of their helplessness, and receive the message that those in the helping professions are paid to be coppers. The agency's belief system is that uncomplaining workers are OK. Myths exist that trained staff should act logically, rationally and objectively. Gender stereotyping in agencies sees women who express stress as 'hysterical' or 'victims', and men as 'wimps' or 'little boys'. Features of race, disability or sexuality create yet other pejorative stereotypes.

3 *Entrapment and accommodation:* Staff are trapped in a dilemma in which telling the truth about their stress is seen as 'unprofessional', whilst denying that they feel stress is seen as coping and professional. In the face of this, staff are forced to accommodate by then deciding that the fault lies not with the agency's insensitivity, or with the nature of their work, but with themselves for feeling as they do, failing to cope, and generally not being sufficiently robust. The answer appears then to lie in suppressing their feelings, invalidating their experiences, and working harder.

4 *Delayed or unconvincing disclosure:* Disclosure of the distress may eventually be triggered by conflict, training, illness or talking with colleagues. Where conflict is the trigger, this may be in the form of unpredictable behaviour such as atypical aggression, lateness, sickness or sudden resignation. If this behaviour is only understood at a superficial level, and not as a signal of a more

prolonged underlying distress, it may result in actual or perceived responses such as 'She should never have been a social worker/teacher/nurse anyway' or 'If you can't stand the heat get out of the kitchen'. The difficulty for managers and the agency is that, as Figure 17.4 shows, it is not until this point that any obvious signs of problems appear, and the fact that the presenting behaviour may well be a problem in its own right. The surface behaviour, however, is like the tip of the iceberg, below which there may lie a history of distress which has progressed through secrecy, helplessness and accommodation, and whose diagnostic signs have been both subtle and ambiguous. If the worker does leave the agency, he or she may well take to their new job these unresolved experiences, which will, unbeknown to their new employer, render the worker additionally vulnerable to stress. Some career patterns seem to be driven by a series of ever more rapid cycles of delayed disclosure-flight.

5 *Retraction:* The delayed or confusing nature of the disclosure, if followed by insensitive, ignoring or disbelieving responses in the agency, leaves the worker psychologically and professionally abandoned, fearing that he or she will now be written off as incompetent. In the face of this threat to their whole career the only solution appears to be retraction: 'I'm fine now, it was just the time of month' or 'I'm fine now, it was nothing to do with work'. Secrecy resumes and the entrapment deepens as a result of the experience of being punished for disclosing, which, of course, confirms the original belief system about the agency.

This model suggests that, with the exception of traumatic forms of primary stress, for example assault by a client, the critical dimensions of stress in child protection work do not arise primarily from work with clients, but in the agency's responses to the strong but normative feelings and fears which such work engenders. Normative anxieties become pathologized in such agency cultures, and solutions, if restricted to the provision of counselling, serve to reinforce the same message - that only 'inadequate' workers complain.

**(5) RETRACTION** I' am fine now

**(4) DELAYED or UNCONVINCING DISCLOSURE** Resignation, sickness

**Behaviour surfaces**

- - - - - - - - - - - - - - - - - - - - - - - - -

**Small pre-disclosure signs?**

**(3) ENTRAPMENT and ACCOMMODATION** If I was a better worker...

**(2) HELPLESSNESS** Uncomplaining workers must be OK

**(1) SECRECY** I dare not share my feelings

**Figure 17.4**: Professional Accommodation Model (Morrison, 1990, adapted)

## Towards emotionally competent organizations

Although approaches to organizational theory have tended to stress directional and structural aspects as being crucial to organizational well-being, other literature (Menzies, 1970; Vince and Martin, 1993) has emphasized the emotional and cognitive life of the organization operating at both conscious and unconscious levels. These approaches, drawing from group analytic and open systems theories, explore the impact on the agency of group interactions, and the acting out of the images and fantasies about the institutions which are carried by the members of the organization and which influence much of these members' organizational behaviour. To put it more simply, such approaches integrate the *feeling* and *thinking* aspects of the agency's life with the *doing/task* focus. Indeed, the premise is that more rather than less is achieved if feeling and thinking are attended to, because the organization and its staff are not wasting precious energy and resources on organizational, social and personal defence systems (Menzies, 1970), such as denial or projection which in fact only worsen existing problems and demotivate the workforce.

One way of conceptualizing the nature of healthy organizations is to return to two of the models already described, namely Vince and Martin's Dysfunctional Learning Cycle and the Professional Accommodation Syndrome, and explore strategies for the creation of positive agency cultures which need to underpin child protection work. Thus, if we look again at the Professional Accommodation Syndrome, from this angle we can begin to identify a number of strategies:

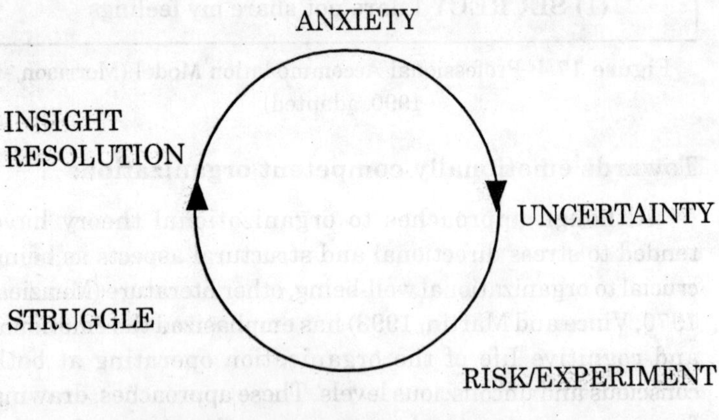


**Figure 17.5**: Functional Learning Cycle (Vince and Martin, 1993; reproduced with permission of Management Education and Development)

1 *From secrecy to openness:* If secrecy is where problems start, then the promotion of openness, by a variety of means, is the first objective in a healthy organization. This can be linked to Vince and Martin's Functional Learning Cycle (Figure 17.5).

In this culture, anxiety and stress are openly acknowledged and seen as normative, allowing for the expression of healthy uncertainty, and difference, where problems and 'mistakes' are opportunities for learning, not punishment. Risks are taken and innovations are attempted. The unresolvable nature of many issues is openly acknowledged and struggled with, from which unexpected or creative resolution may come. In consequence of this, staff are empowered to tackle further demands.

In other words, the organization is managed in ways that acknowledge anxiety as an institutional, and not just an individual, phenomenon. This approach is therefore not primarily about the provision of staff counselling services, although this has a place, but is much more about the quality of management, so that the organization knows what its job is, knows where it is going, and equips its staff to get there. This happens through the provision of an effective infrastructure for practice: goals; values; leadership; structures; polices; resources, and effective human resource management. Time does not permit a discussion of these elements but, clearly, agency culture and structures are interdependent. Healthy processes will not happen in agencies that do not know where they are going or how they want to get there.

However, one specific element that does require mentioning is the critical role of supervision in the creation of a positive climate for practice. It is essential to reaffirm, as a profession, that supervision is the worker's most important helping relationship, and is, for the organization, the most important process by which thinking, feeling and doing are integrated. At an individual level, supervision is the vehicle through which anxiety is contained and held. It is also, far more so than training, the primary means for the development of competence and self-efficacy in staff. Openness cannot thrive in the absence of skilled and sensitive supervisory processes (Morrison, 1993).

2 *From helplessness to empowerment:* Helplessness needs to be combated through a range of empowerment strategies, central to which must be the notion that a primary buffer to stress and burn-out is self-efficacy. It is of little value to allow staff to ventilate feelings if they are not enabled to acquire sufficient knowledge and skills to do the job. They will remain hapless in the face of their incompetence. However, empowerment is also about acknowledging, valuing and utilizing difference within the workforce, and therefore it is concerned with making explicit issues of inequality and power. Working together means contact between differing emotional realities, different systems of meaning and different types of bias. Consequently, women and men, black and white, disabled and able-bodied, gay and straight have to address differential experiences of power and powerlessness as aspects of the organizational practice and learning (Vince and Martin, 1993).

3 *From accommodation to clarity:* Entrapment and accommodation is essentially a process of cognitive distortion whereby responsibilities and distinctions between 'me' and 'not me' become blurred and confused. The result is individuals taking too much responsibility for processes that are not within their control: 'If I had visited that child, she wouldn't have been abused.' However, because these are cognitive processes they may be well hidden, revealing only the most subtle of clues. The underlying strategy here must be about making the

worker's thinking, beliefs, assumptions, fantasies or fears explicit so that they can be tested against external realities, facts, values, limitations, policies and expectations. Only by doing so can clarity and an appropriate sense of role and responsibility be regained. At an organizational level, continuing attention to role clarity is essential, given that role ambiguity and confusion are highly correlated with stress and burn-out.

4 *From delayed disclosure to restoration:* At this point there is a dual need. First, the presenting behaviour needs to be understood, as a potential sign of distress, and as a consequence of the worker going through the previous stages. However, it is also possible that the worker's problems in fact do not originate within the workplace, but eleswhere such as at home. It is very important, then, that a sensitive and intelligent analysis is sought as to the reasons for the behaviour, in order that the worker feels that any cry for help is heard, and to identify any organizational/supervisory deficits or problems that have contributed to the behaviour. Secondly, it is vital to restore the worker to positive functioning as quickly as possible, even if this includes making clear the need to change the behaviour, alongside the provision of support, training, co-work or possibly counselling where appropriate. The overriding aim is to prevent a move to retraction.

5 *From retraction to prevention:* Once retraction has occurred, the aim is primarily preventative, to open up communication and make opportunities for openness and sharing of feelings more accessible in the future, accepting the worker's current statement that everything is now OK. Particular attention should be paid to the quality and safety of the supervisory relationship, and any specific support needs required by the worker. For example, black workers should be entitled and assisted in establishing support groups. It may be useful to examine with the

worker whether they have had similar experiences in other settings which have not been resolved. However, as with the previous stage, every effort needs to be made to enable the worker to regain their confidence and sense of self-efficacy in the workplace as soon as possible. This may mean a sensitive review of the size and appropriateness of their workload.

Many of these strategies need to be implemented at a corporate level, for Pearlin and Schooler (1978) state: 'Work problems are intertwined with the social structure and organisation of the workplace, and thus require collective, rather than individual solutions.' These must start at the organizational level, and clearly senior managers have a major responsibility, but the strategies must also work their way down to smaller work units. At a strategic level, there are four priorities as far as combating stress is concerned:

1 Raising awareness.
2 Developing interpersonal management skills.
3 Redesigning unhelpful structures.
4 Training. (HEA, 1988)

At a team level, one simple suggestion is for each local work unit/team to use the Professional Accommodation Model to analyse unhelpful processes, and then to generate a Team Health Plan based around the five stages described above: openness, empowerment, clarity, restoration and prevention.

## Conclusion

Plainly there are no quick fixes or standardized remedies for the complex emotional turbulence of child protection work. What is clear, however, is that such processes are best understood as a triangular interaction involving agency, clients and workers. As such, the question is not whether organizations should be concerned for their emotional health but how to grow healthy organizational environments. This chapter has sought to provide models that may catalyse discussion, energy and action towards a vision of emotionally competent organizations. But, through it all, we should keep Tonnesman's words in mind:

> The human encounter in the helping professions is inherently stressful. The stress aroused can be accommodated and used for the good of our clients. But our emotional responsiveness will wither if the human encounter cannot be contained within the institutions within which we work. Defensive manoeuvres will then become operative and these will prevent healing. By contrast if we can maintain contact with the emotional reality of our clients and ourselves, then the human encounter can facilitate not only a healing experience, but also an enriching experience for them and us. (1979, cited in Morrison, 1993)

# XVIII

# MEN, MASCULINITY AND CHILDCARE

## Introduction

This chapter discusses the nature of masculinity, particularly in relation to men and their relationship with women and children, and in their roles as workers in the personal social services. In terms of safety and the risks involved, the issue of the appropriateness of men working with children is not a new one, as Pringle has noted:

> a recognition of the role of gender in the occurrence of sexual abuse calls into question the safety of children in any welfare setting where males are present as carers and/or therapists, not merely the residential sector. The implications for such an analysis in terms of policy and practice may be dramatic as regards the future role of men in welfare systems. (1992)

Nevertheless, this chapter begins with the premise that tighter guidelines for men working with abused and 'damaged' children may only be one part of a more complex issue. This complexity arises from a recognition that many aspects of the social and psychological construction of masculinity are highly problematic in the ways in which they are manifested within the personal social services. The chapter explores some implications of this recognition and concludes with a selection of strategies for working which attempt to begin the process of revising and realigning the nature of men's work with men, women and children.

**The development of awareness**

During a recent workshop on anti-discriminatory practice a male residential childcare worker related an interesting story. He was an experienced worker in a senior position who was wrestling with the complex issues around practising in an anti-discriminatory way. He was attempting to challenge traditional stereotypes and introduce practices into his unit that were less oppressive to both the young women residents and his women colleagues. On duty one day, he was asked to intervene after several of the other staff had failed to calm a disturbed young man who had become abusive and violent, and who had begun to mutilate himself. Although the worker was a gentle man and physically small, the young man's behaviour became so risky that it became necessary to resort to physical restraint. After some time, when the young man had calmed down and been reassured. The incident appeared to be over. However, later on, three colleagues (two women and one man) came to him and complimented him on his actions in restraining this difficult resident. Superficially this might seem unremarkable but for the fact that their praise was not for his social work skills but for his physical prowess, and by implication his masculinity. Over the next few days, this scenario was repeated as several other of the young male residents also appeared to reassess their perceptions of him in a similar fashion.

The worker's experience was confirmed by other social workers in the discussion group, who also anecdotally confirmed the predominance of the perception that residential childcare was primarily a masculine activity, with women workers often being regarded as being too weak and fragile for the rigours of the job. This chauvinistic perception has been noted by other writers. Ruxton, for example, reports one male worker as stating: 'they didn't want me because they wanted a caring man, they wanted me primarily as a strong disciplinarian father figure . . . wait 'till your dad gets home – that's what it felt like' (1992). Similarly, Bowl observed that: 'residential social work can be an aggressively male ritual, revolving round strong masculine father figures' (1985).

Within the workshop, the discussion moved to the alarming number of scandals over recent years, mostly involving men abusing children in their care. All of the participants had at least one recollection of abuse being committed by welfare professionals on children they had worked with. Their concerns about men as abusers are confirmed by studies both in Britain and the United States (NSPCC, 1992; Nunno and Rindfleisch, 1991; Rosenthal et al., 1991). For example, Finkelhor (1990) estimated that 98 per cent of abuse on female children and 83 per cent of abuse on male children was carried out by males, and McFadden and Ryan noted that one of the few factors to show a reliable relationship with the incidence of sexual abuse is the gender of the head of the household. They stated that 'there was a very low incidence of sexual abuse in families headed by a single woman' (1991). Rosenthal et al. (1991), in their study of abuse in residential homes, found that the perpetrators were predominantly men. Of course, some women do abuse, and this is an aspect which needs more attention, but, as a proportion set against male abuse, it remains a very small part of the picture.

The male participants in the workshop expressed their deep unease at the apparently unending series of scandals which had been revealed during the 1980s and 1990s. Events in Clwyed and Leicestershire children's home and other incidents in schools, church organizations, residential units for people with learning difficulties and youth clubs had created a sense of despair and despondency amongst many of the workers. They felt that much of what was good about their services and their jobs was being devalued by this procession of malpractice and abuse. However, their unease had deeper roots. In part, it stemmed from a growing awareness that perhaps these events were not simply the actions of a few bad apples, but derived from more complex roots. They were beginning to realize that neither the problems nor the 'solutions' lay solely with other people, that they themselves might be implicated in the need for change. This, as Pugh has noted, is a characteristic feature of anti-discriminatory perspectives on practice - that is, the realization by social workers that 'their work is not automatically beneficial in its consequences: that they might be part of the problem, not the solution' (1996). The influence of feminist theory is clear: the decentring of the worker dramatically switches the focus from workers 'as the agents of change', to their becoming 'the subjects for change!' (Pugh, 1996).

This glimmering of consciousness in the male participants in the workshop heralded the realization that perhaps they were embarking upon an uncomfortable exploration of the patriarchal values and sexist ideologies embedded in their own personal, social and cultural patterns of identity and existence. As Mason and Mason have noted:

> While men who work in the 'helping' profession are not stereotypical macho heroes and may appear to be more sensitive than many men, we have not escaped this socialisation ... men in the helping profession are probably just more subtle about sexism. (1990)

**Cause and culpability ?**

Clearly, the group were beginning to realize that these problems of abuse involved much broader issues of causality and, ultimately perhaps, a reframing of the very nature of masculinity. As the facilitator, my role was to build positively upon this insight and keep the group from getting stuck in an overly simplistic position of blaming. While blaming may seem like an attractive proposition, especially to those who have suffered the depredations inflicted by men, it is ultimately futile. Instead of stimulating positive change, it encourages either defensiveness or hopelessness. Nevertheless, as these men were beginning to realize, sexism is not a phenomenon constructed solely by 'monsters'. They, like all men, had a responsibility to examine their own actions as well as those of other men.

Many men still prefer to consider male abusers as aberrant 'perverts', beyond the boundaries of normal experience, and that stricter professional criteria, better training, clearer rules on appropriate touching and more rigorous police checking should be sufficient to eliminate abuse. However, this can be seen to be a mistaken conceit, one which may be employed to avoid any self-critical examination of the nature of masculinity. For, as Cameron and Frazer suggest, there is a common thread uniting male abusers: 'a shared construction of masculine sexuality, or even more broadly, masculinity in general' (1990). Teague (1993), in a study of convicted repists, showed the 'normality' of most rapists' personalities. For the most part, they were not the 'beasts' portrayed in the media, but men alarmingly like the rest of the male population. Teague accepts the premise most notably stated by feminist writers like Brownmiller (1975) and Chesler (1990), that rape is not primarily about sexual satisfaction but is about power. It is about men demonstrating and inflicting their power on women. From this premise, it is possible to see how rapists, while committing apparently deviant and depraved behaviour, can be conceptualized as being merely at the furthest extreme of a continuum of attitudes which also encompasses 'normal' behaviour. Teague quotes Ussher (1991):

> [these men]... don't sprout horns. Rapists, sexual murderers and paedophiles do not look like monsters. They cannot be identified by . . . their marked difference from other men. (1993)

This is supported by Wyre (1986) who, in his direct work with sexual offenders, has noted that many of them hold views about women which reflect the views of most men in society at large. Of course, there might be other common factors but, as Pringle (1992) found in his review of the research into perpetrators, there do not appear to be common predictors of future perpetrators. For example, he challenges the notion that a history of abuse in childhood is in itself a reliable predictor of future behaviour. It is probable, therefore, that it is the feminist and social constructionist views of masculinity which offer more convincing accounts of the reasons for male violence and abuse. In these accounts, contemporary representations of masculinity are seen as intrinsically supporting the subjugation of women through the objectification of sexuality and, ultimately, through violence or the threat of it. The following section begins to unpack some of the strands of representation which tell particular 'stories' about men and women in our society.

**Unpacking the narratives**

The roots of the dominant masculine culture can be found in what Smart and Smart refer to as the:

> prevailing material conditions, cultural values, customs and social practices, such as the differential socialisation of male and female children within the family, schooling, forms of speech and language, media propagated stereotypes and other numerous seemingly innocuous processes. (1976)

Many social scientists who write about male violence on women and children often present a narrative that belies blame or fails to attribute responsibility. Lamb, in a review of journal articles on men who 'batter' women, suggests that many social scientists tend to use the 'ubiquitous passive voice . . . which presents acts without agents, harm without guilt' (1991). Often the severe injuries inflicted upon women were referred to as being the result of 'domestic' or 'spousal' violence, as if there were joint responsibility for what has occurred, rather than a violent act inflicted by one person upon another. This type of masking of actions by the use of language is frequently used to obscure the exercise of power (Pugh, 1996). Similarly, Hooper (1987) shows how the language used about incest often portrays men as 'victims' of their families. She notes how women are variously described as 'setting up' the conditions for incest by 'keeping themselves tired', or going to work, or into hospital. Hooper, describes how some perpetrators who had been cast into the role of primary carers by unemployment gave masked accounts of their behaviour, in which they suddenly found themselves touching their daughters' genitals. In this way the sought to avoid culpability. Alternatively, the facts of abuse may be hidden behind the language of disease, being seen as a 'symptom' of family dysfunction rather than holding men responsible for the choices they make about their own behaviour.

The significance of language in constructing particular narratives or accounts of events cannot be underestimated, for not only can it be used to mask events, it can also be employed in ways which, intentionally or otherwise, disempower women. French (1992) refers to research into women's refuges and points out that the implications of portraying women as 'victims' when seeking funding continues to present them as being weak and 'helpless'. One further consequence is that such narratives conveniently support the mushrooming of professionals who become experts on 'family violence'. French points out that the clear association between masculinity, violence and indecency is rarely commented upon. In much of the media coverage of the horrendous murders of women by Frederick West, there was relatively little discussion of West's misogynistic views, and little analysis of the culture which may have shaped him. While some commentators did wonder how this apparently ordinary man could be capable of such vile acts, West was largely presented as an aberration, as someone beyond the normal realm of society. In terms of the scale of his atrocities, he clearly was 'abnormal', but in terms of the nature of his actions and his own accounts of them, his comments revealed that he was much like other perpetrators. During the trial, for example, tape recordings of West revealed his belief that all women were just interested in sex and that his victims had forced themselves on him. Teague's (1993) work with rapists revealed that many of them made similar comments, variously stating that they believed that women 'need to be raped'; 'want to be raped'; 'it teaches them a lesson'; 'shows them who is boss', and that 'they provoke it anyway so they deserve to be raped'. Teague develops this point by stating that: 'If these are simply cognitive distortions then the whole of male culture would appear to be distorted', because these views seem to be widely held beyond the ranks of convicted rapists and murderers.

Analysis of the actions of the media indicates some fundamental ambiguities in the representations of sexuality and gender. These were exemplified during the horrowing court proceedings in the West case. On one day in court, a frightened young woman gave evidence that Fred West had tried to look up her skirt whilst she was cycling home from school, and the media duly reported this as evidence of his perversion. Yet, the very next day, several newspapers pruriently printed a photograph of Hillary Clinton sitting down in a manner which accidentally revealed her underwear (Campbell, 1995). How is it that editors who reported the terror and embarrassment of a young schoolgirl failed to make any connection between the indecencies of West and their own actions in printing the photograph ?

This was not an isolated instance of public dissociation and ambiguity. There have been many cases of horrifying violence perpetrated by men on women and children in which an insensitive judiciary and media thoughtlessly continue to present derogatory views of women. Teague (1993) cites the grotesque comments of the judge who, when sentencing Nicholas Boyce to imprisonment for manslaughter after killing his wife, described him as a *'man of reasonable self control'* (emhasis added) who had been provoked into killing her. The full obscenity of this description can only be fully grasped with a knowledge of what was said of Boyce's actions - that: 'You cut her up with a saw and boiled her skin and bones. You bagged up the pieces and over the next two days disposed of the boyd.'!

There have been numerous other examples of victim-blaming, especially in the reporting of offences against women. In one notorious case, a man received a light sentence because of the 'contributory negligence' of the victim who was portrayed as being reckless, as she had worn a short shirt. While these examples are conspicuous, in the sense that they were noted and remarked upon publicly, much of what the judiciary does passes without comment. Teague speculates that the judiciary have a structural role in maintaining the gender-based uneven distribution of power, and that their actions often implicitly legitimate male violence towards women.

## Constructing gender and constructing masculinity

The constructionist analysis of gender adopted in this chapter is one which rejects the notion that there is any biological or innate disposition to attitudes and behaviours. However, it does recognize that this social differentiation is constructed upon the base of the biological distinction of male and female secondary sexual characteristics. Masculinity is therefore intrinsically a social construction which stratifies gender-specific roles and expectations by defining what is 'normal' behaviour for both men and women (Thompson, 1993), and this social structuring essentially subjugates women. This subjugation or derogation of women occurs in many different ways, but primarily it operates, not from the initial distinction of sex - that is, of male and female - but from the gender distinction, of masculine and feminine, of men and women. As Miedzan indicates, there is a prevailing 'sociocultural assumption, often unconscious, that male behaviour, is the norm and constitutes a paradigm for human behaviour, female behaviour being viewed as deviant or defective' (1992). From the outset, femininity is often defined as the absence of masculinity. This form of gender apartheid does not lead to perceptions of women as separate but equal, but to a perception of them as separate and inferior. The problem, of course, is the apparent 'normalness' of masculinity. Like the wallpaper, it is no longer noticed, so why bother to examine something that seems so self-evident ? The answer is: because it is highly probable that male socialization and masculine culture are contributing factors to abusive behaviour by men.

Masculinity is a complex cluster of expectations that lay out the ground rules of how men should behave (norms), and how they should think (attitudes). The following subsections examine three of the most powerful aspects of masculinity.

### Emotional 'hardness'

The reluctance of men to explore their feelings and express their vulnerability is well documented. Hite's (1987) survey of 4,500 women in the USA found that 98 per cent felt the biggest problem in their current relationship was a lack of emotional closeness with their male partner. For many men, the idea of masculinity revolves around the perception of being 'in control' of themselves and of other people and things. Thus, the direct expression of 'tender' emotions exposes their potential vulnerability to being hurt by other people. The implications of this are obvious. Because men are unlikely to expose their feelings if they think these will be abused, they may not only find it difficult to express the full range of emotions, but they will only do so in particular circumstances, and then often only with great difficulty. Hence, relationships with women and other men, which are not primarily sexual ones, will frequently be obstructed by the lack of direct expression of those feelings which could enhance trust, and facilitate support. Instead, men cultivate the carapace of 'hardness'. The iconic behaviour conveyed by Clint Eastwood in most of his earlier films epitomizes this desired persona.

This 'hardness' can also restrict close associations with children and colleagues, especially when combined with men's fears about their own sexual identity. Thus, while there may be sound reasons for being wary of emotionally close relationships with children in childcare work for fear of wrongful allegations, some men nevertheless often approach their work in ways which preclude even the possibility of effective relationships. Thompson (1995) has noted how the fear of being labelled as homosexual if a close relationship develops with another man also operates to limit the possibilities.

### The instability of male identity

It has been argued that male identity is inherently unstable, being built around elements of masculinity that are themselves oppressive (Jackson, 1982; Bowl, 1985; Thompson, 1995). The centrality of competitiveness, competence, aggression and objectification creates a masculinity characterized by anxiety and instability. Failure to impress, complete or acknowledge competence, particularly in areas of sexuality, may well lead to inadequacies and fears which, not surprisingly, can then be projected onto women and children.

Other writers, like French, suggest that this instability is due to the fact that men strive for the appearance of manhood which involves postures of dominance and oppression. She continues:

> Such behaviour suggests men believe 'manhood' is not inherent in a man, but depends on both the opinion of other men and the existence of a subjugated person. Male identity is therefore extremely unstable, and this instability creates anxiety, often expressed as rage. (1992)

## Socialization, stereotyping and derogation of women

The role of stereotypes in maintaining oppression and disadvantage is well documented (Thompson, 1993), and similarly the transmission of these stereotypes through the media, education and childrearing is also well known (French, 1992; Burck and Speed, 1995). The net effect, as Schein has suggested, is that: 'Boys and men are taught to despise and control the values and behaviours that are not considered masculine. As feminine traits are clearly not included in this category, this hatred transforms male behaviours and attitudes into violence and misogyny (hatred of women)' (1977). The stereotyping of men and women into commonly accepted gender roles is clear for all to see in social work agencies and in children's services particularly. Ruxton (1992) talks of men working in caring situations who are afraid of being labelled homosexual. The perception that they have in some way 'failed' to make it in a real man's job is a fear acknowledged by Savage, writing of the male nurse:

> He is emasculated by taking on 'women's work' in which he is expected to demonstrate 'feminine qualities' such as caring and gentleness and, in which, at least to begin with, he will be subordinate to women. And if his masculinity is in question, so too is his sexuality. (1987)

## Resume

Before considering how we might change our practice, it is worth recapitulating the main points covered in the first part of this chapter, namely that:

- the majority of abuse on women and children is inflicted by men;
- guidelines and codes of practice are probably ineffective in protecting children in schools and welfare agencies;
- the profiles of violent and abusing men are indistinguishable from men in general;
- all men have the potential to abuse and violate;
- gender is a social construction not a biological or 'natural' one; because of this it can be amended;
- male workers may have to engage in a critique of the very essence of masculinity at a personal, cultural and structural level, they are to retain credibility as childcare workers.

## Changing our practice

Thompson (1995) argues that childcare workers must acknowledge the central role that male power plays in relationships with colleagues, children and the agencies in which they work, if the status quo is not to be perpetuated and reinforced. The six strategies that follow are based on Thompson's (1995) paper:

## Avoid exclusion

This applies not only to the language men use which reinforces male supremacy but also to the way men behave. Men cannot dominate women without maintaining a unity against them, so it is important that men begin to learn to avoid exclusive male rituals and sexist terminology like referring to women colleagues as 'girls'. When male staff respond to a situation that may require physical restraint, it is essential that this is not done in a way that celebrates macho supremacy, for 'many women struggle to establish their competence as workers, or are hindered in their efforts to maintain or develop alternative forms of positive control when men behave this way' (Pugh, 1988).

For men involved in childcare, it also means rejecting practices that involve the macho (and sometimes violent) initiation of young men into manhood or the treating of them as subordinates. It is grown men alone who initiate young men into masculine adulthood and the worst behaviour is usually practised in the company of other men. Male workers need to involve boys and girls and women colleagues on equal terms by rejecting the notion that men can only find meaning in other man through such things as clubs, cults and games.

Women, of course, also have a responsibility. The job of redefining masculinity and creating a more gentle, equitable society must be a joint activity. The increased divorce rate has ensured that more children are being brought by women on their own, and many children in the welfare system will be cared for by women. Women too must become actively involved in order to try to give boys, in particular, an opportunity to grow and develop in ways which will allow them to become the sort of men our daughters will want to know.

**Debunk stereotypes**

The perpetuation of stereotypes is pervasive. It is vital to examine and challenge stereotypical assumptions such as the traditional roles people play in childcare and the differing expectations we hold for boys and girls. Childcare practitioners should encourage young women to take control of *their* sexuality and not have it decided for them by men. This may mean the discouragement of allowing the display of sexist posters or calendars by young males in children's homes, youth groups and so on.

In addition, social work with children demands that all staff - men and women - have to find ways to support young males in dealing with the impossible contradictory demands of growing up in a sexist society. As Phillips argues:

> What do you say to a twelve year old boy who is afraid to go to school because some kids have threatened him ? How do you encourage a boy to stand up for himself when the only available means of doing so is to hit back ? How do you protect a boy who has refused to fight and, as a result, been beaten up? (1993)

## Involve men in families and family work and women in organizations

The separation and allocation of different roles for men and women are evident. It is important to challenge the divide by encouraging men to become more active in family activities and women to become more involved in organizations. Men should encourage and support women, for example, in promotional struggles and be especially assertive in examining working relationships, pay scales and issues of power and status within the workplace.

The intrinsic sexism in some approaches to counselling and therapeutic models needs to be acknowledged and avoided. As the work of Lamb (1991) cited earlier indicates, some therapists discuss male violence and abuse as if both perpetrator and victim were jointly and equally responsible for the actions of the man. Feminist writers have offered valuable insights in analysing and deconstructing the received truths about family social work, and their work can provide useful material for workshop and discussion groups (Burck and Speed, 1995; Jones, 1995). As Burck and Speed point out, despite efforts to integrate anti-discriminatory practice into practitioners' mind-sets, the acquisition of knowledge does not, by itself, guarantee action. Without a profound change in our orientation to practice, it is likely that the critical insights of feminism will remain:

> a tokenist addendum . . . a superficial nod in the direction of 'gender roles', leaving untouched the difficult and risky territory of the social and political construction of gender, and the role-played by therapists in the maintenance, adaptation or subversion of family systems which may operate to the advantage or disadvantage of some or all of its members. (1995)

## Avoid 'masculinism'

For men to develop and to rethink masculinity, a great deal of unlearning is required. Masculinity provides a sense of personal wholeness or, as Giddens (1993) describes it, 'ontological security'. This holistic sense of a personal integrity becomes challenged at times of stress or when being confronted. The option to retreat behind male defences seems attractive but has to be avoided. As I discussed earlier, a common aspect of male socialization is the need to prove oneself in male company by taking risks, or showing fearlessness. Men in childcare have a unique vantage point from which to begin the process of undoing such damaging behaviour and offering models of masculinity that reject such practices. By giving young males models of manhood that are essentially gentle, non-confrontational and non-violent, there is a hope that this collective courage can begin the process of offering a more acceptable face of masculinity. For example, male workers who do not respond to provocation with macho posturing can offer young men a model of behaviour that shows it is possible to deal with problems without recourse to aggression or violence. Of course, women colleagues also have a responsibility to stimulate the changing atmosphere by reinforcing healthier, less stressful models of masculinity that allow young men to express anxieties and apprehensions without fear of ridicule or humiliation.

Another feature of 'masculinism' is the reluctance of men to seek help. This is already well documented in relation to men seeking help for physical and mental health difficulties

(Cunningham-Burley, 1986; Verbrugge, 1985). Men are also conspicuous by their absence when it comes to families receiving family support (Berg and Rosenblum, 1977). This particular study reported that about 30 per cent of families turned up for their first session without the father and that in general fathers were more resistant than mothers about coming back to the clinic. Harris and Sullivan (1988) suggest that social work has been collusive in supporting the traditional demarcation of roles within the family where the male role is seen as private and inviolable. Many writers have pointed out the costs of maintaining the masculine front and have emphasized the potentially damaging burden of being unable to express feelings, of living in a world of distorted relationships, emotional illiteracy and of communicating at arm's length (Thompson, 1995; Harris and Sullivan, 1988; Bowl, 1985). The result is often an inability to see when things are going wrong, exacerbated by the man's contract with the world of work and the illusory comfort of a trouble-free, compensatory home life. As Tolson argues:

> More often, deeply troubled masculine feelings are swept away by feminine tension management, and the cost of harmony in the home can be a masculine superficiality towards feelings in general, in relationships within the family, and in a man's relationship with himself. (1977)

The reluctance of men to seek medical and social work help spills over into their reluctance to seek support when overcome with stress (Morrison, 1990). For example, child protection work is a stressful activity, yet the culture of masculinity inhibits men acknowledging the heavy price of such work on their emotional homeostasis (Thompson et al., 1994). In addition, childcare workers can encourage young men to break down their emotional barriers and allow them to reveal their vulnerability without fear of humiliation or punishment. In beginning the process of rejecting 'masculinism', men can help each other to 'dump baggage' and begin to communicate their needs to each other and explore parts of their lives that have been traditionally out of bounds.

**Reject heterosexism**

Heterosexism is the received image of masculinity promoted by patriarchal ideology. As heterosexism is based on a typified image of masculinity, it is important for men in childcare to reject any notion of indulging in anti-gay or anti-lesbian activities, language or behaviour. This is especially important when working with young boys who may have been abused (see Chapter 16 in this volume). The acquisition of manhood depends on other men, and so it is especially important that the messages going out to boys and young men is a liberated one and not one which will continue to damage growing boys by initiating them into the destructive world of traditional masculinity.

**Challenge sexism in others**

Sexism is not just a personal prejudice. It is embedded in the cultural and structural building blocks of our society, thus demanding that men challenge the common representations of gender which uphold and reinforce patriarchy. For men in childcare it may involve the routine challenging of sexist language and behaviour through to contesting practice assumptions about the nature of a child's abuse by, for example, challenging an assessment that avoids male culpability. Men and women workers need to recognize the often oppressive nature of many models of family therapy and counselling techniques. Working with families where abuse has taken place demands a gender-sensitive practice. Lerner argues for an approach that 'does not minimise or obscure the role of fathers, the complexity of interlocking relationships, and the impact of culture on women's subordinate status' (1988).

**Conclusion**

If we are to be effective in tackling the issue of abuse, we have to acknowledge that it is not sufficient simply to draw up guidelines about safe practice with children. A more fundamental exploration into the culture of masculinity is necessary if men are to remain credible workers with children. We need to begin what Mezirow terms 'perspective transformation':

> the emancipatory process of becoming critically aware of how and why the structure of psychocultural assumptions has come to constrain the way we see ourselves and our relationships, reconstituting this structure to permit a more inclusive and discriminating integration of experience and acting upon those understandings. (1981)

This involves challenging the dominant assumptions of our culture and background and rethinking 'taken-for-granted' beliefs about our behaviour and the behaviour of others. Men need to understand that patriarchy damages them also. It becomes an emotional constraint that can lead to men failing to take responsibility for the part they play in both their private and public lives in the continuation of oppression and all the horrors that go with it.

Both men and women practitioners need to acknowledge that sexism, and its consequences, is not maintained solely by men. Women too, as recent writers have noted (Phillips, 1993), as well as being victims, are also participants in the everyday activities which either challenge or reinforce and reiterate our stereotypical images and patterned responses. As Thompson states: 'like any social formation, sexism has to be maintained, reinforced and consolidated if it is to remain a living force and not pass into history' (1995). Failure to understand that the reconstruction of male roles and behaviour within social work is part of a much bigger project - the reconstruction of gender - means that we must comprehend that this is a joint enterprise between men and women, its remifications going far beyond the realms of our day-to-day practice.

# INDEX

■■■